THE PERSONALITY OF THE CRITIC

YEARBOOK OF
COMPARATIVE CRITICISM

VOLUME VI

The Personality

of

The Critic

Edited by

Joseph P. Strelka

THE PENNSYLVANIA STATE
UNIVERSITY PRESS
University Park and London

Library of Congress Cataloging in Publication Data
Main entry under title:
The personality of the critic.
    (Yearbook of comparative criticism, v. 6)
    Includes bibliographical references.
    1. Criticism—Addresses, essays, lectures.
I.   Strelka, Joseph, 1927–   ed. II. Series.
PN85.P45   801'.95   73–6880
ISBN   0–271–01120–3

Library of Congress Catalog Card Number 73–6880
International Standard Book Number D–271–01160–2
Printed in the United States of America

CONTENTS

PREFACE   vii
Joseph P. Strelka

A CRITICAL STANCE   1
Eugene H. Falk

THE CONCEPT OF STRATA AND PHASES IN ROMAN
INGARDEN'S THEORY OF LITERARY STRUCTURE   10
John Fizer

FAR EASTERN EXISTENTIALISM: *HAIKU* AND THE
MAN OF *WABI*   40
Toshihiko Izutsu and Toyu Izutsu

THE CRITIC AS PERSON AND PERSONA   70
Murray Krieger

ABSOLUTISM AND JUDGMENT   93
Paul Ramsey

THE PERSONALITY OF THE CHINESE CRITIC   111
Adele Austin Rickett

KANT AND THE PERSONALITY OF THE CRITIC   135
Hans H. Rudnick

LITERARY CRITICISM IN THE FIELD OF
ISLAMIC POETRY   155
Annemarie Schimmel

WALTER BENJAMIN'S LITERARY CRITICISM IN HIS
MARXIST PHASE   168
René Wellek

LIST OF CONTRIBUTORS   179

INDEX OF NAMES   183

PREFACE

THE AIM OF LITERARY CRITICISM—COMPREHENSION, ANALYSIS, AND
evaluation of a literary work of art—can be accomplished only by a
living subject, a person. Otherwise the text will remain dead, whether it be spoken, written, or printed. This plain fact has led to some
theories which maintain that literary criticism must be subjective, in
a relativistic and completely nonobjective fashion, or alternatively
that criticism is identical with, or at least indivisible from, a subjective psychological experience. The experience theory—"Erlebnis," as
the famous German critic Wilhelm Dilthey defined his key term—is
representative of such views, as are the psychoanalytic theories of
Jacques Lacan in France or the hypothesis of the English critic Ivor
Armstrong Richards which holds that future triumphs of neurology
will settle all literary problems.[1]

Despite the kernel of truth in their initial premises, all those theories are wrong. As the first critic of modern times to establish definitely and convincingly the uniqueness and autonomy of the aesthetic
realm, Kant long ago pointed out that critical judgment is neither
completely subjective nor completely objective. And from Kant down
to Roman Ingarden, the Polish philosopher and aesthetician of our
time, we can find the same insight in the works of all great literary
theorists and critics: that despite the fact that a literary work must
initially achieve a concrete personal form, the critical act itself is
nevertheless by no means hopelessly subjective. As René Wellek
phrased it: "Criticism is personal but it aims to discover a structure of
determination in the object itself."[2]

The striving for exactitude and scholarly objectivity has repeatedly
led to the opposite extreme of arbitrary subjectivity, that is, to either
frozen absolutism or the exclusion of all criticism and to a limitation
of literary studies to ordering and establishing textual evidence and
the external circumstances of literary history. Although a rather extreme form of factual positivism and a concomitant endeavor to emu-
late the methods of natural sciences reached a peak in the nineteenth

century, the same dangers are implicit in some contemporary approaches to literary studies—especially those stressing the methods of mathematical statistics in the use of computers and of linguistics. There is no doubt, however, that extension of such methods to the extreme of total scientific explanation and "objectivity" would mean the death not only of criticism but also of any possibility for comprehending a work of art. One can argue, of course, whether Kant's approach leaves too much to subjectivity or whether the contemporary phenomenological approach provides a more satisfying theory; the fact remains that René Wellek's statement is still valid even if its word order is reversed. Criticism "aims to discover a structure of determination in the object itself," but is nevertheless inescapably "personal."

The personal qualities of criticism which emerge from the personality of the critic in its broadest sense have different aspects at various levels of the critic's tasks. Efforts have been made from various perspectives to develop these "subjective" starting points in a way that provides trans-subjective (i.e., objective) insights and results. The question of how and how precisely this personal approach can proceed then leads directly to the question of how precisely criticism itself can proceed.

There is no uniformity in literary theories about this procedure and even the process itself has been described in differing terms. Morton W. Bloomfield, for example, calls it the "existential" approach,[3] a term clearly implying the personal quality; Philip Wheelwright speaks of "authentic imagining,"[4] implicitly differentiating thereby his concept from arbitrary subjectivity; and although Georges Poulet speaks of "subjectivity," it is a subjectivity that is the personal "consciousness of the critic" coinciding with the consciousness of "the thinking or feeling person located in the heart of the text" in such a way that nothing remains of merely relative or arbitrary subjectivity. This "double consciousness appears less in its multiplicity of sensous relations with things, than prior to and separate from any object, as self-consciousness or pure consciousness."[5] Although these differences may represent differing aspects of the same central problem, they share as their common denominator an insight into the importance of the personal quality of criticism and the personality of the critic.

F. W. Bateson has laid the groundwork of a theory which shows how the interaction of scholarship and criticism—the latter involving the critic's personality—brings about interpretation as the central

activity of literary study. As opposed to the old linguistic cycle of
Saussure ("le circuit de la parole") Bateson calls his scheme the
"literary cycle."[6] He emphasizes the difference between these two
since literary interpretation must extend into prelinguistic and post-
linguistic origins, meanings, implications, and consequences of the
artifact, and in this respect he shares the view of Jean Paulhan that
there is no help to be expected for the central literary questions from
linguistics.[7]

Bateson's literary cycle delineates four steps in the process of creating a work of art out of the personality of the author. Step number
five is the completed text. The steps begin with "theme," of which
the author is only semiconscious, and proceed through "symbol," the
process of fusing image and concept, and "style," the level of personal verbalization in "repeats" of appropriate genre, to "language,"
which covers the conventions of vocabulary and grammar superim-
posed upon an often-muted inner speech. The outcome of this process
is step number five, the "text," the basis from which the reader and
particularly the specialized form of reader must begin. The circle
now closes as the critic takes exactly the same steps, only in reverse,
in order to recognize and to comprehend completely the implications
expressed in the text. Therefore, step number six represents the level
of "language," this time a concern with comprehending standard
meanings as they have been translated from inner speech. Step number seven stands for the level of "style" and involves the recognition
of genre and appropriate, if often unconscious, responses to "repeats."
Step number eight is the level of symbol and involves its deverbaliza-
tion. As Bateson points out: "'Illusion' is now creating its own aesthetic reality, which a reader can describe."[8] Finally, step number
nine corresponds to step number one in the creative process and
stands for the level on which the reader evaluates what he takes to be
the work's theme. Although Bateson does not point it out explicitly,
it is obvious that from steps six to nine the role of the critic's personality increases constantly and that the act of integration at step
number nine can be accomplished only in terms of the critic's (or
reader's) unique personality.

Bateson's literary cycle touches upon some very important problems of criticism in general, problems which reveal that involvement
of the critic's personality by no means requires reducing analysis and
interpretation to a superficial form of "biographism" or to merely
subjective and psychological experiences of essentially private nature. It tries instead, as Croce put it, to visualize the interaction and

identification between intuition and expression or, in Dilthey's terms, the "Strukturzusammenhang zwischen dem Erleben und dem Ausdruck des Erlebten."[9]

To what extent must the critic's insight be personal? What special epistomological problems does it create? Answers to these questions depend not only upon how one defines "personality" but also upon how deeply one carries the investigation. Closely connected with the function of the critic's personality ever since Schleiermacher has been the "philosophical circle" or "circle of understanding" which, in spite of its opposition to "impersonal" and purely scientific logic, has continually been employed in criticism and which, according to René Wellek, "Schleiermacher, Dilthey, and Leo Spitzer have taught us not to consider 'vicious'."[10]

One should perhaps also mention here two major contributions on epistemological problems of criticism, the first one coming from the Polish philosopher Roman Ingarden, the second one stemming from the American philosopher Philip Wheelwright, both former contributors to the *Yearbook of Comparative Criticism*.

According to Ingarden, the scholarly-critical comprehension of a literary work of art is a very complex act consisting of the interaction of three entirely different modes of understanding.[11] The first one he calls pre-aesthetic and observing comprehension; this covers the external collection of facts that lies prior to the comprehension of an aesthetic point of view. The second mode he terms the aesthetic experience: this constitutes the work as it is realized in the critic's mind and is by no means identical with the kind of "subjectivity" which accomplished "nothing for poetics."[12] Finally he refers to the third mode as the concretization of a literary work's value structure.[13] In this system, the second and third modes of cognition clearly involve the personality of the critic to a high degree.

According to Wheelwright "authentic imagining is far more than the play of fancy"[14] and there are no less than four different ways of imagining. Instead of turning to the usual psychological treatments, he deals rather with poetic expression. He distinguishes four main emphases whose subtle interrelation constitutes the literary work of art: the confrontative imagination, the stylistic imagination, the compositive imagination, and the archetypal imagination. Comprehension and analysis of a work of art must therefore be considered in steps which correspond to these four creative forces underlying poetic utterance. Again, at least the third and the fourth steps are decidedly beyond the reach of "scientific methods."

There are two basic modes of approaching and comprehending a literary work: one is more objective, scientific, and external; the other is more subjective, internal, and inseparable from the personality of the critic. In the full act of understanding, analyzing and evaluating a work of art is, of course, not through one form *or* the other; it is not the "scientific" approach *versus* the "existential," to use Bloomfield's terms; it is not the "pre-ästhetic comprehension" *versus* the "ästhetic experience," in Ingarden's terms; it is both together. As René Wellek once stated, the three branches of literary study—literary history, literary theory, and literary criticism—"implicate each other so thoroughly as to make inconceivable literary theory without criticism or history, or criticism without theory or history, or history without theory and criticism."[15] By the same token one can also conclude that the external collection of factual evidence, the scholarly knowledge of theoretical schemes and traditions, and the personal penetration of a given work of art implicate each other so thoroughly as to make any single field inconceivable without the remaining two. And one could perhaps go even farther and claim that in the merging or, more exactly, in the integration of the three forms of cognition, the most important role is played by the "subjective" quality of the critic's personality.

It is in the area of practical criticism, rather than literary theory, that the personality of the critic becomes most evident. It is hardly by accident that the greatest personalities in literary criticism had few immediate disciples—or bad ones. Nor was it accidental that it was quite often simply impossible to formulate the practical insights of a great critic—as for example those of Eduard Sievers about sound-analysis—as a workable systematic theory. Finally, it is for very good reasons that René Wellek is writing his great standard work on the history of criticism in a manner such that he deals with one critical personality after another; not only their practical critical results but also even their theories can be best described in terms of a certain unity shaped by their specific personal structure.

There are of course many more problems involved; the critic's personality has not only possibilities but also limitations. Of these limitations, the most frequent one is especially relevant in the case of great works of art. Kant has indicated that in some strange way such great works outgrow by far the intentions of their authors. They cannot be comprehended completely by any one critic, even one of the highest stature. These works seem to contain such wealth that a succession of changing perceptions of the work, extending over centuries, is needed for inclusive comprehension. This problem is then linked with another more general one, the fact that criticism as well as the body of world literature as a whole is anything but static. In the continuing flux of time while newer works are added to the canon of great literature older works and past knowledge are forgotten and lost, perhaps irretrievably.

The problem of the personality of the critic has many aspects: practical, theoretical, and historical. On the practical side, René Wellek deals with a concrete case. He shows how in the criticism of Walter Benjamin the personality of a great critic transcends any abstract ideological scheme, and why it would be equally ridiculous to claim that Benjamin was an "orthodox Marxist" or "counterrevolutionary and bourgeois." Murray Krieger also shows how even when the critic is dealing with theoretical aspects his personality remains the powerful, primitive force behind all he can do. Eugene Falk and John Fizer take up the theoretical aspects of the personality of the critic, both of them (not by accident) concentrating on phenomenological ideas, circling around the ideas of Husserl and Ingarden. The historical aspect is treated at least to some extent in Hans Rudnik's article about Kant's criticism of judgment from which a tradition comes down to our present time. There are unfortunately no essays in this volume about equally important traditions like the Cartesian one or the Coleridgian one. More important, however, seem the connections between the critic's personality and his evaluation of literary works as pointed out by Paul Ramsay.

There is one more important part of the problem to be covered. As the most universal and greatest literary critic of our time, René Wellek, has pointed out several years ago, it would be ideal if we could include the Orient and if we could create a literary theory based not only on Western literatures but also on Eastern literatures which developed completely independently of the West.[16] Such an inclusion assumes special importance if the problem of the critic's personality is to be discussed, because of widespread belief in an East-West dichotomy: that the importance of individual values and personality is a purely Western quality, and that the East emphasizes only anonymous, collective values and ideals. The contributions of Annemarie Schimmel about Mideastern literature, of Adele Rickett about Chinese literature, and of Toshihiko and Toyo Izutsu about the Japanese haiku and its master Basho prove this belief to be simply a prejudice. They accomplish even more: they show how in Eastern literary criticism and theory some aspects of the critic's personality become visible which in the Eastern traditions easily can be overlooked or not discovered at all.

In spite of the broad scope of the present collection of essays and in spite of the excellence of some of them this volume again is incomplete, not only in the sense in which any book of this kind is imperfect. It is also incomplete because some of the articles originally promised did not arrive at all. Professor Stephen R. Pepper, a former contributor to the *Yearbook*, died during the work on his essay and most regretfully I had to leave out the article of this great American aesthetician. An essay dealing with ancient Greek and Roman aspects of the problem and another one about French literary criticism did not arrive in time and could not be included. There is hope, however, that one of these contributions will fit into the next volume of the *Yearbook, Literary Criticism and Psychology*.

I should like to express my thanks to Dr. John Spalek, my chairman at the State University of New York at Albany, whose understanding for my many obligations in editing and writing is the presupposition for the existence of this *Yearbook*. In addition, I have to thank the Committee on Institutional Funds of my university and especially its chairman, Vice President Louis R. Salkever, for their continuing support.

JOSEPH P. STRELKA

Notes

1. For more on Dilthey and the development of the term "Erlebnis" in German criticism, see Charlotte Bühler: "Der Erlebnisbegriff in der modernen Kunstwissenschaft," in *Vom Geiste neueren Literaturforschung, Festschrift für Oskar Walzel*, ed. J. Wahle and V. Klemperer (Wildpark-Potsdam, 1924), pp. 195–209. J.A. Richards expressed this in his classic study *Principles of Literary Criticism* (London, 1924), pp. 120, 251.
2. René Wellek, *Discriminations* (New Haven and London, 1971), p. 128.
3. Morton W. Bloomfield, ed., *In Search of Literary Theory* (Ithaca, New York, and London, 1972), p. 84.
4. Philip Wheelwright, *The Burning Fountain* (Bloomington and London, 1968), p. 32.

5. Georges Poulet in a letter to J. Hillis Miller, quoted in *The Quest for Imagination*, ed. O.B. Hardison, Jr. (Cleveland and London, 1971), p. 210.
6. F.W. Bateson, *The Scholar-Critic* (London, 1972), pp. 101–110.
7. Jean Paulhan, *Clef de la Poésie* (Paris, 1944), "argument II." Cf. F.W. Bateson, "Linguistics and Literary Criticism," in *The Disciplines of Criticism*, ed. Peter Demetz, Thomas Greene, and Lowry Nelson, Jr. (New Haven and London, 1968), pp. 3–16.
8. *The Scholar-Critic*, p. 106.
9. Wilhelm Dilthey, *Das Erlebnis und die Dichtung* (Leipzig, 1907), p. 218.
10. *Discriminations*, p. 252.
11. *O Poznawaniu Dzie a Literackiego* (Lvov, 1937). An English translation is being prepared by Northwestern University Press.
12. *Discriminations*, p. 252.
13. Morton W. Bloomfield also speaks briefly of a threefold act of cognition: *In Search of Literary Theory*, p. 89.
14. *The Burning Fountain*, pp. 32–55.
15. René Wellek, *Conceptions of Criticism* (New Haven and London, 1965), p. 1.
16. René Wellek, "Einige Grundzüge der Literaturkritik," in *Kritiker unserer Zeit* (Vol. I), ed. Hans Mayer (Pfullingen, 1964), p. 44.

Eugene H. Falk

A CRITICAL STANCE

EVERY CRITICAL STANCE, BE IT THAT OF AN INDIVIDUAL CRITIC OR THAT OF
a more or less identifiable public, presupposes some concept of "beauty." It is therefore advisable that we realize what such a concept is
before we assign to it the role of a determinant of a critical stance. It
may suffice to state that beauty is a concept of variable value judgments which depend on the view of what a literary work is and on
the particular intellectual and emotional dispositions with which the
critic or the public perceives it.

We know, for instance, that an essential aspect of French classical
doctrine is based on the belief that there is a necessary relationship
between "nature" and the literary work. According to this doctrine
nature is the object which literature is supposed to imitate: literature
is an imitation of nature. For this imitation to be pleasing and pleas-
ingly useful in the broadest sense, definite and absolute criteria of
choice determining both the imitated object and the process of imitation had to be observed, for only thus could the beauty achieved
fit the evolving expectations of seventeenth-century French literary
taste. In the eighteenth century Marmontel made the important
distinction between the beauty which we may find in nature and the
beauty which is the result of art. This distinction was destined to
point out the independence of the beauty achieved by artistic means
from the nature of the object of imitation itself, an independence
which is particularly striking in a nonimitative, nonrepresentational
art form.

Further, this distinction had the considerable merit of ultimately
deflecting aesthetic perception and appreciation from verisimilitude,
i.e., from the search of correlations between the object of imitation
and its artistic representation, and of directing aesthetic apprehen-

sion to the artistic means by which intrinsic correlations within the work of art itself are manifested.

About half a century earlier, towards the end of the famous *Querelle* between the ancients and the moderns, the abbé Dubos maintained that beauty was exclusively the result of our thoughts and conceptions. Aware of the newly emerging notions of the relativity of taste, of the belief that time and place dictate man's predilections and aversions, he concluded that man will at all times produce varying concepts of beauty and hence a variety of critical judgments with regard to one and the same work of art. This view largely prevailed in the past and has been frequently held to this day.

As long as this view determines aesthetic vision and thus the criteria of literary evaluation, it remains concerned less with essential—and therefore timeless—qualities of art, and more with the prevailing tastes of critics. Such an aesthetic vision tells us more about the view of life, the values, the preoccupations, or the idiosyncrasies of the critic at a given time, and less about the essential mode of being of the work of art. Thus the work serves to reveal social and personal views, values, and tastes, instead of being the focal point of a critical exploration of its inner structure and of the world determined by that structure.

We noted initially that for the French classicists literature was at first considered to be an imitation of nature and that, for it to be pleasing and edifying (in the sense of Horace's *dulce et utile*), both the subject-matter and the execution had to satisfy standards of beauty that were considered absolute. However, the criteria for what was perceived as beautiful were actually formulated in large measure by conventions dictated by the increasingly pervasive and dominant taste of a social and intellectual elite.

In retrospect it seems almost natural that by the beginning of the eighteenth century the rules determining the criteria of beauty should no longer have been considered absolute, dictated as they were by more or less intuited "proprieties" imposed by taste which critics helped to create and to defend. It became evident, then, that the choice of the subject-matter as well as of the manner of execution already presupposed a certain cultivated notion of beauty.

Although Marmontel made the distinction between the beauty (or lack of it) in subject-matter itself and that in the artistic form, which was independent of the content, he yet focused his attention first and foremost upon the natural beauty of the subject-matter and upon its impact on our emotions, while relegating to a secondary level of importance the beauty that lay in variety within unity, in harmonious proportions of parts fused into a cohesive whole. Furthermore, he seemed to assume that the natural beauty of force and grandeur had universal appeal unaffected by fluctuations in taste, and failed to appreciate the insights of the abbé Dubos, who denied the universality of any aesthetic appeal and taught that all experience of beauty was the result of an activity of the mind, governed by taste, and not of a direct impact on our emotions.

The abbé Dubos and Marmontel—at least as far as form was concerned—shared in principle the view that beauty was the result of a projection of the mind, yet for different reasons both failed to perceive the implications of this insight. For the abbé Dubos, who denied any existence of beauty in nature, that projection was not an activity of "pure consciousness"—a concept he could not have known —but of a consciousness molded by prevailing tastes. For Marmontel, beauty was either the result of an accomplishment of the mind, or an existentially independent phenomenon perceived as a result of its impact on us—beauty perceived not because of what it is, but rather by virtue of the effects it has on our dispositions. Regardless of whether these dispositions are universal and immutable or whether they are relative, no phenomenon is identical with its effects and hence cannot be so defined.

There is an interesting affinity between these views and those expressed by T.S. Eliot in his *Essays Ancient and Modern*. His statement there recalls the judgment of Solomon, for while he admits that literary standards must be used to determine whether literature is literature, they cannot suffice to see and measure its "greatness." It is of course that "otherness" which is conceived of as the *utile*, whereas the artistic form is the *dulce*.

If this is the critic's stance toward literature (as it has often been, for centuries), then it must be conceded that a work—in the ideas it contains, its materials themselves, or both—will be found edifying only if the critic's intellectual and emotional attitudes predispose him to such a response. He must in his views, his sensibilities, and his tastes—all of which he brings to the perception of the work—be sympathetic to the particular edification it offers, and he will judge its greatness by the extent to which it coincides with his particular notions of greatness. This means that works will have to be reevaluated with each change in taste. It also means that certain works will lose their "relevance" in spite of the critic's sense of historical perspective.

In all these considerations the personality of the critic towers over the work. Since the critic faces his task not only with necessary historical knowledge, but also and especially with his conditioned view of life, emotions, and tastes, his experience of the work is always colored by them. It would be belaboring the obvious to list the great works of literature whose early reception was characterized by misconceptions originating in just such a stance, or to enumerate the even longer list of "great" works which, though best-sellers on publication, are soon thereafter condemned to oblivion. The critic's taste, his emotional response, his edification based on his particular *Weltanschauung* and attitudes are not relevant criteria for the apprehension of a literary work of art if the subject-matter, the ideas, the message, and the structure are viewed and judged from preconceived notions to which the work is expected to correspond. The beauty of a work is indeed constituted by a projection of consciousness upon it, but this constitution is not to be understood as an identification of aspects of the work with what is already in our consciousness. On the contrary, this constitution is a discovery within our consciousness of uniquely structured patterns of meanings in the work regardless of the edifying impact provided by the subject-matter and regardless of the degree to which the represented materials imitate the reality of "nature."

Many a novel in this century shows a marked disregard for whatever appeal subject-matter itself may have for the reader. It seems as if some authors intend to foster the public's indifference to materials in order to draw attention to composition itself. Some aspects of French impressionist painting (and the more recent abstract art) reveal a similar trend. Regardless of what the immediate historical reasons may have been, it is possible to trace a development that leads away from clearly representational to relatively nonrepresentational paintings in which the subject-matter is underemphasized to such a degree that contours are submerged in mist or shadows, or in a profusion of color.

This trend reveals on the one hand a concern to deflect our inclination to correlate the world within the work of art with that of the exterior world, and on the other hand an even greater concern to deflect our interest from represented subject-matter and to channel it towards the meanings of the materials and towards an appreciation of the manner in which composition itself contributes to meanings which the structured materials carry, as clearly demonstrated in some of Butor's and Robbe-Grillet's novels. Some authors go so far in this endeavor as to distort the materials in such a way that no effort at discovering consistent, or sometimes even conceivable, correlations with external reality could prove successful, as for instance in Kafka.

The most important effect of such artistic devices is, however, not only the induced deflection from our habitual concern with imitation and recognition, and thus from our primarily emotional involvement in the events described in the work, but also the relative suspension of our propensity to approach the work with views, attitudes, and emotions conditioned by the real world of our daily lives. Even the sequential and causal coherences of incidents are often disrupted so as to break the familiarity derived from our life-experience of dealing conceptually with disconnected and often chaotic agglomerations of perceptions that challenge our consciousness when it encounters them. It seems as if we were being urged by such novels to abandon the accustomed, traditional, and deeply ingrained modes of apprehension in order to free our thought processes and our responses so that we may focus, without any prejudgment of taste, without the bias of established views, and without the expectations of our own emotional needs, on the perception and apprehension of that which is presented to us, to see it as it gives itself before it can trigger an immediate emotional response. Our predispositions are thus anaesthetized by sometimes banal, sometimes improbable incidents so that our pure consciousness may reach out to a vision, not of the materials themselves, but to the manner in which they are structured into the world of multiple interrelationships within the harmonious unity of a whole. Thus we may open up to the essential meanings carried by the materials in their own context.

These meanings can elicit in us a special, even an emotional, response which stems from the recognition of our humanity rather than from a feeling of individuality, particularity, and privacy within which our personal tastes and views are nurtured, and from the perspective of which we hastily approve or disapprove of whatever we encounter depending on whether we sense intimate relevance or pleasure. It is in essential meanings that we discover the enticing quality of the materially improbable tale of *Oedipus Rex* or in Kafka's *Trial*, where no identification on the material level is possible and where we are immediately forced into an apprehension of what is essential and timeless in the situations, incidents, and attitudes without being bogged down in the materiality, the "existential base" of such works. These are the lessons great art has to offer for the critic of our time.

We have gained here a vantage point from which the earlier views may be judged in clearer perspective. The abbé Dubos, considering his own vantage point, could not help but claim that tastes change and that beauty, which he saw only as a quality that accords with an ephemerally prevailing taste, is therefore relative. He was right in claiming that beauty was a purely human concept, but all he could see was that it was a concept dictated by transitory tastes. He did not see, nor could he have seen—as Descartes, who was just beginning to be more widely known at that time, did not see—that man could divest himself of the burden of acquired tastes and direct his pure consciousness towards essential structures and meanings. Marmontel almost succeeded in discovering how beauty may be constituted, yet he failed. His notion of "pure beauty" was still largely the result of an endeavor to break loose from the tradition of perceiving beauty in the perfect imitation of a sublime subject, by expanding the traditional concept of beauty—as Corneille had tried to do long before him—so that it encompasses in its range overwhelming, even terrifying, grandeur as well as the sublime. Finally, he failed also because he still believed that beauty was an experience of the emotional, sentient ego. *Mutatis mutandis*, Max Scheler may be considered as an heir of Marmontel's legacy.

The basic difference between Scheler and Husserl lies, it seems, in the manner in which these two thinkers conceive of the transcendental ego. Their similar yet differing concepts also underlie differing criteria of evaluation. In the juxtaposition of these concepts we may finally recognize by which particular aesthetic criteria modern literature and art seek to be grasped and ultimately appreciated.

At the risk of oversimplification it may be stated that various institutions such as law, religion, science, and history have systematized all objects—objects in the broadest sense of the word—in such a manner that we can hardly conceive of anything in its self-givenness. We approach all objects with some such system in mind, not only when we seek to answer as complex a question as what a thing is, but even when we ask questions pertaining to its manner of being. The ultimate and "normally" satisfactory answer leads us back to one or more particular systems, including the order established by causality. We operate within systems, in the terms of which we perceive, understand, and describe all objects without first seeking to ascertain their particular constitutive nature, and in some cases their very essence—that identity which makes an object what it is regardless of whatever changes it may undergo in the course of time or of its even ceasing to exist materially. If we wish to apprehend the "being" of an object, that which it essentially is and what it means by virtue of what it thus is, it is necessary to "bracket" all systems, to suspend them, so that an object may be *clarified* before it is *explained.* As a result of such bracketing the object is put back into what Husserl called the "life-world" upon which all systems are built. On this point there is general agreement among phenomenologists.

There is also agreement on another important point which pertains to the apprehending ego itself. The ego evolves within the systems which are already built, which it perpetuates, and to which it may contribute. The ego, then, is also in this world and thus conditioned by various and varying systems. It is inconceivable how it could fully fathom any object in the life-world if it were to remain encumbered by modes of thinking imposed by the systems under which it has evolved. For the ego to be free in its apprehension of the objects of the life-world, the ego must be "pure," free, unencumbered. Descartes' failure to recognize that led to Husserl's criticism of the great French thinker who after all did carry out the first phenomenological reduction, without, however, completing it. It is this failure which accounts for the lasting confusions or misconceptions mentioned earlier.

A basic disagreement among phenomenologists stems from the question of what sort of ego it is that is capable of a pure and direct encounter between the subject and the object. According to Husserl this ego is pure, unbiased consciousness whose essential function is to be a "constituting" consciousness, i.e., a consciousness capable of fathoming, by its essential activity, the constitutive nature and—wherever possible—the essential nature of the object encountered. For Scheler, however, the unencumbered ego is still an emotional, feeling ego.

This essay has, from the outset, dealt with the very problem of how conditioned and unexamined intellectual and emotional responses may affect our critical stance and determine our criteria and judgments. Obviously, there is no question here at all of denying emotions as moments (dependent parts) of pure consciousness. The important question, it seems to me, is to determine the particular relationship between on the one hand pure constitution, aiming at ascertaining the being of an object as well as the meaning of the object thus constituted, and on the other hand the emotional moment of consciousness. If the act of constitution is to occur as we have understood that act of constitution to occur, emotional responses must be assumed to have no part in the act of pure constitution at all; rather they *follow* the apprehension of the being and meaning of the object.

The situation is of course just the reverse if, instead of a constitution by an unencumbered ego, a worldly ego whose conditioned emotions govern his apprehension were to encounter an object. In this case criticism is based on the emotional impact of the incidents or descriptions, and of the ideas and emotions expressed in the work. It is of course the verisimilitude of characters, actions, and situations that makes immediate empathy possible, and it is exactly the spontaneous identification and the reliving of represented emotions that impair the quality of our aesthetic perception and may even preclude any application of aesthetic criteria, regardless of whether we respond positively or negatively to a work. To say that the greatness of literature cannot be judged solely by literary standards is tantamount to saying that literature is great only if it is also nonliterary. And this also means that its greatness depends not on what it is, but on its effects on our already nurtured sensitivity, which obviously varies with each individual and the particular forces that have conditioned him.

What modern more or less nonrepresentational literature and art can teach the critic is to see the mode of being of the material existential base of the text, instead of becoming involved in the materials themselves. This insight may then be also applied to works whose realism derives from verisimilitude. We can thus learn to bring into relief the structure of the literary work regardless of the enticing and gripping quality of its familiar this-worldly materials. We can thus enter the world created by the work without regard for the immediate "relevance" of its materials to our lived world, and see in the structured world of the work what we cannot see through the chaotic experience of our lived world: the essential features of life, those that remain identical, universal, and eternal whatever our existential bases happen to be. We can thus also apprehend the nature, the potential, and the adequacy of the materials as carriers of essential meanings and the significance they achieve by virtue of that function, regardless of how banal and insignificant they may appear in themselves when judged from the point of view of the turbulent, important, overwhelming, and moving experiences lived life may sometimes have to offer. These experiences however, cannot offer essential insights, exactly because the lived experience precludes the distanced apprehension of essential meanings.

No attempt has been made here to come to grips with problems of evaluation. The focus of attention was the stance that is the prerequisite for aesthetic insights without which aesthetic judgments cannot be made.

John Fizer

THE CONCEPT OF STRATA AND PHASES IN ROMAN INGARDEN'S THEORY OF LITERARY STRUCTURE

I

FOR REASONS WHICH ARE HARD TO COMPREHEND, ROMAN INGARDEN'S aesthetics, one of the most sophisticated attempts of our time to conceive artistic structure in terms of its constitutive components, has as yet not been accorded sufficient attention. His principal work, *Das literarische Kunstwerk*, is unavailable in the other major European languages, and his incisive observations are still treated merely as intellectual marginalia. Among the few literary scholars and philosophers familiar with Ingarden's aesthetics, René Wellek[1] and Anna-Teresa Tymieniecka[2] in their respective works viewed Ingarden's concept of strata and phases with a great deal of discernment and acquiescence.[3] Yet, in spite of this, Ingarden's theory still remains relatively unknown.[4] For this reason, instead of studying some of its aspects in depth, I want to review it as a whole.

In his two principal works in aesthetics, *Das literarische Kunstwerk* and *Vom Erkennen des literarischen Kunstwerks*, Roman Ingarden dealt a great deal with an aesthetic process which he called "concretion," whereby the perceiver of literary art expands, alters, or elaborates the skeleton of literary art and thus renders it existentially viable. In my rendering of Ingarden's theory, I am afraid that because of its complexity and some inconclusiveness,[5] I may offer too many concretions and not enough presentation of it. However, I will try to do my best to curtail any excessive interpretations of my own. Before speaking of Ingarden's theory of literary structure and phases, a few words are in order about the conceptual framework in which his theory was conceived. As is generally known, Roman Ingarden was a student and, in the field of aesthetics, the most prolific exponent of Edmund Husserl's phenomenology. Hence, Ingarden's aesthetics as well as his accomplishments in other branches of philosophy (epistemology, ontology, axiology, logic) were treated phenomenologically. To describe this framework in a word or two without oversimplifying it is not an easy task, especially since, as J. J. Kockelmans observes, "anyone familiar with the situation knows that as soon as he uses the term 'phenomenology' he enters a sphere of ambiguity."[6]

At the risk of oversimplification, I nevertheless dare to say the following: In his endeavor to make philosophy a rigorous science[7] Husserl wanted to attain absolutely valid knowledge of things. He believed that in one's confrontation with reality, only phenomena are given and that in these phenomena is given the very essence of that which is. Therefore, if one has described phenomena thoroughly and adequately, one has described all that can be described. In the constancy of this description one reveals the essence of what is described. This description, however, is predicated upon a reduction of things to their invariable, immutable essence. It is only in such a bare confrontation with objects and reality in general that one is capable of getting to their very essences. Hence, there are two such reductions: a) the eidetic and b) the phenomenological. In the first, one proceeds from the realm of facts to general essences, and in the second from the world of realities to their ultimate presuppositions. In the eidetic reduction, the so-called *époché*, one frees the object of perception from all its temporal factuality until one arrives at its immutable, constant components, without which it cannot be conceived. This immutable and unique *eidos* then constitutes the essence of the thing itself. In the phenomenological reduction the attention is turned to the *cogito* rather than to the *cogitatum*, i.e., to the perceiving subject rather than to the object of perception. How this reduction, which is to lead us from the phenomenal "I" to transcendental subjectivity, is to be accomplished is not clear to many students of Husserl. In brief, to use Tymieniecka's apt formulation, Husserl's method "consists of suspending successively certain of the natural, customary aspects and components of our cognition. . . . Thus transformation of our

cognitive attitude from the *natural*—providing only confused, uncertain cognition—to the 'reflexive attitude' (in Husserl's view) opens
the field of *apodictically* certain knowledge."[8]

In what way and to what degree did Ingarden adhere to Husserl's
phenomenology and to what extent did he apply it to his description
of literary structure? Had there been uniformity of views on what
precisely constitutes Husserl's phenomenology,[10] such a question
could be resolved without too much controversy. Such being the case,
it is no wonder that Ingarden himself in his works apologizes on many
occasions for not being certain whether he interprets Husserl correctly. Husserl also stated in a letter to Ingarden dated August 19,
1932: "Versuchen Sie zu verstehen, warum ich immerfort sagen kann,
dass Sie den tieferen Sinn der konstitutiven Phänomenologie nicht
verstanden haben und warum das kein Vorwurf ist, weil den Nie-
mand meiner alten Schule verstand. Es liegt nicht an dem Fehler
der konkreten Untersuchungen. Darin sind Sie selbst weiter als die
Meisten. Aber alle intentionalen Analysen sind in der ersten Stufe der
Phänomenologie doppeldeutig."[11] One thing we are certain of is that
Ingarden, in his works on epistemology and ontology and particularly
in his *The Controversy over the Existence of the World* (*Spór o ist-
nienie świata*), rejected Husserl's transcendental idealism. If I understand this concept correctly, Husserl posited by it that objects,
events, actions, or what have you, are what they are irrespective of
whether or not they are. As J. Q. Lauer observed, according to this
concept "it is possible to know what something is without any reference at all to whether it is or not"—or that the "sense of things, their
signification, is not to be found in a contingent world of things independently of consciousness; it is to be found precisely in consciousness itself where admittedly significance is concentrated."[12]

It is on this focal point of epistemology that Ingarden differs radically from Husserl. Not all reality or, to use Ingarden's term, not all
moments of being are contingent upon consciousness. According to
Ingarden there are four distinct modes of being, of which only one is
purely intentional and hence contingent upon consciousness. The
four modes are: 1) absolute or timeless being, which is characterized
by such existential moments as self-existence, originality, actuality,
fissuration, persistence, separateness, and self-dependence; 2) extra-
temporal being, which is defined by such moments as autonomy, originality, nonactuality, separateness or inseparateness, self-dependence
or contingency; 3) temporal being, which is defined by such moments as autonomy, derivative actuality, fissuration, fragility, self-

dependence or contingency, postactuality, retrospective derivation, heteronomy, empirical possibility; 4) purely intentional being, which is defined by heteronomy, derivation, nonactuality, separateness or inseparateness, and contingency. Of these four categories, the one of greatest interest for the understanding of literary art is the fourth category. Objects in the fourth category, being purely intentional, do not possess an essence of their own as Husserl maintained in his *Ideas*. Ingarden states:

> All their material determination, formal moments, and even their existential moments, which appear in their contents, are in some way only ascribed to purely intentional objects, but they are not embodied in them, in the strict meaning of this word. For example, if, in a poetic vein, we invent some character who is supposed to have such and such properties, to live here and there and to do thus and so, we pretend that this is, among other things, an object that "really exists," and we ascribe reality to it. But all these properties, this manner of behaving, this reality, etc., are only fancied, or invested in this (character) by the text. This strong young man, poetically conceived, is not really (in the sense of being existentially autonomous) young, really strong—he is not "actually" a man. He is only "represented" to be. We attribute something to him which he cannot himself do. . . , for he does not contain *any* immanent competence. His reality is also only ascribed to him, and is ultimately conferred by an act of will and of poetic imagination. Creative imagination has only the effect of investing an intentional object with a certain kind of *habitus* of reality and of *evoking an illusion of it*, and likewise with respect to his youth, strength, manhood, etc. . . . . In other words, a creative poetic act cannot create a self-existent object. It is "impotently creative." What it creates lives by its grace and its support, and cannot become something "spontaneous, independent, autonomous." If it may be so expressed, it cannot "rebel" against the acts of consciousness that produced it, it cannot have any other properties in its contents, any other identity, arbitrarily chosen, *but those* which have been ascribed to it. It does not have its own existential foundation in itself. Its existential foundation is in the conscious act that produced it intentionally, or, more exactly, in the psychic subject who performed the act.[13]

In brief, all purely intentional beings, and in our case all poetically conceived objects, are contingent upon the intending consciousness. It seems that this definition of purely intentional being proves that Ingarden deviated substantially from Husserl's transcendental idealism.

All in all, Ingarden accepted Husserl's basic analytical results and phenomenological method but remained skeptical about his transcendental idealism. Unlike many followers of Husserl who interpreted his phenomenology as a special version of idealism, Ingarden used it in a realistic exploration of *eidos*. In his introduction to *Das literarische Kunstwerk* he described his disagreement with Husserl in this way:

> Meine Ausführungen stimmen mit den Husserlschen in der "formalen und transzendentalen Logik" in der Ansicht überein, dass die Wortbedeutungen, Sätze und höhere Sinneinheiten Gebilde sind, die aus den subjektiven Bewusstseinsoperationen hervorgehen. Sie sind also keine idealen Gegenständlichkeiten in dem Sinne, wie sie Husserl selbst in seinen "logischen Untersuchungen" bestimmt hat. Während aber Husserl den Terminus "ideal" an den meisten Stellen seiner "Logik" beibehält und nur manchmal in der Parenthese das Wort "irreal" hinzufügt, verzichte ich ganz auf diese Benennung und suche diese Gebilde der idealen Gegenständlichkeiten in strengem Sinne scharf gegenüberzustellen. Darin zeigt sich die erste sachliche Differenz: Husserl hält jetzt alle, ehemals für ideal—in dem alten Sinne—gehaltenen Gegenständlichkeiten für intentionale Gebilde besonderer Art und gelangt dadurch zu einer universellen Erweiterung des transzendentalen Idealismus, während ich heute die strenge Idealität verschiedener idealen Gegenständlichkeiten (der idealen Begriffe, idealen individuellen Gegenstände, Ideen und Wesenheiten) aufrecht erhalten und sogar in den idealen Begriffen ein ontisches Fundament der Wortbedeutungen sehe, das ihnen ihre introsubjektive Idealität und seinsheteronime Seinsweise ermöglicht.[14]

II

Ingarden's application of the phenomenological method to literature is attested to by the fact that in his intensive exploration of literary art he bracketed or eliminated from the object of his investigation that factuality which was not essential for its description. I have in mind that complex sociopsychological context in which literature and, for this reason, any art supposedly originate. On that factuality Ingarden performed the methodological *époché*, i.e., put it in brackets and thus suspended its relevance to the thing itself. For this reason also Ingarden was opposed to Marxist, psychologistic, psychoanalytic, mythical, and existential criticism. Even stylistic criticism (*Stilforschung*), which elevates its method almost to a concept, was unsatisfactory for Ingarden. It was for this reason that, although one encounters in his two principal works myriad references to Walzel, Vossler, Spitzer, and other representatives of this criticism, Ingarden attempts to remain free from any theoretical bias which could sway him from a direct confrontation with his subject matter or limit his vision of the

totality of artistic "givenness." That he was fully aware of this trend
could be seen from the following observation:

Diese Diskussionen waren im allgemeinen wenig ergiebig, weil sie
sich oft auf die Verteidigung der einen Methode beschränkten. Man
diskutierte über die Methoden der Forschung oder der "Kritik," ohne
sich überhaupt die Frage gestellt zu haben: einerseits, wie das gebaut
ist, was untersucht bzw. erkannt werden soll, d.h. das literarische
Kunstwerk selbst, andererseits, worin die Verfahrensweise, die zur
Erkenntnis des literarischen Kunstwerks führen soll, besteht, d.h. wie
das Erkennen dieses Kunstwerks vor sich geht und wozu es führt,
bzw. führen kann.[15]

In order to arrive at an objective knowledge of literary art, one
must, according to Ingarden, clearly distinguish between two separate areas of intellectual concern: pre-aesthetic and aesthetic. The
pre-aesthetic area involves rigorous intellectual preoccupation with
those structural elements that constitute the skeleton of the artistic
work or, as Ingarden states, "welche den Grund für die Konstituierung der ästhetisch relevanten Qualitäten in den ästhetischen Konkretisationen bilden" and which ". . . von den Wandlungen un-
abhängig sind."[16] The aesthetic area of concern relates to those
relevant addenda to the structural skeleton through which the skeleton is concretized or actualized.

Structural strata and time phases as issues of scholarly analysis
belong to the first area of concern. Although these strata and phases
are also discernible in the aesthetic concretions, they can be delineated and described with greater precision as artistic rather than aesthetic issues. The purpose of conceiving the artistic whole, the artistic
polyphony, in terms of its structural components, i.e., strata and
phases, is to arrive at the "Wesensanatomie" of the literary work itself, which in turn opens the way for its aesthetic treatment.[17]

In all literary works we distinguish at least four structural strata:[18]
1) the stratum of the language sound patterns (*die Schicht der sprach-
lichen Lautgebilde*); 2) the stratum of the unified meanings (*die
Schicht der Bedeutungseinheiten*); 3) the stratum of presented objectifications (*die Schicht der dargestellten Gegenständlichkeiten*);
and 4) the stratum of schematized aspects (*die Schicht der schematisierten Ansichten*). All these strata, as far as their eidetic specificity
is concerned, are distinct from each other. At the same time they are
components of an organic structure in whose unity alone they can be
actualized. This type of literary structure precludes the following
issues: 1) the author and his biographical, psychological data and ex-

periences, even though the literary work under scrutiny might originate in them; 2) the irrelevant emotional or intellectual projections
or identifications that readers have or might have while exposed to
literary art.

The first stratum contains three distinct elements: 1) individual
words, 2) sentences, 3) combinations of sentences. In the first case a
problem in point is the choice of words intended to express (*Aus-
drucksfunktion*), actualize (*Aktualisierung*), or both; in the second,
the rhythm, tempo, tone, and the manner of syntactical modeling on
which an endless variety of the so-called manifestative qualities
(*Manifestationsqualitäten*) depend; and in the third, the varying
and various types of verbal polyphonies (genres, styles, trends, and
the like).[19]

The polyphony of this stratum is of utmost importance since its
suspension entails various alterations in the structure as a whole.
"Reading literature," Ingarden observes, "in its graphic form is connected with some changes in its general structure as well as in the
character of the reader's perception." Hence, "strictly speaking, a
work read aloud achieves the fullness of its devices."[20] The structural
relevance, i.e., the centrality of the marginality of this stratum, depends upon the intentional literary genre. In a work in which this
stratum is rhythmically organized, e.g., poetry, the verbal enunciation
is central to it. This stratum is completely replaced when it is translated into another language since its uniformity and constancy "permeated the longitudinal cross-section of the work itself."[21]

The second stratum (unity of meanings) in Ingarden's analysis is
a complex phenomenon, inasmuch as it involves "verschiedene Modi-
fizierungen ihres intentionalen Richtungsfaktor und ihres formalen
Inhalts—verschiedene *Modi* der Aktualität und Potentialität." The
verbal structure contains a series of factors which sway its meaning,
in one direction or in several directions. These factors are: 1) "der
intentionale Richtungsfaktor," 2) "der materiale Inhalt," 3) "der
formale Inhalt," 4) "das Moment der existentialen Charakterisie-
rung," and 5) "das Moment der existentialen Position." In brief, the
meaning is always multidimensional and always has a specificity of
its own. Being intentional, it cannot be general, typical, universal,
abstract. As a rule, it has a special and specific reference and in this
way deviates from an ideal model. At the same time, in order to be
recognized, it contains in its material and formal content those elements which do imply its generality or its universality. Thus, while
the meaning stratum "sich gerade auf diesen und auf keinen anderen

oder—in anderen Fällen—auf einen solchen Gegenstand bezieht," at the same time it does invoke qualities which transcend its specificity or individuality. Thus, unlike Husserl who conceived of meanings as ideal *speciei*, imbued in words, Ingarden thought of meanings as lent to words. As Tymieniecka defines it, "a meaning intentionally 'signifies' (symbolizes) an object, determining it materially and formally. This significance is rooted in the physical word, but it is not the property of the word. It is, in a way, 'lent to it' by the signifying act of consciousness; thus, it is not a physical entity. Neither is it identical with the individual act of consciousness; thus, the meaning is not psychic. Although it is brought about and sustained by an act of consciousness, it is *transcendent* to the act. The same meaning can be repeatedly concretized in new conscious acts. In spite of the alteration a meaning can undergo, it does not make a substantial part of our psychological acts of the stream of experience (in the sense of William James)."[22] This definition of meaning, which defies both idealistic and psychologistic positions, is of great significance to creative acts because it postulates infinite possibilities for them but at the same time emphasizes their identity as a basis for intersubjective communication. To further take advantage of Tymieniecka's interpretation of Ingarden's concept of meaning, "meanings are . . . created and can be modified by the conscious act of the one who conceives them, intentionally 'lending' identical context to them, while in the concretions the performer or spectator incorporates them into his actual experience."[23]

This approach to the "Bedeutungseinheiten" in literary art differs from that of many scholars, both in concept and in extenso. In concept it differs in that it does not relegate meaning to some mysterious, everfluctuating "inner form," as was the case with the neo-Platonic theories of Winckelmann, Goethe, Wilhelm von Humboldt, or Alexander Potebnia, to name only a few. Nor does it posit an empirically verifiable reference, as was the case with the positivists, the neopositivists, and the Marxists. In extenso it differs in that it conceives of meaning multidimensionally (verschiedene *Modi*), distributed between the aesthetic *variables* and formal *constants*.[24]

The stratum of the objectifications (*Gegenständlichkeiten*) embraces things; persons; all possible and impossible, potentially plausible, or fantastic events or occurrences; situations; personal acts; and the like. All such objects, irrespective of whether they have correlates in reality (*Realitätshabitus*) or lack such correlates, are purely intentional. Thus such objects are presented or conveyed (*dargestellt*) by quasistatements (*quasi-urteilsmässigen Charakter der Behaup-tungssätze*)[25] rather than by logically and scientifically valid statements. These quasistatements are valid within the limits of the work in which they exist. Of course, there is always a possibility that some of them do or might transcend their literary context and become universal judgments. This is especially true of works which are not pure fiction and which deliberately aim at establishing thematic proximity with some extraliterary reality. There are also instances when logically and objectively valid judgments must be reproduced and used along with quasistatements. For example, when a mathematician in a work of art explains some mathematical theorem, he, being an intentional object, is presented by quasijudgments, but his theorem, in order to retain believability, must be reproduced as an ideal object.

Literary objectifications have their own temporal and spatial dimensions. The time and space in which these objects exist mathematically and geometrically are not objective; they depend upon what Ingarden calls *Orientierungszentrum*.[26] This center could be the author-narrator or any protagonist or protagonists who stand at the focus of the literary work and through whose eyes we perceive the temporal sequence and spatial arrangement of the presented objects. Take, for example, in Tolstoy's celebrated novel of the same title, the death of Anna Karenina. The objective time in which her suicide could have occurred would have lasted a few minutes. However, the time determined by the *Orientierungszentrum* in the novel, that is by Tolstoy as the narrator, lasted immeasurably longer. Here is the description of her death:

> She wanted to fall half-way between the wheels of the front truck which was drawing level with her. But the red bag which she began to pull from her arm delayed her, and it was too late: the truck had passed. She must wait for the next. A sensation similar to the feeling she always had when bathing, before she took the first plunge, seized her and she crossed herself. The familiar gesture brought back a whole series of memories of when she was a girl, and of her childhood, and suddenly the darkness that had enveloped everything for her lifted and for an instant life glowed before her with all its past joy. But she did not take her eyes off the wheels of the approaching second truck.

Although Tolstoy uses such words as "suddenly" and "for an instant," the reader cannot accommodate Anna's experiences of her girlhood and childhood in these expressions; he must extend them far beyond their meaning. Thus, while objectively indeed only an instant would have passed between the first and the second truck, subjectively for

Anna, and intersubjectively for us readers, a whole period of Anna's life has been evoked.[27]

In addition to being cast in a nonobjective time and space, literary objects have a great many undetermined places (*Unbestimmtheits-stellen*). Because of this, in comparison with real objects they are only schematized images (*schematische Gebilde*), which in artistic perception lend themselves to creative fulfillment (*Ausfüllung*) or a closer determination (*Näherbestimmung*). Without such undetermined spaces creative perception would be seriously curtailed. The schematization of objects emanates out of several sources: a) the limited or finite linguistic means which are at the disposal of the creator; b) the limited number of aspects (*Ansichten*) that he can have about the object; c) the creator's physical limitations to presenting the object in its totality; d) the existing aesthetic conventions as well as the writer's own aesthetic preferences which force him to conceive of objects in a schematized way.[28] The character of schematization also depends upon the genre, style, and artistic peculiarity of each individual literary work. While the determined places in literary art force our consciousness to form the proximity or affinity between the presented and imagined images, the undetermined places allow it to project into the presented images addenda of its own. Hence aesthetic concretions are never one-directional, i.e., never only identification or projection, but always both.

Finally, literary objects, much more than nonintentional objects, might be submerged in the metaphysical qualities, such as the sublime, tragic, terrible, shocking, inconceivable, demonic, holy, sinful, sorrowful, exciting, grotesque, etc.[29] These qualities "sind keine gegenständlichen Eigenschaften im gewöhnlichen Sinne, aber im allgemeinen auch keine Merkmale dieser oder jener psychischen Zustände, sondern sie offenbaren sich gewöhnlich in komplexen und oft untereinander sehr verschiedenen Situationen, Ereignissen, als eine spezifische Atmosphäre, die über den in diesen Situationen sich befindenden Menschen und Dingen schwebt und doch alles durchbringt und mit ihrem Lichte verklärt."[30]

The fourth stratum, that of aspects (*Ansichten*), "in respect to the mode of reading and the actualization of the work relatively possesses the greatest emotionality."[31] Hence, it is because of this stratum that literary art differs from nonliterary discourses. While scientific or scholarly presentations tend to conceive of these objects in abstracto, most of the literary presentations do it in concreto. The concreteness of objects in literature is achieved through aspects, i.e., through such visual, auditory, or kinesthetic imagery which emerges in our consciousness during our imaginary confrontations with intentional objects. A tree, for example, in a literary work is not given in terms of its scientific abstractions but in terms of its myriad aspects. It is these aspects which arouse in us the sensation of phenomenological tangibility. These aspects, occurring as fragmentary and incomplete images, are not given in a uniform and uninterrupted flow. As Ingarden stated, they occur *intermittando*.[32] This fact casts some doubt upon the theory of stream of consciousness as conceived by William James and as applied by James Joyce and other practitioners of the "stream of consciousness novels."[33] According to Ingarden, this stream contains many dry places and many deliberate stops.[34] While such a stream might be found in a noncreative state,[35] in a creative state, in which the *Orientierungszentrum* subordinates most of the psychic processes to certain goals, the existence of such a stream is highly problematical.[36]

Frequently aspects are given through the so-called duplicity or iridescence. Many a time, especially in poetry, an image is perceived through a juxtaposition of two aspects. Traditionally this juxtaposition or duplicity is called a metaphor or figure. The function of a metaphor is twofold: it operates in respect to the presented objects and to the presented aspects.

> In the first case the issue at hand is to endow the presented object, without using a special epithet, with a feature which the object of the figurative word usage *always* possesses . . . and does not always possess but in this case the object of expression which is being replaced by a word in a figurative sense must possess. As a result of this, the object in question is as if it were dressed in a given feature of that object which is being used indirectly for its definition. It is as if one object were making the other object translucent and thus acquired its most protruding features. This simultaneous presentation of two different but actually related objects (provided that in the final analysis only one of them is important and only that one arouses the reader's imagination) is precisely the thing that facilitates the actualization of aspects. And at the same time it helps the creation of the "iridescent aspect." In it, on the one hand one sees distinctly those components of an aspect which refer to an object of *direct* meaning of the word, and on the other hand those which refer to an object of the *figurative* meaning of the word. . . ."[37]

While the aspects of tangible reality (*äusseren Ansichten*) are relatively easy to present and to perceive, the aspects of psychic experiences are not.[38]

III

The problem of phases in literary works has received less attention from Ingarden than the problem of strata.[39] By "phases" Ingarden means the time sequence (*Aufeinanderfolge*) of the individual components of the literary work. In his opinion this sequence "darf nicht in dem gewöhnlichen Sinne verstanden werden, in welchem wir von der Aufeinanderfolge realer Ereignisse in der konkreten Zeit sprechen."[40] While events in actual time are rarely, and only on occasion conceived in a tripartite time dimension (past, present, future), literary events are seldom conceived one-dimensionally. Each phase (with the exception of the first), in addition to being grounded in itself, is grounded in the previous as well as in the subsequent phases. This phase interchangeability creates an internal dynamic (*innere Dynamik*) of the literary work and enhances its dramatic possibilities. Without this phase interchangeability the unfolding, the enlargement, and the completion of literary objects would be impossible. In artistic perception the tripartite time dimensionality relies upon the reader's memory retentiveness and his mental anticipations (Husserl's *Vergegenwärtigung*). While the memory retentiveness corresponds to or approximates previous phases, the mental anticipations do not on the whole necessarily correspond with the subsequent phases. It is for this reason that one must speak of two distinct phases of reading literary works, one during the reading and another after the reading (*die Phase während der Lektüre und die Phase nach der Lektüre*).[41] Since, however, time phases are, so to say, enmeshed in the structure of literary objects, once completed they become non-recurrent. They cannot be absolutely repeated. "Only a certain other process, identical in some respects, can occur after it as its repetition. Then, however, certain disparities are always involved."[42]

In short, one must distinguish two sets of time concepts in literary works—one in which the presented objects are given and one in which they are structurally arranged. While the first, because of the *Orientierungszentrum* discussed earlier, deviates considerably from empirical time and often disregards the conventional time sequences (flashbacks, the reverse order of time, time amplifications, slowing or quickening of the time tempo, alterations of present, past, and future), the time or phases of the structural arrangement of objects, although also subject to the author's and the reader's intentionality, depend upon the ontic position (*die ontische Stelle*) of the structural components of the literary work in question. In a word, the time of objects and the time of individual components of literary works are not necessarily the same.

IV

What are the practical feasibilities of Ingarden's concept of literary structure? Unfortunately, to date this concept has not been treated in its entirety. Ingarden himself, save for some illustrative purposes, did not put it into practice. In exploring literary art his purpose was philosophical rather than critical. In the introduction to *Das literarische Kunstwerk* we read: "So sehr aber meine Untersuchungen das literarische Werk bzw. Kunstwerk zum Hauptthema haben, sind die letzteren Motive, die mich zu der Bearbeitung dieses Themas bewogen haben, allgemein *philosophischer* Natur und gehen über dieses besondere Thema weit hinaus. Sie stehen mit dem Idealismus-Realismus, der mich seit Jahren beschäftigt, in engem Zusammenhang."[43]

Therefore, to answer our question properly, we should remind ourselves of the ontic character of literary art as Ingarden understood it. Unlike the followers of psychologism or of various versions of formalism, who correspondingly thought of literary art either as an exclusively psychic experience or as an exclusively physical object,[44] Ingarden proposed a more sophisticated definition of literary art. Being an intentional object and having both the creative act of its author and its own physical properties, the literary work is thus grounded in both ideal notions and ideal qualities and in word signs. It is between these two foci that the ontic basis of literary art is located. While its first focus transcends its sphere of influence (*Machtbereich*), it nevertheless forms the basis for its sentences and thus becomes the regulative principle of its structure.

This concept of the ontic position of literary art seems to open myriad new possibilities for the scholarly and aesthetic exploration of literary art. By not conceiving of it as exclusively psychological and hence as an extremely elusive phenomenon, or as exclusively physical and hence a quantitatively fixed phenomenon,[45] this concept justifies philosophical, structural, linguistic, comparative, and historical studies of literary art.

This ontic position of literary art relieves it from being logically, scientifically, or ethically apodictic. Thus defined, literature is not expected to have utilitarian solutions to man's social, political, and psychological predicaments and is not to be exploited for the advancement, elucidation, or confirmation of issues, causes, or problems which are not contained in it.[46] Should it, however, in addition to its quasijudgments, contain scientifically valid judgments, they should be treated as an extra stratum.[47] Briefly, Ingarden's concept of literary structure suggests that the stratum of sound patterns should be studied as having its own artistic raison d'être. Its morphological, syntactical precision or indefiniteness, its stylistic conventionality or unconventionality should be judged from the standpoint of its own polyphonic harmony rather than from the standpoint of the phonological conventions outside it. This stratum should be studied in the original and not in translation, paraphrase, summary, synopsis, or the like. The stratum of meaning, appearing on various levels (*Wortbedeutungen, Zusammenhänge von Sätzen, höhere Sinneinheiten*), could be studied in its progressive growth, from simple to complex or vice versa, or in its mode of progression: dynamic, light, lucid, heavy, ambiguous, or subordinate to one another. The stratum of objects, frequently thought of as central to literary art, offers many issues for analysis, such as the progressive or rapid emergence of an object, its relationship to other objects, its centrality or marginality, its metaphysical qualities, its open and hidden elements, and, above all, its schematic composition. The undetermined places in all four strata represent a very complex and fascinating problem in our study of literature. On the basis of this problem alone, one can study comparatively various authors, literary trends, and indeed literary epochs. By undertaking such a study one can see the difference between the literary schemata preferred, for example, in the baroque, neoclassic, or romantic period. The stratum of aspects can be studied from the standpoint of its constancy, alteration, interruption, appearance and disappearance, harmony, and contradiction, and finally its fusion into some sort of a superimage.

These possibilities within each literary work by no means exhaust the range of artistic issues. The issue of aesthetic concretion could also be a fascinating object of scholarly exploration. But while in the first set of issues one is relatively safe from the danger of psychologistic monism, in the second set of issues one is not. Ingarden writes:

Literary works may be concretized from principally different positions, for example, from the naive position of a simple consumer of literature, from the specifically ethical position, from the position of a man who has definite political or religious interests and who searches in artistic literature for propagandistic means, and finally from a purely research position favored (at least in definite stages of his work) by a literary scholar. In each of these cases one encounters different modes of completion of the indeterminate places, different modes of actualization of qualitative moments and aspects, and finally different modes of realization of phenomena and constructions of the sound stratum. Therefore, the corresponding concretions differ considerably from one another. But adhering to an aesthetic position, we favor only one of these different types and only this one answers the purpose of artistic literature.[48]

Finally, after a somewhat lengthy exposition of Ingarden's concept of strata and phases in the literary structure, let us look at the main quarry of this study: Ingarden's view of the role of the critic's personality in the realization of his scholarly objectives. Let us begin by observing that any criticism, whether it is highly conceptualized or loosely improvised—i.e., whether it operates from previously known premises or not—is contingent upon some sort of general idea that the critic has in regard to art as a whole. For an intentional evasion of such an idea by itself is tantamount to certain ontological predispositions toward literary fact which facilitate the adoption of specific epistemological categories. In this case, ontic "nothingness," in the same way as its positive counterpart, calls for specific modes of perception, validation, and evaluation which in turn greatly predicate the ensuing judgments on an object of inquiry. Otherwise, if in the intellectual process which precedes the purely sensational processes "nothingness" were indeed tautological with itself, epistemologically it would have to remain unproductive. However, "nothingness" which produces something must ipso facto be something.

In the history of criticism there have been many critics and scholars who claimed no ontological predispositions of any sort toward literary art and who thought to conceive it through some sort of "intellectual innocence." Yet the very moment they began dealing with it, this "innocence" or "ontological nothingness" turned into "ontological somethingness," which in turn precipitated a set of specific modes of critical inquiry. Roman Ingarden, as his views on strata indicate, held a well-defined position as to the role of theoretical coordinates in criticism.[49] In turn, this position had a determinate effect upon his method of research and analysis. Consequently, he knew not only what to expect from criticism but also how to go about it. Unlike many theorists of literature whose theories and criticism often resulted in an insoluble dichotomy, Ingarden consistently did what he postulated. Hence his general propositions and his critical evaluations are highly integrated.

What, specifically, was this position? Since Ingarden's critical epistemology is dependent upon his view concerning the ontic nature of literary art, let us recapitulate this view. Unlike the psychologistically or formalistically oriented critics who correspondingly thought of literature either as a psychological datum or as a physical construct,[50] Ingarden conceived of it as a purely intentional phenomenon.[51] Although this phenomenon originates in the consciousness of its creator, who alone determines its structural identity, this phenomenon upon its completion begins to exist in its verbal signs (*Wortzeichen*) and in its corresponding ideal notions and qualities (*ideale Begriffe und Qualitäten*), as well as in its aesthetic concretizations. These notions and qualities do not form the empirical part (*Bestandteil*) of the work's structure; they transcend it. At the same time, however, these notions constitute the foundation of the work's being (*Seinsfundament*) and the work's regulative principle. They ontologically support it. Without them the work would be incapable of "living" aesthetically and of assuming an intersubjective significance.

> Gäbe es keine idealen Begriffe und weiterhin auch keine idealen Qualitäten (Wesenheiten) und Ideen, so wären nicht bloss die Sätze, bzw. die realen und intentionalen Gegenständlichkeiten unmöglich, sondern es wäre zugleich unmöglich, eine echte sprachliche Verständigung zwischen zwei Bewusstseinssubjekten, in welchen von beiden Seiten der identische Sinngehalt des Satzes erfasst wird, zu erlangen.[52]

In terms of its empirical datum, a literary work is "ein ganz starres Gebilde, das in dieser Starrheit auch hinsichtlich seiner Identität völlig gesichert wäre."[53] This "starres Gebilde," or perfectly organized lexical minimum, is endowed with readiness (*Parathaltung*) to evoke or suggest its corresponding semantic maximum. Although this skeleton is not immanently determined in itself, it nevertheless has its temporal and spatial permanence. Therefore, neither readers nor critics invent its heteronomous existence or provide it with what it already possesses. That heteronomy, irrespective of the critics' particular intention or the work's mode of being, lies outside their invention. They can discover it and endow it with adequate aesthetic addenda or they can falsify it by ascribing to it inadequate addenda. But in neither of these cases do they resolve or dissolve the structural identity of the literary work. It is "something which transcends the sphere of our experiences and their contents, it is something completely transcendent in relation to ourselves."[54]

This view of the ontic nature of the literary work, as was to be expected, predicates well-formulated literary criticism, scholarship, or even ordinary reading (*die schlichte Lektüre*) as well as a special emotional attitude toward the literary fact. In other words, it demands a distinct pattern of the critic's behavior, a special organization of his cognitive, effective, and emotive functions. It insists that such facts be rationally comprehended as something given as well as intuitively grasped as something aesthetically evoked. In short, in addition to intellectual preparation for such a task, the mode of apprehending a work of art "demands a special attitude and exertions if the critic is to withhold himself from all arbitrary completion of qualitative indeterminacies, while at the same time taking full account of the special character of its every moment of potentiality."[55] Only such an integrated approach toward the literary work guarantees the optimal effectiveness of the critic's endeavors.[56] On this point Ingarden differs substantially from the formalists and relativists of various types.

The formalists supposedly care little about the critic's intuitive grasp of the work's ideal qualities, since by their contention the literary work does not transcend its empirical dimensions and therefore is conceivable exclusively *via vis cognitativa*.

The relativists care little about objective knowledge since in their opinion a literary work does not have any enduring objectivity and therefore is apprehended only as an immediate subjective experience.[57] Since, however, a literary fact is much more than a mere empirical fact or a mere stimulus, the critic's attitude toward it must be neither strictly formal nor strictly "laboratory." In order to arrive at the intersubjectively valid judgments concerning literary fact, he must be cognizant of: a) its permanent structural identity, b) its myriad aesthetic potentialities, and c) his own cognizing mind. The first is acquired through careful analysis; the second is acquired through the evaluation of his own and other readers' aesthetic concretions; the third is acquired through "pure conscious experience" or self-awareness. Only by exploring these phenomena,

> lässt es sich zeigen, dass die Sätze und Satzzusammenhänge trotz ihrer Seinsrelativität auf subjektive Operationen eine intersubjektive Identität besitzen und eine der Bewusstseinsakten gegenüber heteronome Seinsweise haben, die ihnen ermöglicht, auch dann zu existieren wenn sie—einmal konzipiert—durch kein Bewusstseinssubjekt gedacht,

resp. 'gelesen' werden, so ist damit auch die intersubjektive Identität des literarischen Werkes als eines von uns herangestellten *schematischen* Gebildes gerettet.[58]

What specific methodological procedure does Ingarden propose for such a complex study of a literary work? Basically, there are two distinct but mutually complementary procedures: the pre-aesthetic and the aesthetic. By the first

> handelt es sich vor allem darum, diejenigen Eigenschaften und Elemente in ihm (literary work) aufzufinden, welche es zum Kunstwerk machen, d.h. welche den Grund für die Konstituierung der ästhetisch relevanten Qualitäten in den ästhetischen Konkretisationen bilden.

> Die vor-ästhetische, forschende Betrachtung eines literarischen Kunstwerks wird gewöhnlich unternommen um—wie man sagt—eine 'objektive' Erkenntnis von ihm selbst zu erziehen.[59]

The pre-aesthetic procedure deals with those structural peculiarities which are free from the aesthetic variations ascribed to them. For example, the stratum of language can be conceived from the standpoint of its semantic clarity or ambiguity, its syntactical regularity or irregularity, its referential or evocative character, its direct or metaphorical presentation, and the like. It can be examined from the point of its "axiological neutrality" or "axiological potency," i.e., from the point of its "givenness," or from the point of the artistic quality of this "givenness." In the first case, one limits himself to pure description; in the second instance one concentrates on those elements which render it artistic and substantially different from nonartistic discourses. These are only a few of the possibilities open to a researcher. In all strata, the researcher may attempt to establish the number of undetermined places and classify them in accordance with their artistic importance. He may compare them internally or externally and thus determine their artistic novelty or stereotype. He may watch their mutual completion or diversion. In short, the first procedure concerns itself with what:

1. is neither a part nor an aspect of our empirical experiences or mental states during commerce with a work of art and therefore does not belong to the category of pleasure or enjoyment.
2. is not something attributed to the work by virtue of the work's being regarded as an instrument for arousing this or that form of pleasure.
3. reveals itself as a specific characteristic of the work itself.
4. exists if and only if the necessary conditions for its existence are present in the qualities of the work itself.

5. is such a thing that its presence causes the work of art to partake of an entirely special form of being distinct from all other cultural products.[60]

The pre-aesthetic study is thus concerned with the actual rather than the potential, with the given rather than the implied. It is a highly exacting reconstruction ("die meistens auf das Quantitative gerichtet ist")[61] of the work's constitutive strata. In order to achieve such a reconstruction, the critic must free his perception of all emotions which hinder it from functioning *sine ira et studio*. These emotions are hatred, anger, jealousy, desire, gratitude, and unrestricted attachment. In studying the work's structure one must "sich abspielen," one must perform on oneself a "bewussten und konsequent durchgeführten Ausschluss aller Gefühle,"[62] which gives preponderance to the perceiving subject, i.e., to oneself, rather than to the perceived object. This does not mean, however, that the researcher must become completely emotionless. In fact, emotions cannot be purged entirely from the total state of consciousness since they accompany, as a rule, all cognitive and conative acts. Therefore one must exercise conscious control over his emotions and permit only those that facilitate and further his objective knowledge. By an act of this control, emotions become a means of rather than an end to one's comprehension. What is important in this regard is sympathy (*das Mitfühlen*) which can help the researcher grasp the "intentional feelings" of the presented object. Sympathy, unlike the emotions mentioned above, or affects, is "keine gefühlmässige Reaktion, sondern ein Mittel, gewisse psychische Tatsachen in ihrer Lebendigkeit zu enthüllen und sie auf diesem Weg zu einer rekonstruierenden Konstituierung zu bringen."[63]

However, sympathy too must be rationally contained so as not to lead into an upsurge of obstructive emotions. Throughout the cognitive processes the discerning "I" must remain fully in control. The critic's behavior on the level of research must resemble that of the stage director who, while identifying himself or his actors with the specific emotional reactions of the dramatis personae, remains constantly aware of his artistic goal. Via this identification he reconstructs the protagonist's emotions as artistically given. The audience, on the other hand, concreticizes them as aesthetically intended. In his case, emotions are subordinated to rational control; in the case of the audience they are relatively free of such control. His "I" and "me," or his transcendental ego and the empirical self, are concomitantly delineated and intentionally juxtaposed. In pre-aesthetic criticism a similar attitude toward the object of one's attention is not easy. On one hand, it requires "a cool aesthetically neutral position" and, on the other, it calls for a controlled emotional identification with the presented objects. But it is precisely due to this psychologically complex character that the pre-aesthetic inquiry becomes "dynamically functional,"[64] and thus differs from an emotionally indifferent quantification. Thus having neutralized his consciousness from the impeding emotions, the critic enables himself to: a) become clearly conscious of *what* is given to him (what kind of object and what kind of properties); b) realize that what is given to him is given in such a way and in such circumstances that he is right in acknowledging it to appertain to an object as its property, immanent in it; and c) apprehend that in an act of cognition, besides perception itself, there are also judgments and comparisons of the results of particular perceptions. On the basis of these checked perceptions, the critic may ascribe to a cognized object only those properties which are *independent* of irrelevant circumstances (those beyond the object perceived).[65]

In sum, the whole process of pre-aesthetic cognition is composed of many cognitive acts and is directed, "if it proceed regularly, by the idea of an exact *adjustment* of the cognitive results to the object to be cognized and of the exclusion of all those elements which admit the slightest suspicion of having issued from factors *foreign* to the cognized object."[66]

The pre-aesthetic inquiry cannot be ideally complete and correct. No matter how diligent and objective the critic tries to be, his reconstruction of the essential components of the work in question only approximates it. "Wir können," Ingarden stated, "keine absolute Gewähr haben, dass die von uns gewonnene Rekonstruktion eines untersuchten literarischen Kunstwerks ihm absolut getreu ist, bzw. in diesem oder einem anderen Punkt noch ungetreu (unkorrekt) ist."[67] This is not, however, in itself detrimental to literary scholarship, since

das Erkennen des literarischen Kunstwerks, das zu einer bestimmten Rekonstruktion desselben führt, bildet nur einen Spezialfall des empirischen Erkennens überhaupt, in welchem wir nie eine absolute Gewähr für die Objektivität der erzielten Ergebnisse gewinnen können. Von der Literaturwissenschaft brauchen wir nicht mehr zu fordern, es kommt nur darauf an, dass die aufgestellten Behauptungen möglichst gut in dem gegebenen Material (d.h. im literarischen Kunstwerk und in seiner Rekonstruktion) gegründet werden.[68]

Thus, although incomplete or unevenly balanced, this pre-aesthetic
inquiry can nevertheless elucidate the identity of a literary work.
This elucidation can be achieved neither through ordinary reading
nor through indiscriminate aesthetic empathy, but only through a
careful pre-aesthetic reconstruction.

The aesthetic inquiry which probes beyond the "unwandelbare
Skelett" of the literary work is incontestably more involved than the
pre-aesthetic one. As we have repeatedly stated, the literary work,
according to Ingarden, is suspended in that ideal ambiance of notions
and qualities which give it a permanent aesthetic sustenance. But
since these ideals and qualities are not and cannot be definitely articulated, only endlessly approximated through the varying aesthetic
concretions, the aesthetic treatment of literary art assumes great
importance. Specifically, this treatment concerns itself with those
aesthetic addenda which the reader ascribes to the work as it is in its
schematized form. However, while pre-aesthetic treatment operates
with only one set of objectively verifiable data, the aesthetic treatment often operates with multiple sets of data or concretions. This
multiplicity of concretions results from the perceptive act which
could be expressed by the following formula:

$$C = a < A$$

in which C stands for concretion, a for the empirically given literary
work, and A for the ideal notions and qualities. Should a be conceived
of in terms of A, concretion will be adequate; however, should A, for
various reasons, be replaced by B or any other quantity, concretions
will be inadequate. Thus, the relationship between the empirically
given structure and its ideal notions, expressed in aesthetic concretions, can oscillate between live vividness and marked obliteration.
In the first case, one may speak of the adequate aesthetic concretion,
and in the second case, "tatsächlich handelt es sich hier entweder um
reine verschiedene Verdeckung oder um eine bewusste Schaffung
eines neuen Werkes das dem ursprünglichen nur mehr oder weniger
verwandt ist."[69] Should the work's structure, however, lose its vitala-
bility to evoke any ideals and qualities, it turns into a historical artifact. Semantically, its verbal signs become sterile. The work thus
ceases to live as an aesthetic phenomenon. Such a supposedly dead
artifact can be newly resuscitated through the discovery of its new
ideal notions and qualities, i.e., through new aesthetic concretions.
In short, the literary work lives or dies because of its potency or lack
of potency to evoke ideal notions and qualities, or, as Ingarden stated,
it lives "indem es *in einer Mannigfaltigkeit von Konkretisationen zur*

Ausprägung gelangt, 2) indem es *infolge* immer neuer, durch Be-wusstseinssubjekte entsprechend gestalteter Konkretisationen *Ver-wandlungen unterliegt*."[70]

The task of the literary critic, as far as this second procedure is concerned, is to discern between adequate and inadequate aesthetic concretion. This task cannot be accomplished by an ordinary reader since even if he concreticizes correctly, he often does not know how to evaluate his own concretions properly. He is content with his aesthetic experiences, irrespective of whether they are within or out-side the appropriate limits (*charakteristische Grenzen*). He would rather listen to the evaluative judgments of the competent critic.

What formal options or criteria are open to the literary critic in respect to aesthetic concretions? Should he have any or should he simply rely upon a "trial and error method"? Ingarden is of the opin-ion that there are no options and that there cannot be any definite criteria which set up specific antecedent conditions, since such criteria "bilden etwas dem zu bewertenden Kunstwerk Äusseres, nicht einen aus dem Wesen des betreffenden Kunstwerks stammenden Faktor, der apodiktisch vorschreibt, was im Kunstwerk erfüllt werden muss." "Die Berufung auf die herrschenden Kriterien ist im Grund eine Flucht vor der Kunst und ist auch für diejenigen bestimmt, die für Kunstwerke und ästhetische Werte blind sind."[71]

While we do not have and cannot have any definitive set of criteria for the evaluation of aesthetic concretions, the research into them must not be haphazard or random. The critic must be appropriately educated for such a task. He must familiarize himself with critical articles, scholarly treatises (*Abhandlungen*), discussions, interpreta-tions, historical assessments, and the like, which bear in any way upon the work in question. Through this study he prepares himself "das Werk auf bestimmte Weise zu verstehen und somit in bestimmt gearteten Konkretisationen zu erfassen."[72] The critic must read this material with continuous discrimination and discernment, since more often than not it contains factual errors or favors a particular bias. Out of this total intellectual involvement with the particular literary work and its aesthetic contact the critic stands a good chance of ar-riving at an adequate knowledge of the aesthetic concretions. His chances are also enhanced by the fact that both the literary work as a schematized structure and its corresponding aesthetic concretions originate and exist in the same "literary atmosphere" (*die literarische Atmosphäre*[73]) which shapes the critic's intellectual apparatus. There-fore, the critic's intellectual apparatus and the work itself are two correlated variables with a relatively small alienation coefficient. This atmosphere, however, has to be thoroughly studied. In studying it, the critic must discriminate between his scholarly aims and his subjective predilections, so as not to favor one set of values (*Wert-qualitäten*) and overlook the other. He must also distinguish between the work's ideal notions and qualities and those imbued in "the literary atmosphere." These two are not necessarily identical. Otherwise he might engage in pseudosociological or pseudohistorical study rather than in aesthetic concretions.

In sum, to establish the permissible "limits of variability" (*Grenzen der Variabilität*) of aesthetic concretions and to determine their adequacy, the critic must follow several general guidelines. These are:

1. to find out to what extent the structural identity of the literary work in question has been preserved or obliterated in aesthetic concretions;

2. to discover in what sense these concretions are novel expressions of the work's aesthetic potentialities or are concealments of such potentialities (*Verdeckungsphenomäne*);

3. to distinguish between one's own critical evaluation of the aesthetic concretions and one's own aesthetic experience of these concretions, i.e., to treat the former as a "nüchterne, gewissenhafte und vorsichtige intellektuelle Betrachtung"[74] and the latter as a creative completion or alteration (*Ergänzung oder Verwandlung*) of the work's undetermined places;

4. to establish which of the strata yield to the largest variability of the aesthetic concretions[75] and why they do so;

5. to differentiate between the subjective and the intersubjective concretions.

Finally, on the basis of all this, the critic may determine the artistic and the aesthetic value of the work under consideration.[76]

In conclusion, aesthetic concretions, contrary to psychological or neopositivistic criticism, do not by themselves make up aesthetics or criticism. They are merely the subject matter of their "besonderen, neuerlichen, oft sehr komplizierten wissenschaftlichen Erkenntnis-bemühungen."[77] Therefore, literary criticism, both in its pre-aesthetic and aesthetic approaches, "ist kein rein intuitiver, sondern ein ausgesprochen intellektueller Akt."[78] To engage in critical inquiry in the sense described below one must not necessarily be "ein angebildeter Literaturwissenschaftler, aber er sollte fähig sein, eine getreue Rekonstruktion des Kunstwerks zu erzielen und für seine künstlerischen Werte empfänglich zu sein, und damit die von ihm konstituierte

Konkretisation in ihren wesentlichen Zügen zu erfassen."[79] In the light of all this, it is obvious that literary criticism is not anybody's folly,[80] even though he might have adequate aesthetic concretions. The right to engage in literary criticism, as Ingarden stated, "stellt jedem zu, der fähig ist, eine entsprechende Überlegung überhaupt durchzuführen."[81] This ability, like intellectual ability in any other scientific discipline, "kann nur durch die Entwicklung, d.h. durch *Erziehung zur Kunst* gewonnen werden." It requires

> besondere Übung am analytischen Erkennen des literarischen Kunstwerks so wie eine grosse Erfahrung bezüglich der möglichen Konkretisierungen des Kunstwerks, ihrer verschiedenen Typen und Stilarten, usw.—alles was ein verantwortlicher Literaturforscher zuerst erlernen muss, bevor er zur Bewertung einzelner literarischer Kunstwerke kommen kann . . . Den Anfang dieser Erziehung bildet das Erkennen der einzelnen literarischen Kuntswerke vermittels einer richtig durchgeführten Lektüre und eines adäquaten und ergiebigen ästhetischem Erlebnis, das zu getreuen und wertvollen ästhetischen Konkretisationen führt. Alle weiteren Probleme der Literaturwissenschaft . . . hängen schon in ihrer richtigen Formulierung und im Ausgang ihrer Lösungsversuche von diesem Anfang ab.[82]

In Ingarden's opinion, any other way leads either to the anarchy of *de gustibus non est disputandum* or to the deadening positivistic circumvention of the transcendental qualities of literary art—in brief, either to purely monosubjective declarations or to a never-ending accumulation of empirical facts.

Notes

1. René Wellek and Austin Warren, *Theory of Literature* (New York, 1956); R. Wellek, *Concepts of Criticism* (New Haven, 1963).
2. A. T. Tymieniecka, *Phenomenology and Science in Contemporary European Thought* (New York, 1962).
3. Michel Dufresne critically assessed Ingarden's theory in *Phénomenologie de l'expérience esthétique*, vol. 1 (Paris, 1953), pp. 266–273.
4. Strangely enough, the multilayered structure of literary art had not been elaborated before Ingarden. As he himself observes, "the multilayered character of literary art (especially in tragedy) was noticed by Aristotle in his *Poetics*. But judging by the components which he enumerates . . . Aristotle failed to perceive its structural basis and only empirically caught

some of its peculiarities . . . (But) in spite of the century-long influence of Aristotle's *Poetics*, regretfully nobody had developed these Aristotelian views and nobody created a theory which could have summed up his concrete judgments." *Issledovaniia po estetike* (Moscow, 1962), p. 24. Considerably later than Ingarden, Nicolai Hartmann in his *Ästhetik* (Berlin, 1953), written in 1945 in besieged Berlin, speaks also about strata in literary art. To a certain extent his views resemble those of Ingarden but they are not as elaborated and as concisely demarcated as those of Ingarden.

5. In a concluding statement to *Das literarische Kunstwerk*, Ingarden stated: "Wir verhehlen uns nicht, dass wir trotz des grossen Umfangs unserer Analysen bloss die Hauptzüge, die Grundstruktur des literarischen Werkes gezeight haben . . . Unsere Mühe wird reichlich belohnt wenn unsere Leser die Resultate dieses Buches zum Ausgangspunkt weiterer Forschungen nehmen können und wenn es ihnen gelingt, die Untersuchung nicht nur weiterzuführen, sondern auch die etwaigen von uns begangenen Fehler durch *bessere* Einsichten zu ersetzen." (p. 399).

6. Joseph J. Kockelmans, ed., *Phenomenology: The Philosophy of Edmund Husserl and Its Interpretation* (Garden City, 1966), p. 24.

7. "Philosophie als strenge Wissenschaft," *Logos: 1*, 289–341, 1910–11.

8. A. T. Tymieniecka, *Phenomenology and Science*, p. 9.

9. A. T. Tymieniecka's study *Phenomenology and Science in Contemporary European Thought* examines the relationship of phenomenology to anthropology, psychology, psychopathology, sociology, law, and economics. A similar aim is pursued in a symposium edited by Joseph J. Kockelmans, *Phenomenology: The Philosophy of Edmund Husserl and Its Interpretation*.

10. "For over thirty years," writes Joseph J. Kockelmans, "scholars have been unable to agree in their interpretations of it (*Cartesian Meditations*). Some interpreters hold that Husserl's phenomenology is 'realistic' in its essence; others see his work as a whole as one or another form of 'idealism,' the exact nature of which they cannot, however, determine or agree upon." See "Realism and Idealism in Husserl's Phenomenology," *Tijdschrift voor Philosophie 20*:395–442, 1958.

11. Roman Ingarden, ed., *Briefe an Roman Ingarden* (The Hague, 1968), p. 80.

12. J. Q. Lauer, *The Triumph of Subjectivity* (New York City, 1958), p. 21.

13. Roman Ingarden, *Times and Modes of Being* (Springfield, Ill., 1964), p. 64.

14. *Das literarische Kunstwerk*, p. xii.

15. *Vom Erkennen des literarischen Kunstwerks* (Tübingen, 1968), p. 2.

16. Ibid., p. 243. This type of inquiry into the artistic structure without recourse to historical knowledge or for that matter to any external information is similar to that proposed by New Criticism, Russian formalism, and Polish and Czech structuralism.

17. *Das literarische Kunstwerk*, p. 2.

18. "In order to be a part of artistic literature, the work has to contain a minimum of four strata. There are cases, however, where the number of strata in some works or in some of its parts increases to eight or twelve."—*Issledovaniia po estetike*, p. 38.

19. Today, an interesting question is in what sense, if any, this concept of sound patterning differs from the views of scholars who were concerned with this stratum but were not phenomenologically committed. As we know, Russian formalism and Czech structuralism (Cercle linguistique de Prague), as well as such eminent scholars in the field of stylistics as Karl Vossler, Leo Spitzer, Fritz Strich, and Damaso Alonso, to mention only a very few, concentrated on this stratum and offered many observations which stand in close proximity to those of Ingarden. However, what is novel in Ingarden's concept and what sets him apart from these scholars is his proposition that

this stratum, like the other three strata, is highly schematized and often deliberately incomplete, and that this incompleteness is as important as its given parts. Its ever-new aesthetic potentialities lie precisely in this attribute. In brief, while the formalists and stylists thought of form in art, so to say, one-dimensionally, Ingarden on the other hand indicated in his *Studia z estetiki*, vol. 1 (Warsaw, 1966) that there are nine different notions of form which should be differentiated.

20. *Issledovaniia po estetike*, p. 24.
21. Ibid., p. 25.
22. Tymieniecka, *Phenomenlogy and Science*, p. 26.
23. Ibid., p. 27.
24. On the basis of this Ingarden developed a highly sophisticated view of different types of truthfulness in artistic works. He proposes eight variants of truthfulness. See Roman Ingarden, "O razlichnom ponimanii pravdivosti (istinnost') v proizvideniiakh isskusstva," *Issledovaniia po estetike*, pp. 92–113.
25. *Das literarische Kunstwerk*, p. 263.
26. Ibid., p. 243.
27. Her death and the accompanying experiences might have an analogue in the epileptic aura, in which objective time is vastly amplified by subjective experiences.
28. In my short study on schematism I added a fifth concept, the psychologically determined patterning of our perceptive processes which for a variety of reasons prevents us from seeing, perceiving, and conceiving of objects *in toto*. (See John Fizer, "Schematism: Aesthetic Device or Psychological Necessity," *Journal of Aesthetics and Art Criticism* 27(4):417–423, 1969.
29. "Metaphysische Qualitäten (Wesenheiten)," *Das literarische Kuntswerk*, pp. 310–319.
30. Ibid., p. 310.
31. *Issledovaniia po estetike*, p. 59.
32. Ibid., p. 59.
33. Robert Humphrey, *Stream of Consciousness in the Modern Novel* (Berkeley, 1954).
34. I might add that such interruptions are of great psychological significance. They guard the work against monotony, against oversaturation with superfluous details, and against excessive exposure. They open endless possibilities for seeing an object from many positions and many points of view. "Stream of consciousness" in literature postulates a passivity and helplessness to do anything with the flow of one's creative imagination.
35. William James, "The Stream of Consciousness," *Psychology: Brief Course* (New York, 1892), pp. 152–175.
36. Perhaps in some sense James's notion of the fringe corresponds to Ingarden's notion of undetermined places in meaning, i.e., that both the fringe and the undetermined place are moments in the flow of consciousness in which new twists of thought can occur.
37. *Issledovaniia po estetike*, p. 63.
38. Ingarden himself observed that the inner aspects "wirklich sehr schwer ist, sie für sich selbst und ihrer Funktion zu erschauen und zu beschreiben." See ¶43 in *Das literarische Kunstwerk* and ¶12 in *Vom Erkenen des literarischen Kunstwerks*. See also E. Husserl's *Ideen zu einer reinen Phänomenologie, Gesamelte Werke*, vol. 4 (Haag, 1950); M. Geiger's *Fragment über den Begriff des Unbewussten und die psychische Realität* (Halle, 1930); and E. Stein's *Beiträge zur philosophischen Begründung der Psychologie* (Halle, 1922).
39. There are 326 pages devoted to strata and only ten to phases in *Das litera-*

36 JOHN FIZER

rische Kuntswerk and 52 pages in *Vom Erkennen des literarischen Kunst-werks*.
40. *Das literarische Kuntswerk*, p. 331.
41. *Vom Erkennen*, p. 98.
42. *Times and Modes of Being*, p. 123.
43. *Das literarische Kuntswerk*, p. x.
44. See his "The Physicalistic Theory of Language and the Work of Literature," *Problems of Literary Evaluation*, ed. Joseph Strelka, University Park, Pa., 1969. In this work Ingarden writes: "I cannot reduce the literary work of art to its basic sounds. Nor can I reduce it to mere language, as the formalists do. . . . I simply cannot accept the formalistic theory of language and literature because it contradicts my experience." (p. 97).
45. A. T. Tymieniecka perceptively observes that were the literary art such in all the variations in which it has or could be conceived or reproduced, it would exist forever; thus, the artist would not be creator but discoverer (p. 27).
46. With this approach to literary art it is relatively easy to assume the posture of what the followers of the New Criticism called "an aesthetic or psychic distance," or what the phenomenologists propose to perform on the object of perception—an *époché*.
47. Four strata are the minimum in any literary work. But there could be more. "The presence of more than four strata does not contradict my concept of the multistrata structure of a literary work. It is only its specific version, only one possibility conditioned by it." *Issledovaniia po estetike*, p. 39.
48. *Issledovaniia po estetike*, p. 85.
49. Ingarden's acceptance of theoretical coordinates in criticism should not be interpreted as contradicting his acceptance of the phenomenological reduction or *époché*. As stated at the onset of this study, *époché* to Ingarden did not mean the withdrawal from the world of facts but rather a preparation for the critical assessment of facts. It meant freeing all phenomena under consideration from all transphenomenal elements which inhibit the critic's access to what is indubitably given. In other words, it meant a suspension of all beliefs or commitments which transcend these phenomena and which shield him from properly intuiting, analyzing, or describing their essences. Theoretical coordinates, on the other hand, have nothing to do with such commitments. They are neither concepts nor derivatives of former experiences but merely general guides for the study of intentionality in action. Without these coordinates one can have neither an intellectual clarity nor rigorous scholarship.
50. Ingarden groups the critics into "psychologists," "physicalists," and "formalists." The first group thinks of literary art as something exclusively psychic; the second thinks of it as something purely "physicoformalist," and the third as a "highly organized linguistic expression." (See his "Commentary on Aristotle's Poetics," *The Journal of Aesthetics and Art Criticism* 20 (2):163–167, 1961). In a different context and on a different occasion, Ingarden spoke of psychologistic "rank nonsense and errors" as resulting from the "existential momism" whose "consistent advocacy leads not only to the complete extinction of all cultural creations but also to the incapacitation of science." (*Times and Modes of Being*, p. 49). For different reasons Ingarden was also highly critical of "physicalists" and "formalists."
51. Ingarden distinguishes between "purely intentional" and "intentional" objects. The former "derive their existence and their entire endowment from an intending experience of consciousness (an 'act'). . . . The latter are *chanced upon* by an intention of an act of consciousness." (*Times and*

Modes of Being, p. 47). If we understand this distinction correctly, the artistic object is "purely intentional," while the aesthetic one is "intentional."

52. *Das literarische Kuntswerk*, p. 389.

53. Ibid., p. 381.

54. "Artistic and Aesthetic Values," *British Journal of Aesthetics* 4(3):202, 1964.

55. Ibid.

56. Ingarden does not exclude the possibility of forming pertinent judgments about the aesthetic value of something without being "aesthetically moved" or without the accomplishment of an aesthetic process. In his opinion, however, such judgments are pure intellectual experiences. He stated: "It is only those judgments concerning value which are given *on the basis* of an aesthetic process, and when such a process has been accomplished, that are *justified*. Again, the judgments concerning value which are obtained by professional critics, many times with great routine, are rather a merely *indirect* continuation not of the *value* of an *aesthetic* object itself, but only of a *work of art* as a means which may lead to a positively valuable aesthetic object if an aesthetic experience is accomplished. Therefore, even if they are not mistaken in their valuation of the *works of art*, the professional critics know, and may say many times, very little about the real contents of the corresponding *aesthetic objects*."—"Aesthetic Experience and Aesthetic Object," *Philosophy and Phenomenological Research* 21 (3):308, 1961.

57. Here are a few examples of critical subjectivism in our time: Günter Blöcker and a host of other German critics postulate that literary art in general and poetry in particular is *Magie* and hence forever closed to analytical penetration. "Dichtung ist nicht erklärbar, sie ist nur erfahrbar."—Günter Blöcker, "Literaturkritik," *Kritik in unserer Zeit*, ed. Karl Otto (Göttingen, 1960), p. 15. The existentialist critics, emulating Heidegger, also have conceived of art as a total mystery which does not yield to rational comprehension. "Das Geheimnis eines dichterischen Werkes," Heidegger observed, "ist seine Undurchdringlichkeit als Schöpfung und als Gestalt. Die Poetik kann an es heranführen, aber es niemals gänzlich erhellen."—*Deutsche Philologie im Aufriss* (vol. 1, rev. ed. 2), ed. Wolfgang Stammler (Berlin, 1957–62). The Geneva School or the "critics of consciousness" also want to comprehend literary art through some sort of quasimystical fusion of the critic's consciousness with that of the creator. Yet as soon as they begin to describe their "insights," their defiance of the structural tangibility of literary art assumes a specific epistemological position. It becomes a neosolipsistic theory of knowledge. See Sarah N. Lawall, *Critics of Consciousness: The Existential Structure of Literature* (Cambridge, 1968). On the theory of subjectivity, Ingarden stated: "There exists . . . a sense of 'subjective'—usually not formulated precisely—in which the theory of subjectivity of aesthetic (or artistic) values ought to be rejected outright, despite its popularity. This is the view that the value of a work of art (or an aesthetic object, which is usually confused with it) is nothing else but pleasure (or in the case of a negative value, disagreeableness) understood as a specific psychical state or experience, lived through by an observer in contact with a given work of art. The greater the pleasure he obtains, the greater the value the observer attributes to the work of art. In truth, however, in this theory the work of art possesses no value. The observer indeed announces his pleasure by valuing the work of art, but strictly speaking he is valuing his own pleasure: his pleasure is valuable to him and this he uncritically transfers to the work of art which arouses his pleasure." ("Artistic and Aesthetic Values," p. 201).

58. *Das literarische Kunstwerk*, p. 384.

59. *Vom Erkennen*, p. 243.
60. Roman Ingarden, "Artistic and Aesthetic Values," p. 204.
61. *Vom Erkennen*, p. 331.
62. Ibid., p. 244.
63. Ibid., p. 246.
64. Ibid., p. 263.
65. Roman Ingarden, "Aesthetic Experience and Aesthetic Object," pp. 291–292.
66. Ibid.
67. *Vom Erkennen*, p. 371.
68. Ibid.
69. *Das literarische Kunstwerk*, p. 361.
70. Ibid., p. 370.
71. *Von Erkennen*, pp. 324–325.
72. Ibid., p. 373.
73. *Das literarische Kuntswerk*, p. 374.
74. *Vom Erkennen*, p. 343.
75. Ingarden assumes that the most radical difference between the work and its concretions occurs in the stratum of aspects. He stated: "Der radikalste Unterschied zwischen dem literarischen Werke und seinen Konkretisationen tritt in der Schicht der Ansichten auf. Aus ihrer blossen Parathaltung und Schematisiertheit im Werke selbst werden sie in den Konkretisationen zur Konkretheit gebracht und zu wahrnehmungsmässigem . . . oder zu phantasiemässigem Erleben . . . erhoben. Dabei gehen die konkret erlebten Ansichten unvermerklich über den schematisierten Gehalt der paratgehaltenen Ansichten im Werke selbst hinaus, indem das blosse Sehen in verschiedener Hinsicht durch konkrete Elemente angefüllt wird." *Das literarische Kunstwerk*, p. 362.
76. Ingarden's distinction between artistic and aesthetic values emanates from his differentiation between the work of art and the aesthetic object. This distinction had been elaborated by Ingarden in his various writings on aesthetics and the theory of art, beginning with his principal work *Das literarische Kuntswerk* (1931). The first "is something which arises in the work of art itself and has its existential ground in that" and the second "is something which manifests itself only in the aesthetic object and as a particular moment which determines the character of the whole." ("Artistic and Aesthetic Values," p. 205). Artistic value is immanent in the work itself, while aesthetic value results from the cocreative activity of its observer or reader.
77. *Vom Erkennen*, p. 133.
78. Ibid., p. 425.
79. Ibid., p. 431.
80. On this point Ingarden is very blunt and direct. "Dies wird ja in jeder Wissenschaft gefordert und es ist nicht erlaubt, Beurteilungen auszusprechen, wenn man Analphabet auf dem betreffenden Gegenstandsgebiet ist . . . Aber so, wie nicht alle Mathematiker sein müssen, brauchen auch nicht alle etwas von Kunst zu verstehen, obwohl es bedauerlich ist, wenn die Enthüllung der Kunst und der durch sie konkretisierten Werte in einem besonderen Fall misslingt." (*Vom Erkennen*, p. 437). Ingarden remained undaunted in his conviction throughout his scholarly career. In a lecture before the British Society of Aesthetics in 1963, he again spoke of a "competent observer" capable of apprehending the work of art in one way rather than another. ("Artistic and Aesthetic Values," p. 201).
81. *Vom Erkennen*, p. 436.
82. Ibid., pp. 436–438.

Selected Bibliography of Roman Ingarden's Work

Das literarische Kunstwerk (2). *Verbesserte und erweiterte Auflage* (Tübingen, 1960).

Vom Erkennen des literarischen Kunstwerks (Tübingen, 1968).

"Das Form-Inhalt Problem im literarischen Kunstwerk," *Helicon* 1:61–67, 1938.

"Racourcis de perspective temporelle dans la concretisation de l'oeuvre littéraire," *Revue de Métaphysique et de Morale* 65 (1):19–51 (n.d.).

"The General Question of the Essence of Form and Content," *Journal of Philosophy* 57 (7):222–233, 1960.

"Aesthetic Experience and Aesthetic Object," *Philosophy and Phenomenological Research* 21 (3):289–313, 1960.

"Prinzipien einer erkenntnistheoretischen Betrachtung der ästhetischen Erfahrung," *Actes du IVe Congrès International d'Esthétique*, Athens, 1962, pp. 622–631.

"Das ästhetische Erlebnis," *IIe Congrès International d'Esthétique et des Sciences de l'Art* (Vol. I), Paris, 1937, pp. 54–60.

"Bemerkungen zum Problem des ästhetischen Werturteils," *Revista di Estetica* 3 (3):414–423, 1958.

Untersuchungen zur Ontologie der Kunst (Tübingen, 1962).

"Artistic and Aesthetic Values," *British Journal of Aesthetics* 4:198–213, 1964.

Toshihiko Izutsu and Toyo Izutsu

FAR EASTERN EXISTENTIALISM: HAIKU AND THE MAN OF WABI

INTRODUCTION

To give a reasonable explanation of the personality of the *haiku*-critic, we must clarify in what point *haiku*-criticism is distinguished from criticism in other related fields of literature and art, including various types of poetry other than *haiku*. And in order to do so, we must necessarily clarify first of all the peculiarity of the inner structure of *haiku* itself as a special form of poetry. We shall further have to elucidate the fact that in the world of *haiku* poetic creation and its criticism—or, we might say, the poet and the reader—are related far more closely than in other genres of literature, so much so that the two are in fact fused into a personal unity.

In the world of *haiku* we have professional masters; but there is no room for a professional critic. In other words, a *haiku*-master is and must always be a *haiku*-critic. Since the earliest phase of *haiku's* development, every *haiku*-poet has on principle been expected to function as a *haiku*-critic. The reader who is capable of properly appreciating *haiku* is of necessity himself a poet. And the reader-creator of *haiku* must at the same time be a critic of *haiku*. These three persons—the poet, the reader, and the critic—are equally entitled to be called "*haiku*-man" or, to use more traditional terminology, "a man engaged in the pursuit of poetic truthfulness,"[1] and a "man of *wabi*."[2]

In the view of the school of Bashô[3] (considered to represent the highest stage of perfection ever reached by *haiku* in its history), what is really worthy to be regarded as a *haiku*-poem must be a work directly born of the mind "engaged in the pursuit of poetic truthfulness." This observation leads to one of the most remarkable and original characteristics of the creative world of *haiku*: that prior to the creation of individual *haiku*-poems and their appreciation, there must necessarily exist what might best be described as a common ground between the poet, reader, and critic, at least in its most fundamental form. And this common ground is the very spirit of *haiku*-creation: *wabi*, or "poetic truthfulness."

Wabi is "something" undefinable: it can be an aesthetic as well as an ethical idea. It refers to a peculiar state of mind, a mode of awareness that leads toward the formation of a peculiar view of Nature, a Weltanschauung, and—even more remarkably—can crystallize itself into a sensation immediately connected with the cognitive function of the sense organs. This "something" is a locus which unites the poet, reader, and critic; by the very act of participating in it, they recognize and ascertain in each other the various aspects of its actualization. Thus delving deeply into the inner structure of the spirit of *haiku* is simultaneously an analysis of the personality expected of a *haiku*-critic. And this is exactly what we intend to do here.

THE MAN OF *WABI*

A "man of *wabi* who has exhausted the ultimate depth of *wabi*"—such a man is said to represent the pinnacle of the literature of the Bashô style.[4] The phrase "man of *wabi*" in its nontechnical sense is explained in a Japanese-French dictionary compiled by a Christian missionary in the seventeenth century (contemporary with Bashô) as meaning "a sad, sordid and miserable man."[5]

Bashô himself wrote an explanatory note for one of his *haiku*-poems in his famous "Journey of a Man Exposed to Wind and Rain," saying:

> My straw head-cover has been soaked with rain and worn to tatters during the long travel. My paper-garment has become totally wrinkled, for I have slept night after night without taking it off. A man of *wabi* who has exhausted the ultimate depth of *wabi*—indeed I am! Even I would feel pity for my own self (if I were to observe this state of mind).[6]

It is worth remarking that in this passage Bashô is not using the expression "man of *wabi* who has exhausted the ultimate depths of *wabi*" in a purely nontechnical sense, i.e., in the sense of a "sad, sordid and miserable man." Here the expression has already been given a kind of spiritual interpretation; that is to say, it is already acquiring that special meaning with which it will later become established as a technical term in *haiku*-literature. More important is the fact that the spiritualized understanding here in question of the "man of *wabi*" is far from being dissociated from its original meaning. Quite the contrary; the context itself clearly shows how the two meanings are most closely connected with each other.

As an example of the usage of the word *wabi* which stands still closer to its technical meaning, we may cite an explanatory note which Bashô attached to a *haiku*-poem he composed in 1689. In this note the word is more conspicuously colored with a spiritualizing nuance:

> Saturated with the feeling of *wabi* for the moon, saturated with the feeling of *wabi* for my existence, saturated with the feeling of *wabi* for my imperfection—I am ready to answer to whomsoever would ask me how I am: "I am saturated with the feeling of *wabi*". But, alas, there is no one even to ask me questions! Thus I do nothing other than sinking ever deep into *wabi*.[7]

Here we witness a man who, without being constrained to suffer sadness, loneliness, and misery solely by the material situation of his life, puts himself rather of his own accord into the spiritual state of *wabi*. As a *haiku*-poet whose essential function it is to be engaged forever in "the pursuit of poetic truthfulness," he unflinchingly directs his view toward his self as it has sunken into the depths of *wabi* and dares even to taste his own *wabi* to the fullest. Clearly we see in this passage a positive attitude manifested toward *wabi*.

The concept of man of *wabi* becomes established only on the basis of such a positive attitude toward the state of existential loneliness and misery. The man of *wabi* drives himself positively and consciously into that existential situation into which all men are inevitably destined to fall sooner or later, no matter how hard they might struggle to evade it. Positive and willing participation in the state of *wabi* thus constitutes one of the primary and most essential conditions for the personal formation of a man of *wabi*.

Where does this positive approach to such a negative aspect of human reality originate from? *Wabi*, insofar as it is man's consciousness of the internal as well as external situation in which he finds himself, is part of man's most immediate, physical, and concrete experience. At the same time, however, it has its ground in the recognition, commonly shared by all men, of the intrinsic weakness, fragility, and ephemerality of all life. The tragic nature of existence, however liable it may be to drive man toward pessimism, is an undeniable truth and must therefore be courageously recognized as such. And, such being the case, man must not avert his eyes from it; rather he must look directly into it. Thus the self-confidence which the man of *wabi* has lies in his genuine conviction that this attitude of his is based not on a false image of human reality but on its objective truth. He is convinced that the range of his most immediate spiritual experience is ultimately determined by, and reducible to, the awareness of this fundamental fact about the reality of existence.

Describing the nature of the *bashô*-tree, the poet Bashô wrote:

> Its leaves are as long as seven feet. Some of them half broken by the wind, sadly evocative of the image of the broken tail-wings of a phoenix. Some others remind us of green fans flown to pieces by the pitiless wind. Not that it never blossoms, but even in bloom it does not look flamboyant. Its stem appears sturdy, but (since it is hollow) it does not deserve even a stroke of an axe. It resembles in this respect that big useless mountain tree (of which Chuang Tzû respectfully writes in his book); it has an intrinsic nobility. No wonder the famous Chinese calligrapher Kai-so[8] used its leaves in place of paper, and the philosopher Chô O-kyo[9] related to have learnt a great deal by observing the nature of its leaves. As for myself, I do not exactly follow in the footsteps of these two (diligently productive) masters. I do nothing with the tree, but pass my time at leisure under its leaves, loving their fragility and their vulnerability to the onslaught of the wind and rain![10]

"I only love their fragility and their vulnerability to the onslaught of the wind and rain"—a remarkable statement! The practical merits such as usefulness, strength, and the like, have for the man of *wabi* nothing to do with the metaphysical significance of human existence itself.

From about 1689 Bashô begins to refer to himself as "the wind-driven gossamer, Bashô." At the outset of his work *Oi-no Kobumi*,[11] he explains the reason why he has adopted for himself this peculiar nom de plume, saying that it is because he considers his own existence as ephemeral and vulnerable as thin clothes that set up no resistance against the wind and rain. The word *bashô* means a special plant of the musaceous family.[12]

The nature of this "tree" attracted the attention of a number of famous artists and thinkers. The genius of Nô drama, Zenchiku Komparu,[13] chose this "tree" as the title of one of his masterpieces; the Buddhist monk Genshin[14] refers to it in his celebrated religious work *Ôjo Yôshû*.[15] In every case the name of this "tree" symbolizes the

ephemerality of life. The uselessness of its stem, the vulnerability of
its leaves (as soon as the fresh roll-leaves are unfolded and exposed
to the wind, they are broken to tatters), the tragic appearance of
the long broken leaves as they flutter in the merciless wind as if they
were broken pieces of a black-dyed garment of a beggar-monk—all
these characteristic features of the *bashô*-"tree" make the emotion of
attachment to and sympathy with this "tree" something symbolic of
the very nature of the man of *wabi*.

"I only love their fragility and their vulnerability to the onslaught
of the wind and rain"—in these short concluding words we see a
typical verbal crystallization of the subtle *poésie* characteristic of
the man of *wabi* who appreciates truth more than beauty, and who is
too seriously involved in the actuality of human life to be given up to
purely aesthetic emotions. Here we notice at the same time the
psychological and existential aspect of the aesthetic ideas peculiar to
haiku of the Bashô school, such as *wabi, sabi,*[16] *shiori,*[17] and *hosomi.*[18]

Sometimes showing hesitant self-complacency mingled with self-
derision, sometimes manifesting self-commiseration coupled with
bold self-confidence, the man of *wabi* is filled with contradictions
with regard to his own self. This contradictory psychological structure naturally discloses an even more complicated inner inflection
when he stands face to face with other men who have nothing to do
with *wabi*. We must remark, however, that this peculiar psychological
structure itself of the man of *wabi* constitutes one of the main sources
of his poetic creation.

From the point of view of the man of *wabi*, the mode of being of
those who are not of his kind and who therefore stand opposed to him
is conceivable in two forms. On one hand, there is a category of people who adopt as their own the conventional values that happen to be
dominant in the society in which they exist, who live without sober
reflection on anything, taking the purely phenomenal or this-worldly
reality for the only reality, sharing innocently the smiles and frowns
of human existence with all others. On the other hand, there are those
who are commonly adored as saintly men, those whom Bashô calls
"spiritual men without any human attachment"—in short, those religious men who have already attained to the supreme stage of
Awakening.

It will be clear without any explanation that the ethics and Weltanschauung of the man of *wabi are* not compatible with those of the

"ordinary" people (the first of the two categories described above). The standard of values which is usually recognized by the "ordinary" man is in the eyes of the man of *wabi* devoid of an existential basis and is therefore in the majority of cases nothing but a source of false values. And many of what are considered negative values in the commonly accepted way of thinking are for the man of *wabi* positive values. Furthermore, the man of *wabi* often suggests and even openly declares that being entirely valueless and useless in the society is a means of man's getting into immediate contact with true reality.

If such be the case, it would only be natural for the man of *wabi* to deny and reject, at least in his consciousness, the "ordinary" man in the most straightforward manner. In reality, however, the attitude taken by the man of *wabi* to the "ordinary" man is apparently not as simple as that.

> Once my (desolate) straw-hut,
>   Now with new dwellers
>   Is a house (adorned) with festive dolls![19]

This is a verse composed in 1689 by Bashô when he parted with his old house in which he had lived alone for about ten years. He turned over his house to a stranger in order to cut off the root of attachment to things of this world so that he might be able to taste to the full the emotion of being a solitary traveler, starting on a wandering journey to the deep north—the descriptive diary of this journey is the famous *Oku-no Hosomichi* "The Narrow Road to the Deep North." [20] The poem may be paraphrased in the following way. What was until just yesterday a humble dwelling-place of a "man of *wabi*" is now a house inhabited by a man who has moved into it with his wife and daughters. The house is filled with an atmosphere of sprightly human life. The impression of cheerfulness is particularly strong to-day—so says Bashô—because it is the day of the Girls' Festival. One can see from outside the whole family, blithe and happy, in their festive garments gathered together before the tier-stand for dolls.

The color of *wabi* is traditionally considered to be grey. From the very midst of a dark, ash-grey world of his own, a man of *wabi* is quietly gazing upon the sprightly pink world of the Feast of Dolls—pink because the flower symbolizing this Feast is the pink peach-blossom. Here we see the lonely man of *wabi* who is about to start on a long wandering journey, contemplating and marveling at the very process by which what has once been a grey, somber house is suddenly transformed into a vivaciously colorful place, resplendent with glowing colors, so symbolically characteristic of ordinary human life. This mode of existence remains quite alien to the man of *wabi*. The *haiku*-poem just quoted of Bashô vividly reflects the mood of an open and unreserved approval of this alien world. We sense in this poem even, we might say, a sort of cheerfulness which the poet as a man of *wabi* feels for the innocent mode of human existence in the phenomenal world as he observes it out of his own greyish world.

The man of *wabi* observes the "ordinary" people (as well as the men of the highest spiritual enlightenment) as those belonging to an entirely different world from his own, as men of an alien world. However, he is aware of the whole weight of the sight of those people observing him from outside, as much as the weight of his own self. Thus into the consciousness of the man of *wabi* the sight of others directed toward him is incorporated as parallel to his own sight directed toward his own self. The self-consciousness of the man of *wabi* is itself the converging point of these different sights. It will be but natural that the self-confidence or self-affirmation of such a man should invariably be accompanied by a tragic sense of humility, critical reflection upon himself, and even self-derision, which disclose themselves sometimes openly, sometimes stealthily, like a shadow accompanying a moving figure. Bashô gives the following description of this aspect of his existence as a poet of *wabi:*

> Having been enthusiastically fond of the poetry of folly and derision [i.e., *haiku*] for many years, he finally decided to make it his lifework. Since then, he has sometimes grown weary of it and even thought of abandoning it for good. Sometimes, incited by emulation, he has tried to establish an undisputed superiority over others. Pros and cons have in this way constantly been fighting each other in his mind so that he has never felt free from disquiet of the mind. There was once a time when he seriously entertained a desire of advancement in life, but the desire was curbed by the attachment to poetry. At another time he cherished an intention of studying Buddhism in order to overcome his folly through enlightenment, but the intention was defeated again by his attachment to poetry. Thus, incompetent and inefficient in every respect, he has ended up by holding on to this single rope [of *haiku*].[21]

In the eyes of those who remain outside of the world of *wabi*, *haiku* is after all nothing more than a kind of "poetry of folly." In their eyes, the man of *wabi* is but a lazy fellow incapable of rising in the world, while in the eyes of the enlightened, he is but a blind fool who, being unable to sever the ties of the flesh, goes on being tossed about on the waves of passions and attachments.

The phrase "incompetent and inefficient in every respect" is not to be taken as a rhetorical expression of modesty and humbleness. Rather, it must be understood as referring to the objective and descriptive reality of the man of *wabi* as it is reflected in the observing eyes of those who exist outside the world of *wabi*. Nor is it exactly correct to take the expression to signify self-derision on the part of the man of *wabi* himself. Rather, it refers to the reality of the man of *wabi* who positively assumes others' critical sight and evaluation of himself from their standpoint, as if it were his own.

Having thus assumed to his own self the criticism of him by others, the poet declares that he has nothing more to hold on to except the single rope (of *haiku*-poetry). The self-confidence entertained by the man of *wabi*, originating as it does from his own choice to go on living as a man of *wabi*, is comparable to a single rope which is sustained by his power alone. Because it is not strengthened by being intertwisted with other ropes, it is a single, feeble rope. Feeble indeed, but at least it is pure and genuine—this awareness clearly asserts itself in the concluding sentence of the passage. There is observable here a very peculiar kind of tenacious self-confidence. This self-confidence supports itself, not being sustained by anything else. The self-confidence is unwaveringly strong because it is directly related to the poet's own existence, because upon it depends his own existence. But it is also as feeble and vulnerable as his own existence. Is this "rope" strong? Or is it weak? Is this mental attitude of his a state of sheer passivity? Or is it rather a bold challenge to himself and others? Is it an attitude of boasting? Or of modesty? Each of these—and possibly other—pairs of questions has become only two different ways of expressing the same state of affairs. It would not make any real difference whichever way one may choose to answer. For the reality of human existence as conceived by Bashô, the man of *wabi*, stands above and beyond the dimension of such questions.

Let us now turn to the relation in which the man of *wabi* stands to the spiritual persons who have attained to the height of enlightenment. Here again we find him reluctant to identify himself with others—"others" meaning, in this case, men of enlightenment. The man of *wabi* finds his position between the "ordinary" people and those who have already experienced Awakening.

> How forlorn and lonesome it looks,
> A solitary *asunarô*-tree!
> As the evening falls upon cherry blossoms.

> Lonesome and deserted,
> A solitary *asunarô*-tree
> In the neighborhood of blooming cherries.[22]

The name of the tree which plays the central role in these two verses, *asu-narô*, literally means: "tomorrow-I-shall-become (a ground-cypress)." This curious appellation owes its origin to the fact that the tree outwardly resembles the ground-cypress, which supplies the most highly appreciated kind of lumber. In the explanatory note attached to these *haiku*, Bashô writes:

> A useless tree that grew old in solitude in a deep valley is related to have once proudly declared: "Tomorrow, tomorrow surely, I shall become a ground-cypress!" But alas! the "yesterday" is already gone as an insubstantial dream, whereas the "tomorrow" has no reality yet. Instead of enjoying myself over a cask of delicious *saké* [rice wine] while still in life, I have spent the whole of my life, mumbling to myself: "Tomorrow! Tomorrow surely!" And here I am in a state which rightly deserves being reproved by the sages.[23]

Of the earthly pleasures symbolized here by a cask of delicious *saké* he is deprived. Nor has he yet succeeded in raising himself up to the dimension of spiritual awakening. The position occupied by the man of *wabi* lies in between. And the remarkable fact is that the man of *wabi* chooses rather with self-complacency to remain in such a midway position, beyond the sensual pleasures of the world but without reaching the state of enlightenment.

Bashô composed several other *haiku* indicative of such a halfway attitude. For example:

> Summer has come, and yet
> Still single-leafed
> Remains this one-leave-fern.[24]

> Without becoming a butterfly
> Remains the rape-worm
> In late autumn.[25]

These and other similar verses express the state of self-complacency peculiar to the man of *wabi* who remains attached neither to advancement in the world of the "ordinary" people nor to the spiritual achievement of the enlightened ones. Self-complacency this certainly is. But this self-complacency which finds here an ironical expression is lined with the shame and compunction he feels in remaining in such a halfway state.

> How noble and precious is the man
> Who remains unenlightened
> At the sight of a lightning.[26]

Like a sudden lightning enlightenment is said to come. This *haiku* has an explanatory note which reads: "As a certain monk of high rank remarked, Zen enlightenment, when imperfect and superficial, is itself a world of demons." Rather than attaching a high value to man's attaining a superficial enlightenment, Bashô in this verse seems to be in sympathy with those who remain contented with the state of nonenlightenment, who do not and can never experience spiritual awakening at the sight of lightning (an occurrence symbolic of the swiftness of a lifetime and the ephemerality of human existence as well as the sudden coming of enlightenment), and who innocently continue to live without reflection in the very turmoil of their ephemeral life. What is actually expressed in the verse is a kind of admiration for the simple, naive mode of living which characterizes the life of "ordinary" men in contrast to those "halfway Buddhists" who show no concern except with the attainment of enlightenment. As for men of Awakening:

> The moon do you like? Or cherry-blossoms?
> No answer but loud snoring
> From the four sleepers![27]

This is a colophon written by Bashô over a famous picture of four monks asleep, suggestive of aloofness and detachment from the world. The otherworldly men, men of enlightenment, show no interest in the "folly of the moon and flowers." Sometimes entertaining high esteem verging on veneration, sometimes showing a gesture of decided denial, the "man of *wabi*" in any case cannot help being deeply concerned about the personal make-up of the enlightened men and their enlightened state of mind. But the otherworldly men, the learned and highly accomplished monks, do not show (and rightly do not show) any concern with the man of *wabi*, i.e., the *haiku*-poet engaged in the pursuit of "poetic truthfulness"—such at least is what he thinks of the position taken by the otherworldly men.

The pursuit of "poetic truthfulness" is a "folly of the moon and flowers" also from the point of view of the "ordinary" man.

> Into my folly of the moon and flowers
> Let me drive a pin of reproof
> At the advent of this first day of midwinter.[28]

It used to be the custom with common people in those days to have recourse to moxibustion and acupuncture, on the advent of the coldest season of the year, in order to build up their bodily strength against the rigors of winter. In the verse just quoted reference is made to this popular custom. Instead of physical acupuncture, however, the poet thinks that he should rather "drive a pin" into his own folly of wandering about in pursuit of the *poésie* of Nature as symbolized by the beauty of "the moon and flowers." The underlying idea is that the practical aspect of daily life, too, involves difficulties too seriously connected with existential anxiety to be ignored by the poet. This verse reflects further the introspective reflection and self-admonishment of the man of *wabi* who does not hesitate to give priority to his unremitting search for "poetic truthfulness," entirely ignoring the seriousness of practical life.

In the *haiku*-poem above we have observed the reproving as well as apologetic attitude taken by Bashô toward his own pursuit of "poetic truthfulness" which in its negative aspect appears as "folly of the moon and flowers" to the eyes of both the awakened and the "ordinary" men. It is to be remarked that when to the same ideal of "pursuit of poetic truthfulness" the "man of *wabi*" gives himself up entirely, detaching himself decisively from the world-view of the outsiders and their value judgment, it becomes concretized into the form of an irrepressible longing toward traveling and finds its identity in actual life in the life of a traveler.

Bashô, the man of *wabi*, spent in fact the greater part of his life in traveling and died as a traveler. Traveling stands in the closest relation to the mode of living peculiar to the man of *wabi*. Traveling provides him with a means of eradicating attachment to stabilized things. Through traveling he chooses to go into the very turmoil of uncertainty, anxiety, and anguish of life, for in his view, such is the sole mode of living by which he could remain faithful to the reality of human existence. Traveling *is* the life itself of the man of *wabi*. His life must necessarily assume the form of traveling.

The noblest thing is to keep the mind absolutely void and empty. Utter ignorance and inefficiency are therefore the ultimate realization of the human mode of being. Next to this comes [the state of material non-possession:] having no permanent place to live in, possessing not even a single straw-hut as his own. How could the mind [of a giant phoenix] which, being dependent upon nothing, is of an adamantine unyieldingness, be matched by the feeble wings of a dove?![29]

That is, how could such a mind bear confinement to the tiny space of a house among the petty circumstances of mundane life?

Days go and months pass as eternal travelers. So also are the years that pass by. Those who make a livelihood by working at oars or by driving a pack-horse until they reach the declining years of life, go on traveling day after day and make traveling itself their abode. We know of many famous men in olden times who ended their life on the road.[30]

But what kind of traveling is he thinking of? "Sustaining my life by one walking stick and one mendicant bowl"—this is how he describes his own way of traveling. But whether he goes on wandering in such a manner ("Would that I go on a journey/ Would that I be called a 'traveler'/ In the first drizzling rain of autumn"),[31] or whether he stays for some time in a straw hut, secluded from human society ("Confined in my hut, I would fain/ Lean my back upon the familiar pillar of mine/ To go through this winter"),[32] for the man of *wabi* the whole length of his life itself is, as it were, a segment of a journey which begins without any definite beginning and which abruptly comes to a close without any real conclusion. For his is a kind of life for which no completion is to be expected and from which no conclusion is to be drawn.

Thus guarding himself against being attached physically as well as spiritually to anything whatsoever, and being determined to live every single moment of his life with the whole of his own naked existence, the man of *wabi* ends up by trying to eliminate even the desire to remain attached to his state of being a man of *wabi*. The spirit of the *haiku*-poet, which prizes above anything else the search after "poetic truthfulness," may after all—so he thinks—be a form of a foolish attachment just like all other forms of human attachment to things of the world.

Such is the basic paradox of the very existence of the man of *wabi*. True, he never forgets to view his own state from the negative point of view of the outsiders and describes it by such negative expressions as "folly," "madness." But sooner or later the time comes when he is forced to realize that such a negative gesture itself has been nothing other than the reverse side of his tenacious attachment to his own being a man of *wabi*. And when he does realize this, his basic state or attitude becomes almost of necessity sublimated into that of *karumi*, "lightness,"[33] i.e., an infinite freedom from any fixed ideas and established values.

Thus toward the end of his life, Bashô, the man of *wabi*, begins to propose as the highest ideal of *haiku* the principle of "lightness" which allows one to accept the phenomenal mode of existence of all things, including one's own, as it actually is in the phenomenal dimension of being, to accept it lightly, jovially, and without a shadow of doubt—an absolute affirmation of the reality of the things and events in the phenomenal world. The world of "lightness" is a world in which—as the celebrated Zen adage goes—"The willow is green and the flower is red."[34]

Bashô in this period of his life succeeded, so it seems, in establishing this principle of poetic experience, at least as a theory. Moreover, he did exemplify through some concrete works the state of "lightness."

So he apparently turned from the poetic principles directly stemming from the spirit of *wabi*, such as *sabi*, *shiori*, and *hosomi*, to a principle of a somewhat different nature, *karumi*. But does *karumi*, the poetic principle of "lightness," truly represent the ultimate stage of Bashô's poetic career, in which he could find unalloyed satisfaction? That is highly questionable, for the man of *wabi* who has come up to this stage is a man who has already had a glimpse of the world of Silence and Nothing lying at the back of all phenomenal things, and who, consequently, is no longer able to see all things, including his own self, except against the background of, and in contrast to, the eternal Silence and Nothing. And yet, tragically enough, Bashô, the man of *wabi*, unlike the man of Awakening, was destined to remain to the last unable to overcome this existential polarity and sublate it to a higher dimension in which all contradictions would be dissolved into an absolute Unity.

However it may be, the fact is that Bashô terminated his life as a man of *wabi* and as a poet who had seen the bottomless abyss into which *wabi* could drive him. Instead of going the way of spiritual Awakening, he died the death of a man of *wabi*, the death of a roving traveler, which was exactly the kind of death he had almost expected and of which he had often talked to his disciples as being most suitable to a man of his kind.

BEING AND NOTHING IN THE WORLD-VIEW OF *WABI*

Haiku, whose external structure demands that a complete poem should be made of seventeen syllables arranged in three consecutive units of 5/7/5 syllables, is obviously the shortest of all forms of verbal art, and may therefore be said to have the most strict formal limitations. Whether the poet aims at an objective description of the external world or a subjective expression of his emotions, such formal limitations would seem to make his free creative activity almost impossible. On the other hand, however, we must remember that in poetic creation in general the very content to be expressed demands for itself a special external form. And if so, the content of *haiku* must, we might surmise, also be something very peculiar, corresponding to the peculiarity of its external structure. The poetic content to be put into 5/7/5 syllables should be not an ordinary description or expression, but rather something of a very particular nature.

In the art of *haiku*, we might say, what is to be expressed and how it should be expressed is, at least in its most fundamental form, already determined from the very beginning. This basic content of *haiku*, in the school of Bashô, is constituted by such characteristic aesthetic principles as *sabi, shiori,* and *hosomi*. In other words, one or more of these aesthetic ideas must be realized in some form or other in any *haiku*-poem in its depth-structure, whatever be its actual content in the dimension of verbal expression. As a matter of fact, these basic principles that are expected to be realized in such an extraordinarily short form naturally tend to dictate to a considerable extent what is to be said; so important is the position occupied by these aesthetic ideas in the creation of *haiku*-poems.

The most important point to note about these aesthetic ideas is that in their inner structure each of them is inseparably connected with Nature, and that it is impossible for any of them to be established as an aesthetic value except through the intermediary of Nature.[35]

The inseparable connection of these aesthetic ideas with Nature is shown first of all by the fact that one of the fundamental technical rules of *haiku* demands that every *haiku*-poem should contain among the words of the seventeen syllables (5/7/5) a key word indicative of one of the four seasons, the so called "season-term."[36]

In the second place, we must observe that each of the aesthetic ideas such as *sabi, shiori,* and *hosomi* stands on the basis of the spiritual state of the man of *wabi* as analyzed above, and that the concept

itself of the man of *wabi* is established in reference to the most intimate relationship between man and Nature. It is worth observing
further that the basic inner contradiction which, as we have seen
earlier, is inherent in the very structure of the state of the man of
wabi, is also conceivable only in reference to Nature.

Viewed in this light, Nature is found to play an exceedingly important role in *haiku* and in the formative process of the spirit of
haiku.

It has often been pointed out that the majority of the purely aesthetic
ideas—including *aware*,[37] which, as a representative aesthetic concept of *waka*-poetry, was historically the forerunner of *wabi, sabi,
shiori,* and *hosomi*—are semantically of a negative nature. What is
definitely a positive value is made to assume semantically a negative
form. That in itself is a remarkable fact. For when a semantically
negative expression is made to play a positive role as an indicator of
an aesthetic value, the meaning of the word of necessity becomes partially positive; yet the negativity which the word originally had in
its semantic structure leaves an indelible trace in the make-up of the
concept. Rather, we should point out as a characteristic feature of
these purely Japanese aesthetic ideas that negative expressions were
adopted from the outset with the expectation of their functioning as
indicators of positive values retaining in themselves a negative
nuance.

Let us now analyze the inner structure of this seemingly strange semantic phenomenon. Our analysis of it will bring to light the important fact that the majority of the principal value words in Japan,
whether ethical or aesthetic, owe their formation to a functional relation between two opposing terms: man versus Nature, and Nature
versus man.

A celebrated *waka*-poet of the *Shin-kokin* period was once asked
what he considered the spiritual core of his poetic creation; he is said
to have answered: "withered pampas grass in the desolate field and
the wan moon in the morning sky!"[38] This answer is remarkable in
that it shows that this poet perceived in withered pampas grass in a
desolate autumn field a deeper poetic beauty than in the green exuberance of luxuriant trees and grass in summer, and found the pale
moon in the dim light of the dawn poetically evocative of far deeper

poetic emotions than the brightly shining moon in the middle of the night.

Another representative *waka*-poet of the same period, Lord Teika of the Fujiwara clan,[39] has the following famous poem which reads:

> All around, no flowers in bloom are seen,
> Nor blazing maple leaves I see,
> Only a solitary fisherman's hut I see,
> On the sea beach, in the twilight of this autumn eve.[40]

It is to be noted that in this poem the "flowers in bloom" and "blazing maple leaves" appear in a negative form by their actual existence being verbally negated. This poem and the "withered-grass" statement of Mototoshi are generally regarded by the man of *wabi* of the later ages as the earliest instances of the advocacy of the spirit of *wabi* in Japanese literature. In both these cases, the beauty is made to subsist in a negative form by emphasis on the reminiscence it leaves in its wake after all those things ordinarily considered beautiful have disappeared in the flow of universal impermanence.[41]

Likewise, Kenkô Kimura in his Essay (*Tsurezure-Gusa*)—"As for cherry blossoms, are they only to be admired in full bloom? As for the moon, is it only to be admired gloriously shining in the sky?"— may be said to express the same spirit of *wabi*.[42]

Cherry-blossoms in full bloom, the gloriously shining full moon, the verdant exuberance of grass and trees—these and all other things of Nature are impermanent and incessantly changing; they are all destined to decline and fade. What the *waka*-poets of the period of the *Shin-kokin* Anthology obtained from Nature by intently gazing into its depths, just as they gazed into the depths of their own consciousness, was the idea of the impermanence of Nature as represented by cherry blossoms scattered by the wind and autumn leaves falling to the ground. They discovered therein an aesthetic value, the beauty of ephemerality, the *awaré*.

Here it is to be remarked that the observation of impermanence peculiar to the *waka*-poet is made exclusively in reference to the phenomenal world as it is reflected in the mirror of the observing eyes of the human subject. In such a context and from such a point of view it makes no difference, in terms of a real opposition of metaphysical negativity and positivity, whether one speaks of the immutability or of the changefulness of Nature, for both are concepts belonging to the same ontological level of thinking and opposed to each other on that level. In a similar manner, put in opposition to fresh verdure are withered leaves, and in opposition to full-blown cherry blossoms, falling petals in the wind. Surely, this opposition rests on a clear awareness of the impermanence of existence, but the opposing terms are always in the same dimension; a natural phenomenon versus another natural phenomenon, a form of being versus another form of being.

Otherwise expressed, the *waka*-poets of the period of the *Shin-kokin* Anthology looked at Nature solely in its positive aspects. For them Nature was a world filled with all kinds of things and events, with no space left vacant. Nature was in their view the sum total of innumerable things and events, a picture, as it were, wholly filled with "figures" in relief with a total elimination of the "ground."

Even negative concepts like impermanence and nothingness acquire a certain kind of positivity through linguistic articulation. And in the dimension of linguistic consciousness they turn into something positive; they become positive *things*. In this sense, Nature was for the poets of the *Shin-kokin* Anthology a world-consciousness constituted by linguistically articulated reality and what may be called an externally projected extension of that consciousness.

Thus the negativity of the aesthetic idea of *waka*, i.e., *awaré*, having its basis in such a view of Nature, cannot possibly be a negativity constituted through the intermediary of a Negation belonging to a different dimension. For in such a view being is always opposed to nonbeing, existence to nothingness, on one single level of the perception of universal change and impermanency. In the case of *haiku*, on the contrary, "being" is essentially viewed standing directly against the background of Nothing. The fundamental negativity lying at the basis of *haiku* is of quite a different structure from that of *waka*. For it does not owe its origin to a one-dimensional opposition of two terms; it is established only through the intermediary of the concept of "nothingness" belonging to a higher dimension of human consciousness. It is in this respect that the aesthetic ideas of *haiku* disclose a totally different structure from their historical forerunner, the aesthetic idea of *waka*.

> The most fundamental factor which distinguishes the Mediaeval Age from both the prior and posterior periods in the cultural history of Japan is that by the time the spirit of the former became established, the Japanese had already experienced the process of going through Negation, Nothing and Nothingness.[43]

So says Junzô Karaki. *Haiku*, thus considered, may rightly be regarded in its basic inner structure as representative of the spirit of the medieval arts of Japan.

The *haiku*-poet living in the world of *wabi* regards the phenomenal or empirical aspect of reality as a positive factor. He recognizes as its background Nothingness, and he is keenly conscious of Nothingness as being the negative aspect of reality in a higher, metaphysical dimension. The positive aspect subsists only on the basis of the negative reality, while the negative reality discloses its true nature as metaphysical Nothingness only against the positive reality.

All movements calm down into stillness in the midst of Nothingness; all forms become ultimately lost into it; all sounds go back therein to eternal silence. What is opposed to human existence and all phenomenal things and events of Nature is Nature in its primordial Nothingness as an empty locus for everything in a higher, nonphenomenal dimension of being. Nature in the view of the man of *wabi* may thus be said to be characterized by its two-stratum structure: the stratum of Being and that of Nothingness. In this vision, Nothingness supports and sustains from behind the world of variegated phenomena.

The world of Being, that is, phenomenal Nature, is saturated with movement, change, and ephemerality. The world of Nothingness which is at its back and which constitutes an invisible locus in which all phenomenal things and events become visible, is immovable and immutable because it is in itself an absolutely empty locus. And since it is a world beyond all phenomena, it is eternally existent, or rather, it reposes in its primordial stillness beyond time and space.

The phenomenal reality of Being, however, appears transformed into something of an entirely different nature when it is seen in contrast to the world of Nothingness. We might even go a step further in this direction and say that whatever is observable in the phenomenal Nature—the regular changes of the seasons, "cherry blossoms scattered by the wind and autumn leaves falling to the ground," movement, stillness, ephemerality, eternity—all these things establish themselves as concrete phenomena only in relation to the existential awareness of man and on the basis of the cognitive articulations of his mind. If it were not for this ontological relation with human existence, Nature would lack the human systematization in terms of time and space stemming from the act of cognition through articulation. Rather, Nature itself would not emerge as Nature in its phenomenality. Nature *in itself* would be neither Being nor Nonbeing, neither existence nor even Nothingness. It would be sheer primordial Chaos:

> Stillness is the mode of changelessness. Movement is changefulness. Nothing stops moving if it is not stopped. Stopping here means that the poet crystallizes a moving thing instantaneously in the very act of perception. Falling blossoms, leaves scattered by the wind—they will never be brought to a positive form unless the poet crystallizes them; everything will disappear into nothingness, leaving no trace behind, even those that are alive at the moment. . . . The moment you seize a moving thing flashing upon your mind, you must crystallize it through expression before it goes to naught.[44]

This colorless, formless Nature becomes aesthetically or ethically colored through the intervention of the existential awareness of man. Through it, again, do such phenomenal aspects of Nature as have properly no relation whatsoever with values and evaluation (like the changes of the seasons, local motions, etc.) become linguistically transformed into a negative term *mujô*, "ephemerality" or "impermanency." By a similar process of semantic transformation, special value-terms become established, connoting negative qualities such as oldness, imperfection, frailty, and lowliness. *Wabi, sabi, shiori,* and *hosomi* belong to this group. Note that these "values" are exact contraries of such concepts as perfection, greatness, grandeur, eternity, and the like, that are usually considered values in the positive sense.

The problem now is: Where does this linguistic negativity originate? And if these values are negative, what do they negate?

Let us start by remarking that the Nothingness which plays a central role in the formation of the Weltanschauung of *haiku,* is somewhat different from the transcendental Nothingness as experienced by the otherworldly men in their enlightenment. Rather than being pure Nothingness, it is Nature conceived as the actual background of phenomenal things. In this sense it still remains Nature. But it is felt and conceived as Nonbeing and Nothingness in the particular sense that it is a world from which all phenomenal things have been eliminated, in contrast to the phenomenal things which are, in this case, conceived of in their positive aspect. Thus the negativity in question is a negativity stemming from the negation of the phenomenal world, Nonbeing in contrast to the positive existence of the world of phenomena. It is against the background of transcendental, nonphenomenal Nature whose eternal immutability and constancy have positively been affirmed that the world of phenomena discloses its negativity to our eyes as a world essentially characterized by ephemerality, transiency, and mutability.

Man finds himself faced by these two Natures (or Nature in two different dimensions)—namely, phenomenal Nature and transcendental Nature. On one hand, man as a phenomenal being is placed in the midst of phenomenal Nature which comprises him together with all other phenomenal things. In this situation, he is but a small and weak being liable to be overwhelmed and crushed by the awful grandeur of phenomenal Nature. Against transcendental Nature, on the other hand, he is forced to realize his fatal, absolute inferiority by keen awareness of the transiency of his existence.

Considered in the light of such observation, the world of phenomena, including man and all other sensible objects, is found to be linguistically established as something positive insofar as it constitutes the object of man's sense experience, while in relation to Nothing (i.e., transcendental Nature) it appars in the position of undeniable negativity in terms of value-relation as well as in terms of the comprising-comprised relationship. Nature qua Nothing, on the contrary, is linguistically posited as something negative only insofar as it is non-sensible, but it is in all other respects endowed with an overwhelming superiority as something absolutely positive.

It is to be remembered that the above is but a simplified consideration from the viewpoint of psychological dynamism of the positive-negative relation observable in the dimension of linguistic expression with regard to the two opposing terms "man" and "Nature." The reality of the matter, however, is far more complicated. The "subject" here, to begin with, differs from what is generally posited as the subject of cognition and action in ordinary systems of subject-object relationship. For in the poetic experience of *haiku*, the subject is not a fixed subject. It is rather a flexible and mobile subject that freely changes its viewpoint in accordance with different focuses and various points of emphasis which it may choose to adopt. And this infinitely mobile subjective attitude, reflecting all of man's psychological undulations, forms for itself an extremely complicated system of values having Nothing as the basis and means of cognition and action. Such a complicated structure is faithfully represented by concepts like *wabi, sabi, shiori,* and *hosomi,* which are of an aesthetic as well as an ethical nature.

The "unremitting pursuit of poetic truthfulness," then, means precisely man's effort to come ever closer to the true reality of human existence in the face of Nature and to the true reality of all phenomenal things standing against the background of Nothingness. *Haiku* is a peculiar type of poetry which aims at realizing and expressing the truth of things thus comprehended, in seventeen syllables. And he who is engaged in creating and appreciating *haiku* is the man of *wabi*: the *haiku*-poet who is at the same time necessarily the *haiku*-critic.

DÔ, THE SPIRITUAL WAY OF SELF-DISCIPLINE

It has often been declared that *haiku* is an art aiming at truth rather than beauty. Yoshinori Ônishi, for example, states: "The spirit of *haiku* consists in trying to grasp directly the true reality of life-experience."[45]

Haiku in its inner structure intends to solve two difficult problems. One of them is to transcend the contradictory opposition of the subject and object, and the other is to transcend the opposition of Being and Nothing. As for the first opposition, the man of *wabi* is conscious of it as a pure problem of art. That is to say, he understands it as a basic problem relating to the poetic experience of the poet, his self-expression, and the object to be described.

The second opposition, that of Being and Nothing, is for the man of *wabi* a problem of which he is critically conscious: It is crucial to the very basis of the reality of human existence.

These two kinds of opposition are in the view of the man of *wabi* supposed to be overcome by what is called *dô* (the "way," i.e., the spiritual way of discipline). Let us first consider how the problem of the subject-object opposition is solved. Yoshinori Ônishi, in explaining the characteristics of the creative process of *haiku*, makes the following observation: "*Haiku* grasps the experiential reality of the interfusion of the subject and object at the precise moment of their interfusion."[46] This would seem to suggest that in *haiku* there can be neither a purely objective description nor a purely subjective expression. The self-expression of the poet is always actualized through his describing some object, while the described object is not allowed to subsist independently of the subjective attitude of the poet.

> Our master used to admonish us to learn about the pine-tree from the pine-tree itself, and about the bamboo from the bamboo itself. He meant thereby that we would totally abandon the act of deliberation based on our ego. [Those who are immature] mistakenly take this word "learn" in the sense of learning through deliberation. This is

why they end up by not "learning" in the true sense. What the master really meant by "learning" is our penetrating into the object itself until its inscrutable essence is revealed to us. Then the poetic emotion thereby stimulated becomes crystallized into a verse. No matter how clearly we may depict an object in a verse, the object and our ego would remain two separated things and the poetic emotion expressed would never reach the true reality of the object, if the emotion is not a spontaneous effusion out of the reality of that object. Such [discrepancy between the emotion and reality] is caused by the deliberate intention on the part of our ego.[47]

In producing *haiku* there is a difference between "becoming" and "making." If one constantly cultivates one's own interior, trying to make it correspond to the external object, the hue of one's mind becomes naturally a verse. If, on the contrary, one neglects to cultivate constantly one's interior, the mind does not become a verse; rather, in such a case one *makes* the verse through the conscious deliberation of the ego.[48]

These two passages are found in a work of Dohô Hattori, in which this notable disciple of Bashô transmits the teachings of his master. As is clear from these words, describing a pine tree or a bamboo in *haiku* is not the same objectively describing a pine tree or a bamboo; it means rather that a pine tree or a bamboo as it has been reflected in the mind depicts its own figure in the form of a verse. It must be remarked, further, that the "mind" reflecting a pine tree or a bamboo is not to be taken here as the mind in the psychological sense, but only as the mind which has reached a certain state, or as a certain state of spirituality attained by the mind. This would mean that reaching that kind of state of mind is already an act of *haiku*-production before the actual production of *haiku*. *Haiku*, in other words, does not come into being by the poet's actually describing an object in a verse. Quite the contrary; *haiku* may rightly be regarded as having already come into existence at the very moment when the poet has achieved the realization of this particular state of mind.

In such a situation, the relation between mind and object is clearly not a unilateral relation between the seer and the seen, but a bilateral relation of mutual correspondence between the two terms. The object manifests infinitely varying aspects in accordance with varying states of the cognitive subject. Consequently the object described in this or that way discloses the spiritual state of the subject who has so described it. Self-expression in *haiku* is usually through description with this kind of peculiar structure. And this fact remains the same whether the object described happens to be a thing of Nature, an event, or a human condition.

This point may also be considered from a somewhat different view-point. Man is actually surrounded by innumerable things and events emerging in infinitely various forms. When, out of the chaos of these things and events, something attracts his eyes or something strikes his ears, the man in reality is articulating the chaos in that particular manner. Through the act of articulating the chaos an unconscious choice is made. The mind of the cognizant subject, though apparently in a passive state in the sense that something is reflected in its mirror, is in truth already actively working upon the external world.

The *haiku* poet has an extraordinarily keen awareness of this cognitive process and aims at reproducing it in his creative process. That is to say, there is in the case of *haiku* a positive act of poetic creation prior to the actual production of a poem, and that, precisely, is the most essential part of the creative process of *haiku*. A product of such an inner creative activity is called by Bashô "a verse that *becomes.*" He declares that genuine *haiku*-poems must invariably be "verses that become." In contrast to this, a *haiku*-poem which is com-posed by a deliberate intention on the part of the poet to compose a *haiku* is called by Bashô a "verse that is made." Bashô strictly guards himself and his disciples against "making a verse," that is, composing a verse so that such-and-such aspect of such-and-such an object be deliberately chosen as its motive only after the mind has started to work in the dimension of verbal expression. Quite to the contrary, according to Bashô, that which has already been there in the mind must "come out of the mind to the dimension of verbal expression in-stantaneously, on the spot, without there being even a hair's breadth between the pen and the mind. There is here absolutely no room for hesitation or deliberation."[49]

The peculiarity of the structure which characterizes the subjective attitude of the mind in *haiku* and its mode of expression, is in reality a peculiarity shared by all forms of art stemming from *dô* (the spir-itual way of self-discipline). *Haiku*, it must be remembered, is a typical art based on *dô*. It is characteristic of every art of *dô* that a description of an object is in itself a self-expression of the subject, while a self-expression of the subject in the presence of and in ac-cordance with an object discloses the object itself as he has seen it with his inner eye. By dint of this characteristic, the gap between the subject and object, between "I" and the external world, appears to be bridged—at least structurally—in the domain of the artistic expression of *haiku* as well as in that of the aesthetic experience of the subject.

Once we turn our attention, however, from the relation between the subject and object, i.e., between the interior and the exterior, to the more crucial problem, that of the real nature of the state of mind itself which plays the most decisive role in the creative activity of *haiku*, we find the problem far more complicated.

The peculiar state of mind productive of genuine *haiku* must, first and foremost, be such that it grasps and faithfully reflects the true reality of life-experience. It must be such that it views Being against the background of Nothing, movement against stillness, colorfulness against colorlessness, sound against silence, time against timelessness; in short it must be such that it intuits, grasps, and reflects all things against the background of the transcendental Nothingness.

The focus of attention here is no longer the opposition of the subject and object; it is, instead, the opposition of Being and Nothing. What is at issue now is the opposition of the world of Nothingness and the phenomenal world with all the things existing therein.

The world-view of the man of *wabi* which is characterized by the opposition of Being and Nothing functions as an inexhaustible source of the creation and appreciation of *haiku*. Yet the moment the poet becomes conscious of it as a purely subjective problem directly connected with human existence, the gap once opened between Being and Nothing begins to disclose itself to him as a problem foreboding a serious crisis. The irresistible annihilating power of the omnipotent Nothing which casts its dark shadow upon the colorful and lively world of phenomena, naturally raises for human existence a far deeper and far more immediate problem than the one raised by the opposition of subject and object.

Thus the liquidation of the opposition and the consequent solution of the problem must evidently be sought for in the sublation of the contradictory relation between the phenomenal world and the transcendental Nothing, subsisting each in a different metaphysical dimension, into a unity in a still higher dimension. And such a thing is supposed to be realizable in the art of *dô* only in spiritual enlightenment.

The *dô* in the field of art is a way of leading to spiritual enlightenment through art; the *dô* consists here in making an art a means by which to achieve enlightenment as its ultimate goal. In the artistic *dô*, however, particular emphasis is laid on the process, the way, by which one goes toward the goal. To every stage of the way a certain spiritual state corresponds, and at every stage the artist tries to get into communion with the quintessence of art through the corresponding spiritual state, and to make himself bloom in the art.

In the religious *dô*, on the contrary, that which counts primarily is the attainment of enlightenment and what comes thereafter. The latter kind of *dô* strictly demands that man should eliminate or annihilate his own phenomenal self. Here there is no room left for a man on his way to enlightenment to appreciate the value of living his phenomenal life in the world of phenomena, in no matter how artistically elevated a form it may be. It is only after having attained enlightenment that he allows himself to come back to this world and begin to live again among the phenomena.

For a man aiming at religious enlightenment, therefore, the pre-enlightenment stages are of almost no value. For a man aiming at artistic perfection, on the contrary, the ultimate state of enlightenment will remain a goal which he most probably will never be able to reach as long as he remains attached to his art. He who goes along this road bears upon himself the burden of this destiny. The man of *wabi* is thus a man destined to remain in the state of being "not-yet-enlightened." He is a man who, for the sake of art, has positively chosen such a way. Kikaku tells the following episode:[50]

> There is a *haiku*-poem composed on the theme, "Self-nature":
>
>> Even the enlightened monk in spiritual peace
>>   Is sad and sorrowful
>>   This autumn eve.[51]
>
> Taking an exception against this verse, a certain monk remarked: "An enlightened monk enjoying spiritual peace cannot possibly feel sorrow for anything. The poet should have said: 'Let even the monk in spiritual peace be in sorrow and grief!' Only then the poem would have been acceptable." Against this I retorted saying: "The peculiar wording of this poem does nothing but evoke a cosmic sadness reigning over everything. Here there is absolutely no discrepancy of any sort between the world and the subject. The poem describes the absolute Self in which the heavens and earth are fused into one single unity."[53]

Kikaku interprets the "sadness" mentioned in this verse of Kifû as referring to the metaphysical and cosmic sadness of the absolute Self integrating into itself heavens and earth, that is, the metaphysical dimension of Nothing which transcends and sublimates into a higher unity the opposition of the "I" and the thing, the subject and the object, the seer (the monk) and the seen (autumn), and being and nonbeing.

Surely, we cannot deny the possibility of understanding in this way, at least theoretically and structurally, the concept of Nothing in this verse. But does the "sadness" mentioned in the verse of Kifû really indicate the cosmic sadness of the absolute Nothing as interpreted by Kikaku? Is it not rather the fact that by the "autumn eve" is meant an autumn evening in the phenomenal world—the phenomenal world here being represented as a world opposed to Nothing? And is the "sadness," consequently, not the emotion of sadness pertaining to the world of ephemerality and impermanence? Certainly the monk and the autumn evening in Kifû's poem might be, as Kikaku points out, in a state of perfect fusion. But is it not the case that the opposition of the phenomenal world and the transcendental world, i.e., Being and Nothing, still remains far from being sublated into an absolute unity of a higher order? And if this is true, then this autumn evening as reflected in the eyes of Kifû, the man of *wabi*, must be essentially different from the same autumn evening as reflected in the enlightened mind of the monk. Although this is not the main issue in the present context, the argument of the monk may in this sense be recognized as hitting the mark.

In any case, this is an interesting episode revealing the fundamental difference between the religious standpoint of the monk and the artistic standpoint of the man of *wabi*.

It would seem necessary, though, to touch upon the difference between the Nothing as experienced by the man of Awakening and the Nothing as understood by the man of *wabi*.

> There is Something primordial beyond heavens and earth. Formless and eternally lonely, It works as the Lord of all things, and never withers throughout the four seasons.[53]

It is hard to tell whether the Something (i.e., Nothing) which is indicated in this passage is the Nothing of the enlightened man or that of the man of *wabi*. To such an extent are the two conceptions of Nothing similar to each other in the dimension of verbal description. If, however, one reads the passage more carefully one will feel that the description is in reality a powerful "self-expression" of the Nothing itself as actually experienced by the man of enlightenment, and not a "description" of the Nothing of the man of *wabi*, which, as we have already seen, is conceived of as transcendental Nature functioning as the negative background against which the appearance of the phenomenal world takes place.

Jôshû was once asked by a monk: "Is there Buddha-nature [i.e., Absolute reality or Nothingness] in the dog? Or is there not?" Answered Jôshû: "No!"[54]

The No! of the Zen Master Jôshû is not an ordinary word of negation. It is rather a straightforward presentation of the state of Nothingness. (In Chinese, be it remarked in passing, No, Nothing, and Nothingness are indicated by the same word, *wu* [J. *mu*].) The monk raised the question of whether the dog is possessed of Buddha-nature or not. The question stands in a spiritual dimension in which being is opposed to nonbeing. Instead of giving a direct answer to this question in the same dimension, Joshû through this utterance abruptly manifests his own Self to the monk as an embodiment of the spiritual state of Nothingness itself, transcending both being and nonbeing.

The Nothing of the man of enlightenment is a transcendental unity of the I and the thing, the subject and object, being and nonbeing. It is even beyond the Nothing as conceived of in opposition to the world of Being. As such, it has essentially and in itself nothing to do with aesthetic or ethical values. It has not even the "value" of being the truth. This Nothing which properly lies beyond all values does enter various relations with various values, as soon as those who have not yet attained enlightenment try to approach it.

As for the world of phenomena, it discloses its true reality and true beauty only to the eyes of one who has attained enlightenment and who, after having looked into the absolute Nothing beyond truth and beauty, returns again to the phenomenal dimension of Being, bringing back to it his own self as a form of phenomenal existence. There he finds the opposition between phenomenal Nature and transcendental Nature completely nullified. What he observes is the phenomenal world in its purity and senenity reposing in the bosom of Absolute Affirmation, there being not even a shadow of negation. This is the world of "the willows are green and the flowers are red."

Let us read two *waka*-poems, one of Zen Master Dôgen and another of Zen Master Ryôkan,[56] in which such world-view finds its most candid expression.

> Cherry-blossoms in spring, cuckoos in summer,
>   And in autumn, the moon.
> Winter, the serenity of snow—
> How pleasantly cool this world is![55]

> What shall I leave after me, as a memento . . .
>   Other than flowers of spring,
> Cuckoos in the mountains,
> Maple-leaves tinted in autumn?[56]

Compare the world-view of these two remarkable men of enlightenment with that which is expressed in the following *haiku*-poem of Bashô, composed a year before his death—of Bashô who lived his life as a man of *wabi* and died as a man of man of *wabi*.

> Along this road
> Goes no one
> This aumtumn eve.[57]

The last days of the life of Bashô, the man "who has not yet attained enlightenment," are described in a moving tone by his disciple Kikaku in his *The Record of the Last Moments of Master Bashô*.[58]

> The Master may have faintly heard from behind the wall his disciples muttering a prayer for the prolongation of his life. In a feeble voice, he remarked all of a sudden: "Ah, I have been dreaming!" And a *haiku* fell from his lips:
>
>> Fallen ill on the road,
>> My dream running frantically
>> In the withered field.
>
> Then he said: "It might perhaps be better to change the wording (of the latter part of the poem) to 'A dreamy mind roving in the withered field'." "But", the Master continued, "going to this extent is itself an act prompted by my own ineradicable attachment to this futile illusion. Now that I am going to die in the midst of my 'pursuit of poetic truthfulness,' my heart tormented by regret, is filled with an irresistible longing toward the Way [of religious salvation]."
> The above-given is a *haiku* composed by the Master on the eighth day of the month, late at night.

Bashô, the man of *wabi*, thus ended his life at the age of fifty-one on the twelfth of October, 1694.

Notes

1. "Poetic truthfulness" is a tentative translation of *fûga-no makoto*. As one of the key terms of the Bashô school it has been variously defined and explained. Y. Ônishi, to give a typical example, says: "It is a special spiritual attitude taken by man toward the true reality of the universe so that he might come even closer to its depths."—Yoshinori Ônishi: *Bagaku* (Aesthetics) II (Tokyo, 1969).

2. *Wabi*, one of the most important key concepts which has exercised a tremendous influence on the formation of Japanese culture after the "Mediaeval" times, particularly in the field of literature and art, will be explained in detail later in this paper.
3. Bashô, Matsuo (1644–1695), founder of what is known as the Bashô school of *haiku*. Known as the *"haiku*-saint," he is considered the greatest of all *haiku* poets.
4. *Matsuo Bashô Shû*, Shôgakukan Series of Japanese Classical Literature XLI (Tokyo, 1972), p. 421.
5. Ibid., p. 408.
6. Ibid., p. 421, note.
7. Ibid., pp. 408–409.
8. Kai-so (725–786), a celebrated calligrapher of the early T'ang dynasty.
9. One of the representative philosophers of the Sung dynasty.
10. *Matsuo Bashô Shû*, p. 532.
11. See *Bashô Bunshû*, Iwanami Series of Classical Japanese Literature XLVI (Tokyo, 1959), p. 52.
12. The botanical name is *Musa Basjoo Sieb.*
13. Zenchiku Komparu (d. 1468), a famous Nô actor and also a remarkable theoretician on the spirit of Nô drama.
14. Genshin (942–1017), a monk of the Tendai school in the Heian Period.
15. *Ôjô Yôshû* ("Essentials of Salvation"), the *opus magnum* of Genshin, in which he urged the exclusive worship of Amitâbha (J. Amida).
16. On *wabi* and *sabi*, see Toshihiko Izutsu and Toyo Izutsu, "Poetry and Philosophy in Japan" *Contemporary Philosophy* (IV), ed. R. Klibansky (Florence, 1971), pp. 544–546. On *sabi*, see also Minoru Nishio, *Chûseitekina-mono-to sono-Tenkai* ("Mediaeval Ideas and Their Development"), (Tokyo, 1961), pp. 58–73.
17. *Shiori* means "verbal crystallization of what naturally effuses from the mind as man looks upon the things of Nature and human affairs with the emotion of commiseration"—Dictionary *Shin Kô-Jien*, ed. I. Shimmura (Tokyo, 1971).
18. *Hosomi* (lit. "thinness") is defined as "indicative of the inner profundity of a verse coming from the beauty felt by the poet in an elevated spiritual state of poetic consciousness."—Dictionary *Shin Kô-Jien.*
19. *Matsuo Bashô Shû*, p. 157.
20. Composed in 1689.
21. From *Oi-no Kobumi* (composed in 1691). *Matsuo Bashô Shû*, p. 311.
22. These two poems were composed by Bashô in 1688. See *Matsuo Bashô Shû*, p. 450.
23. Ibid.
24. Composed in 1689. Ibid., p. 142.
25. Composed in 1689. Ibid., p. 187.
26. Composed in 1680. Ibid., p. 206.
27. Composed in 1689. Ibid., p. 172.
28. Composed in 1692. Ibid., p. 235.
29. From an essay composed by Bashô in 1692. Ibid., p. 535.
30. From *Oku-no Hosomichi*, Ibid., p. 341.
31. From *Oi-no Kobumi*, Ibid., p. 312.
32. Composed in 1688. Ibid., p. 152.
33. *Karumi* (lit. "being-light") is defined as "a spiritual attitude to actualize the light flexibility of the mind so that it might go on responding to the ever-changing reality without remaining attached to any particular aspect of it."—Dictionary *Shin Kô-Jien.*
34. The adage originates from Su Tung P'o (J., So Tô Ba), a famous poet-painter

of the Sung dynasty. It refers to the things in their original "Suchness," un-contaminated by any artificial activity of the human mind.

35. See "Poetry and Philosophy in Japan," pp. 533–535, 541–546.
36. *Ki-go.* A number of special books, called *sai-ji-ki,* have been compiled in which key poetic words are classified in terms of the seasons.
37. *Aware,* established as a technical term in the Heian Period (794–1185), means primarily a deep emotion evoked by the observation of some particular situation, human or natural, and secondarily such a situation itself. In most cases, and particularly in the later ages, the word connotes profound sadness and the feeling of loneliness. See also Y. Ōnishi, *Yūgen-to Aware* (Tokyo, 1943).
38. The poet is Mototoshi. See Iwanami Series of Classical Japanese Literature LXVI (Tokyo, 1961), p. 175. See also Riichi Kurimoto, *Bashō-no Haikai Bi Ron* (The Haiku-Aesthetics of Bashō), (Tokyo, 1971), pp. 104–105.
39. Teika Fujiwara (1162–1251), the greatest poet of the *Shin-Kokin* period.
40. For a detailed analysis of this poem from the point of view of *wabi,* see Toshihiko Izutsu, *The Elimination of Color in Far Eastern Art and Philosophy,* Eranos Lecture, 1972, to be published in the Eranos-Yearbook 1972.
41. This interpretation of the poem is based on that given by the monk Sōkei in his *Nambō Roku,* Chikuma Series of Japanese Thought VII (Tokyo, 1971), pp. 302–303.
42. Kenkō Kimura, 1283–1351(?) See Iwanami Series of Classical Japanese Literature XXX (Tokyo, 1957), p. 201.
43. Junzō Karaki: *Mujō* ("Impermanency"), (Tokyo, 1965), p. 278.
44. A remark made by Bashō as it has been transmitted to us by one of his disciples, Dohō Hattori (d. 1730), in his *Aka Zōshi* ("Red Book"). Classical *Haiku* Literature Series X (Tokyo, 1970), p. 303.
45. Y. Onishi, *Bigaku* II, p. 480.
46. Ibid.
47. Dohō Hattori: *Aka Zōshi,* p. 302.
48. Ibid., p. 303.
49. Ibid.
50. Kikaku (1661–1744), an outstanding *haiku*-poet of the Bashō school.
51. The name of the poet who composed this *haiku* is Kifū.
52. From *Zōdan Shū* by Kikaku, Classical *Haiku* Literature Series X, p. 36.
53. See T. Shirota; *Bukkyō-ni okeru Chie-no Kōzo.* . . . ("On the Structure of Wisdom in Buddhism. . . .") in *Risō* (July 1972, Tokyo), p. 13.
54. *Pi Yen Lu* (J., *Heki Gan Roku*), Koan No. 1.
55. Dōgen, 1200–1253.
56. Ryōkan, 1178–1831. Composed at his death-bed.
57. Composed in 1694.
58. *Bashō-ō Shūen-no Ki,* in Shōgakukan Classical Japanese Literature XLII (Tokyo, 1972), p. 488.

Murray Krieger

THE CRITIC AS PERSON AND PERSONA

IN WILLIAM FAULKNER'S *Light in August* THERE IS A DRAMATIC TURN-
ing point when Reverend Hightower, until now trapped in the weakness of sterile self-torture and a withdrawal from life, delivers Lena
Grove's child and is thereby transformed into a newly vigorous be-
liever in fecundity and action. The change in him is made manifest
by his laying aside the Tennyson he had been reading previously, for
Shakespeare's *Henry IV*, which he now pronounces "food for a man"
—that is to say, *his* food. This example of literature as "food" suggests
clearly enough the notion that a reader uses his literary work,
matches it to his prior needs, and then absorbs it into himself, forcing it to serve his own bodily functions. We choose our literature and
in choosing make it ours, instead of discovering it and forcing ourselves (or rather allowing it to force us) to respond to it on *its*
grounds, transforming ourselves as we go. It is there to accommodate
us, and will be forced to, since we will not do what we must to ourselves in order to accommodate *it*.

But Hightower, we can argue, is not a critic; he is just a common
user—or rather a common misuser—of literature. And we might like
to say that the critic knows better, since his is the task of discovering
the literary work on its own terms rather than remaking it to serve
his. Yet there is a nagging skepticism that tugs at every honest critic,
even after he has done his best. He must candidly ask himself, as a
stand-in for all critics, Are the literary works we read our teachers,
shapers of our visions and our persons, or are they reflections of our
needs? Do they seize upon us and mold us, creating for us and in us

This essay was written under a research grant provided by the National
Endowment for the Humanities. I am grateful to this organization for its support
of my work.

the forms which become the forms of all our imaginations, or do we seize upon them, forcing them to be what our persons require them to be, putting them into a rude service for us? And, if the latter, do we then, worst of all, read these caterings to our needs back into the works and claim that they have been there all the time for us to discover them where they lay? Are we doomed only to project our own imaginative forms outward, peopling all works with the single cast of monsters created by our own imagination, and so turning all works into essentially the same work, even though we persuade ourselves we are but responding to a variety of external features whose uniformity of pattern seems to confirm our hypothesis about them? In his hermeneutic circularity, does the critic's every claim to objectivity reduce to this charade played out by his own personality in order to deceive—most of all—himself?

I

It is with such issues as these in mind that I turn to the matter of the critic as person and persona. In these days, when academic fashion increasingly prescribes that interior consciousness be regarded as the principal characteristic of the literature the critic studies, it is natural for him to dramatize his own position by discovering himself in his work, both as persona and as person—even to find a voice for himself that can speak with, or in competition with, the voice of the author under study. This may be only a perverse reaction to his inheritance from the New Criticism, with its exacting pretensions to objectivity. And it may very well be that such pretensions, insofar as they sprang from a notion of criticism as an impersonal would-be science, called for a reaction that celebrated the cult of the critic's personality in order to save criticism as an art. The candor about the critic's epistemological limitations, which makes him aware of his hermeneutic circularity, leads him to the artful delicacy with which he surrounds and invades his object with himself. Further, he sees himself as doing so and recognizes that his criticism, to the extent that it will be artful and delicate, must embrace the surrounding and the invading, as well as the object itself. All this his criticism may now do, although he cannot distinguish between the object and the self which has both marked it off and filled it.

Can the critic save anything of the object once he faces the logical consequences of his candid admission of the self's role in constituting the object it needs and wants? The problem is an obvious but troublesome one, as old as criticism. To the extent that the critic owes his primary fealty to the object that calls him into existence, he must obliterate himself to explain and exalt *it*. Thus the object would seem to define him rather than he it; it justifies his role instead of his prescribing its nature. But to the extent that he must call into question the very possibility of his finding and marking the objective qualities of the thing itself, he must keep himself self-consciously in the midst of his operations—all for the sake of candor and in flight from self-deception—since he is trapped within his version of the work and is unsure whether there can be a knowable work out there against which that version can be checked, or only other versions deriving from (and responding to) other personalities. The problem is what I elsewhere called the conflict between the play and the place of criticism: the need for the critic humbly to know his place, as subservient to the work, is challenged, embarrassed, and thoroughly undercut by his need for an arrogantly free play that inflates himself and our awareness of him.

How does the critic persuade us that he is dealing with a work, then, and not only with a reflection of his own personality? After we make all our hermeneutic admissions, it will be quite a trick for the critic to skirt his way between—on the one side—the sheerly and randomly personal, the private and idiosyncratic, and—on the other side —those responses which, in spite of his personal intrusions, still do refer roughly (how roughly!) to an object, the same object that arises out of those varied experiences of them within which each of us is trapped. It will be quite a trick because it courts logical, indeed epistemological, inconsistency to try to save the object we experience out of our random experiences of the object (or rather our experiences of the stimuli that we constitute as an apparent object).

The personal elements that significantly condition (at least!) what the critic chooses to criticize and how he then does so are not to be regretted—as these post-New Critical days have taught us to acknowledge—since they help him to function within criticism as an art, which is to say a humanistic discipline. But so long as we also think of it as a discipline, we must try to guard whatever normative and sharable element may yet be saved out of the critical procedure. It is our epistemological fate to have only versions of objects rather than objects themselves, and our selves are, obviously, self-protective about the versions they will permit. In our criticism, then, we should want—since we must have—the intrusion of the critic's person, as well as his persona. If we dig him out of his criticism as a self-conscious presence, we are the better able to deal with him, and perhaps (but only perhaps) to separate him (and his "version") from the work that claims his attention. So we search for the fellow behind the position-taking critic who maintains his system and his allegiance to it; for the fellow behind may, at times almost perversely, demur. And out of the holding back may arise a new awareness of all that the literary work may demand of us, a humane disaffection with universal systems and all that *they* demand of us, all that they make us give up. The only half-intended revelations of the critical persona, by thus opening up our responses, can make a virtue out of our hermeneutic necessity.

Let us try to summarize the distinctions I have been trying to make among the work (or rather the critic's attempt to speak normatively about his version of the work), the critic's persona, and his person. The literary work, with its beckonings, is what presumably stimulates the critic and what his discourse claims to be "about": it is to be at once the object and the objective of the discourse, both its material and its final cause. But hermeneutic candor requires him to confess that he has access to no works but only to versions of works. And what intrudes and distorts is the critic's self, his person and his persona.

The critic's persona I take to be the public personality he comes to adopt, and adopts with considerable conformity (we may flatter him by calling it consistency) as he moves from critique to critique or to a general statement of his critical principles, his claims about the nature of literature. However implicit or explicit, this is his system, the primary aesthetic assumptions and criteria he brings to every work to precondition it. He must fear, of course, that he may be reducing every work to *it*, with a severity that hammers consistency or conformity into mere uniformity. In this way all works would come to look the same (as do Nature and Homer for Pope in *An Essay on Criticism*). Though in the confrontation with every superior work there is a challenge for him to open his closed system, the critical persona tends to resist, in the interest of integrity and systematic fidelity. (After all, if his system represents *the* theoretical solution to problems in poetics, then it ought to account for whatever comes along.) So arises the party critic (and which of us is altogether innocent of the charge of being one, at least on occasion?) who must maintain his allegiance to whatever his aesthetic principles may be. For he sees that the alternative possibility—that of being *un*principled—is not merely eclectic (in trying to put together several conflicting principles) but rather is utterly *ad hoc*, responding randomly to the errant occasion. And this alternative is as undesirable as it is—given our critical egos—unlikely, unless one is to hold out for a naive empiricism, an experiential openness, that denies the censoring activity of the persona as he controls the critic's perceptions. It is, then, this allegiance, felt by the reader as much in the critic's tone as in his claims, that defines the critic's persona, his public personality as critic, the official and authorized—the dominant—voice, representative of his system and his perspective, that appears to be speaking to us—or rather at us—pedagogically. Indeed, more than ego, it acts as the critic's theoretical superego.

For the most part we see the individual critique as the intersection of the literary work (which we can speak of by extrapolation even if we cannot reach it as a neutral, independently beckoning entity) and the critic's system, represented by the persona. The yield for us, usually, is what that system permits to be grasped by perception in the work, what it permits to be grasped *as* the work. But in the sensitive critic there is a restiveness which leads him to struggle to let his system be shaped anew by the superior work, to try once more for objectivity and an open empirical encounter that breaks the circle. This struggle, thanks to the censoring persona, may finally turn out to be vain; but behind the struggle between the work and the critical persona, the sensitive critic can also permit us to see what I term his "person" striving to mount the doubly resistant beast compounded of work and system. If we think of the persona as the critic's superego, we may think of the person as his id. When the person succeeds in relaxing the persona more than most of us normally can, the persona's system opens itself (and us, as its readers) outward in order to embrace alien and challenging elements, which, as embraced, enlarge its (and our) capacity. This possibility of a free openness may finally be an illusion, though it is just this illusion that prompts and continues the considerable effort we put into critical debate with our fellows, debate which—just sometimes—persuades, and changes minds.

It may be, of course, that the person, as an antagonist of the persona—as the persona's critical underside, is really no more than a second, antisystematic persona. He would then be not the person himself, closer to the critic's self and an expression of his inner consciousness, but simply another, more subtle, trickier public personality which the critic has created out of his self-conscious awareness of the limitations of his public role. Rather than theoretical superego and the id that would overcome it, the critic now is seen as setting up a strategy of dialogue, a public drama between two created roles, his apparent persona and the resistant person behind. This alternative formulation does not bother me, so long as it does not disguise our sense of the critic's doubleness. For, regardless of which locution we prefer, the totality of the critic is to be seen by the shrewd reader as compounded of both persona and person or of the two antithetical personae. And we witness the critical performance as a drama between them, while the work, alternatively obscured or revealed, but assaulted, hides in the wings.

II

Yet we must continue searching to see, out of these epistemological and phenomenological shambles, what is left of the work for us to try to share with one another. Enough must be saved so that the work, in the end, is more than a private psychological episode, a "happening" in the critic's autobiography that he records in confessional prose. It is probably true, after all, that such confessional and rhapsodic criticism as we are often now given as a recital of self-consciousness, is not essentially different from that old impressionistic criticism which Anatole France termed "the adventure of [the] soul among masterpieces" (or would more philosophical candor require us to say "among the sensory stimuli we honorifically term masterpieces"?). As they promulgated the New Criticism, René Wellek and others often reminded us, always derogatorily, of this characterization. It is, perhaps, poetic justice that so-called critics of consciousness should have succeeded the New Criticism with their new—and philosophically more guarded—version of that subjectivism. But whether we see with the New Critics, the dominance of external system that reduces works to itself, or with the critics of consciousness, the dominance of the private sensibility that would absorb itself into each work, we must face the need to have some common residue which we can refer to as the work, even though we know how hard it is to get around ourselves to point to it.

The fact is, as I have been suggesting, that even the most systematic critic (if he is also a sensitive one) reveals some struggle with the reading self that is confronting *this* poem and—on the other side— that even the most subjective critic (if he is also a responsible one) reveals some allegiance to universals that precondition (and thus mediate) his immediate encounter. This is why we find the great critics in our tradition inevitably—if quite variously—at odds with themselves at certain key points in their work. My suggestion of the conflict between persona and person[1] was meant to give us some handles with which to grasp the sometimes wayward consequences of the drama that unfolds out of the critic's dialogue with himself. As he seeks to modify his theoretical obligations with his obligations to the new and utterly unique work at hand, and seeks further to keep himself at the center of what is to remain a human and humanistic experience, the critic may be seen not only as courting inconsistency, but as married to it, though he may struggle against his fate as do most husbands. This is why I think of the history of literary criticism in the West as deriving from what could be termed the consistent inconsistency of literary theory, if I may reword a phrase from Aristotle. Consequently, even a superficial study of the work of some representative "great critics" would reveal a rich complex of major and minor modes (or moods).

Even in the austere Plato himself, we find a grudging admiration—though accompanied by awe—for the poet's powers of vision and of profoundly moving his audience, an admiration that Plato occasionally permits to intrude upon his dominantly puritanical denials and prohibitions. It is as if the poet in Plato, responding as writer to the writings of others, is forcing the ascetic philosopher now and then to make his moral and metaphysical system give way to more weakly and warmly human requirements. We may thus see the damning judgment he passes upon the arts as the other side of his fears that acknowledge the full range of its powers. It is in accord with this tradition that the Platonic Augustine unhappily recalls how he "wept for Dido slain," in what is a tribute to the poet as much as it is a condemnation of himself. And in the Platonic rejection of poetry we find a formulation that, however wavering, must allow any anxiety about poetry's effects to be accompanied by an implicit tribute to its powers.

The Renaissance Neoplatonism of Sir Philip Sidney may be seen as betraying an even more marked duality. His dominant philosophical allegiances require him to treat the poem as a reflection of moral and metaphysical universals, so that the poem must serve the "foreconceit" which is its lord. But Sidney is a poet too, and a fine one, with a commitment to the poet's creative powers. This commitment requires him to treat the poetic imagination as sovereign, creator, and lord of its own domain and servant to no other. Yet his fidelity is a wavering one, so that the particular creatures of this imagination, far from arbitrary, end (in typical Renaissance Neoplatonic fashion) by finding their home in the heaven of Platonic universals. His affiliations to the conservative Italian tradition require that Sidney's native liberal tendency to exalt the poet as a free agent be directed into the safe channels of imitation, imitation metaphysically sanctified.

Even as doctrinal a critic as Alexander Pope betrays a wavering that was common among the best of the neoclassicists. In one passage he can make the most dogmatic equation among the rules, the ancients, and Nature as proper (and identical) objects of imitation; but he follows this passage immediately with the call to the poet to be a liberated Pegasus, deviating from "the common track" in order to "snatch a grace beyond the reach of art." And he can defend Shakespeare while he chides him, giving him the right to ignore the rules of one kind of art since—with an immediate access to Nature— he was practicing another. Thus does the Longinian concern with original genius intrude itself upon the Horatian strictures, with an unrestrained openness that threatens to break in upon the closet of the neoclassical system. Despite such momentary lapses, the dominant fidelity to the system holds.

Of course, in all these cases but most obviously in Pope's, the duality of attitude could spring from conflicting theoretical and philosophical traditions rather than from a conflict between the person and his theoretical tradition. The very tightness of the neoclassical system, its total inhibition of creativity, required its defender —if he were at all sensitive to what the poet's mind is capable of—to provide an antisystematic annex to accommodate some exceptions that the system would normally have to reject: any system that wanted to stay in business could not afford summarily to reject these. In this way what was potentially subversive was made to serve the system, by providing—at the cost of inconsistency—for what had to be provided for. Thus the notion of original genius, of the *lusus naturae*, at once *un*natural and within nature, breaks in, as an errant particular, upon a closed doctrine of Nature as a perfect artifact that permits no particular aberrations. What should threaten to destroy the system is made, through the psychological comfort it provides, to reinforce it. Pope has, then, an alternative theoretical tradition with which to counter the tradition to which he owes his primary allegiance, though it may also be his person as poet that, having sensitized him, induces him to invoke it so forcefully. Surely, that person must be called upon to create a single critical personality out of such antithetical strains. It is a tribute to Pope to say that he achieves in his work a personal unity that overrides its internal theoretical conflicts.

The conflict in Dr. Johnson seems more clearly traceable to the struggle of the person to resist accepting the dogmas which his system, represented by his majestic critical persona, sought to impose. Johnson's usual insistence on the poem's need to adhere to general nature, at whatever sacrifice of particularity, is undercut at moments here and there (though at strategically important moments) by his antibookish, antiartificial interest in the chaotic way events actually (and accidentally) occur in "the real state of sublunary nature."[2] In the midst of his dedication to the moral notion of how things—by universal design—ought to be, he wants to dedicate the poet to the realism of how things—just happening, without design—in fact are. It is as if Johnson would claim that an orderly pattern contains the world's errant particulars, except that he at times doubts that these particulars can be so confined, doubts that the ordering universals are more than conventions imposed by men. His claim to the rational order is what characterizes the critical persona that is our monumental picture of Dr. Johnson as the high priest of neoclassicism, and his doubts are the voice of the late eighteenth-century person who can no longer be constantly appeased by the well-made moral and metaphysical schemes to which both person and persona are supposed, in the eighteenth century, to owe their fealty.

By the time of Samuel Taylor Coleridge, the theorist is free to postulate the power of imaginative vision to create its world. So the Coleridge persona, in accordance with Kantian and post-Kantian (largely Schellingian) epistemology, can dedicate itself to the life-infusing power which the imagination (as the I AM) bestows upon every object, thereby destroying its status as mere object. But Coleridge (perhaps via his person as working poet) wants also to modify this epistemological freeing of imaginative vision with the poet's mundane struggle to convert his materials into the constructed object that is his poem. Thus Coleridge introduces the dual notion of primary and secondary imaginations, with an indecisive effort to determine which of them has the dominant responsibility for the making of the poem. These partly conflicting definitions lead to an equally confusing pair of definitions: the essentially psychological definition of "poetry" as resulting from the author's power of vision, and the essentially aesthetic definition of the "poem" as resulting from its author's power to produce an organic whole. Coleridge, like so many after him, must reconcile man's generally epistemological power of life-bestowing vision, granted him by Transcendental Idealism, with the poet's special power of making, granted him by aestheticians concerned with what forms and language can create and embody. The first of these he shares with his philosophic contemporaries; the second undercuts their epistemological foundations by introducing questions about the formative function of the literary medium, questions that become central issues in poetics for the century and a half that follow. Although Coleridge could not reconcile the divergent elements in this self-dialogue that persists through most of his work, the very doubleness of his attitudes and theoretical attachments deepened the possibilities for all Romantic theory that is influenced by him.

Both Shelley and Benedetto Croce, in considerably different ways, extend the Romantic Idealism that runs through Coleridge, though neither can escape being troubled by Coleridge's own restraints. Shelley is of course far less inhibited than Coleridge in the claims he makes for the purely visionary power. For him the seeing is itself the guarantor of the infinite and eternal validity of what is seen. Yet even Shelley cannot consistently avoid the responsibility of the poet as maker-in-language; what poet could? So he can accompany the most universalizing concept of the poem as "the very image of life expressed in its eternal truth" with the insistence that a poem is untranslatable, its sounds and meanings creating a unique and fixed entity, hence utterly particular.[3] The poet who is the maker of the finite thing itself thus arises (if only momentarily) to challenge the Platonizing mystic who travels through all human and supernal orders to the all-absorbing unity of Godhead itself.

Croce's struggle is similar in kind. Because he is a thoroughgoing Idealist, Croce must feel contempt for the material embodiment of the vision he refers to as "intuition." The intuition must be self-sufficient, so that the "externalization"—the making of the object itself—takes place only as a translation of the intuition into a sensory stimulus for the aesthetic experience of others. The externalization, then, is aesthetically unnecessary in that the form of the intuition is already complete without it. But earlier in his treatise[4] Croce, recognizing the symbolic nature of human thought, identifies intuition with expression: to intuit is to express, so that there can be no intuition without its accompanying and enabling expression. Here most of us would see Croce as conceding the dependence of the visionary side of poetry upon its making side, since we would assume that "expression" includes (or is essentially one with) "externalization." Since the symbolic medium is that in which and by means of which we intuit, then the expression that is simultaneous with the intuition must be simultaneous also with its externalization. Who but a most driven Idealist could see these (expression and externalization) as two rather than one? Such is Croce, whose Idealistic persona cannot permit expression to depend upon the material fact of externalization but must make a factitious distinction between them. He must claim a difference (which he can hardly demonstrate) between internal expression and the technical feat which permits the external physical fact that he thinks of as the aesthetic object ("the physical stimulus for reproduction"). Yet Croce, in the person of the sensitive critic, has sufficient respect for the symbolic nature of expression to persuade himself to identify intuitive vision with it, even if he must back off from acknowledging (as the non-Idealist would) that the poet's manipulation of his medium is at once symbolic-expressive and technical. So the inconsistency for him remains: he cannot reconcile the part of him that grants the immediacy of the created poem with that more ideologically restrained part of him which insists on the immediacy of interior vision itself, self-sufficient and disembodied.

With several of these critics I have suggested a pattern in which a more sensitive person, sometimes a poet's person, celebrates poetry's magical powers that undo the critic-theorist's systems. In Matthew Arnold we find a striking variation upon this pattern. His important criticism is written after he turns from the primary pursuit of writing poetry, so that his person helps turn him into an apologist for criticism, although there will be another person in him who will turn again. From what Arnold the theorist tells us of the poet's plight in periods like his, when the shortage of available ideas forces the poet to be idea-maker as well as maker of poems, we may gather that he is condemning his own poetry as too flat and overly philosophical, and is encouraging himself to concentrate on writing criticism rather than poetry.[5] For at such a time, and with such limits placed upon what poetry can do, why not invent ideas directly—as criticism does—and prepare the way for future poets? With this suggestion Arnold has created the theoretical framework in which the critic turns out to have the more significant—indeed even the more creative—role in our culture, more creative than that of the "creative power" of the poet, who creates objects but not ideas, the essential ingredients of poems. So Arnold thus persuades himself that he has done well in his own commitment to vocation. But the dedication to poetry also persists in Arnold, as does the awe with which he contemplates its power to move its reader. Hence, although he may often overemphasize poetry's dependence upon the ideational content, which it is to borrow from criticism, he is able later to declaim in behalf of its almost apocalyptic nature, in the opening pages of "The Study of Poetry": "The future of poetry is immense, because in poetry, where it is worthy of its high destinies, our race, as time goes on, will find an ever surer and surer stay. . . . Without poetry, our science will appear incomplete; and most of what now passes with us for religion and philosophy will be replaced by poetry. . . . The day will come when we shall wonder at ourselves for having trusted to them, for having taken them seriously; and the more we perceive their hollowness, the more we shall prize 'the breath and finer spirit of knowledge' offered to us by poetry." Here is a magnanimous gesture to poetry's superiority to idea, to its omnipotence by one who, in straying from its calling, had severely denied the extent of its power.

III

What I have presented is not intended to be a thumbnail sketch of the history of criticism; it is rather intended to indicate the continuing need for theoretical inconsistency—for major and minor strains sustained at considerable cost—in the work of a few obvious, though representative, major critic-theorists in our history. And I have tried to suggest the theoretical impatience that accompanies any major critic as he confronts the complexity of his particular experience and its resistance to the theoretical universals that are supposed to govern it. Yet in each case the critical persona returns persistently enough to dominate the discourse, though the unsettling intrusion of the critic's person (or apparent person) gives it the special mark, the signature, that we associate with a major critical personality: it breathes the warmth of human relevance into the system which it seeks to undo.

The persona says, "I am right about this object and about our general experience with literary objects, of which this object is an instructive example. You ought to agree with me." The person (or the apparent person) rather insists, "It is exclusively *I* who is having this experience, which has never occurred before. I must guard its authenticity and my private investment in it, whether or not others will agree with what I find in it and even whether or not it accords with other experiences of my own." If what the person finds undermines the commitments of the persona, so much the better; for it is then more likely than an inviolate human encounter has occurred, with its subjectivity intact. But I have more than once suggested that it may only be an apparent person—a counter-persona—who is the alternative to the persona. I have done so because such a partial withdrawal from theoretical commitment is often only a shrewd tactic which the critic-theorist uses to persuade (perhaps to persuade himself as well as us!) that he will keep his critical operation open and human, at whatever cost to its self-assuredness and its certainty—these latter hardly being humanistic virtues. In so doing he would be creating a second voice for himself that is no less fictional than his first. This device can make his criticism more persuasive, and even more just to its object, though at a tremendous cost to his theoretical allegiance.

But the person of the critic—and here I mean the true, inward person—does have another kind of function, one which often serves to reinforce rather than to undermine the dominant theory he espouses. Indeed the person often provides the internal, existential pressures that lead to the theoretical espousal or even invention. We could take one obvious case, like Hegel's theory of tragedy, which clearly derives from his general system, both his metaphysic and his philosophic method. The relation of the tragic hero, as individual, to the "ethical substance," his drive to alienation and the cosmic insistence on reabsorbing him—these basic notions in Hegel's theory of tragedy clearly reflect his systematic philosophy of history and the role of universals in it. Hegel's favorite play, *Antigone*, is the work by means of which his theory of tragedy develops. It becomes an almost inevitable choice for him—especially given his interpretation of it, which is equally inevitable. Despite his concentration on this play, we can hardly charge him with being inadequately empirical, pinning too much on a single case, since his procedure is so openly the opposite of empirical, with the system dictating the theory and the theory dictating the work and his reading of it. Using the terms I have introduced here, we could argue that the person, having created the system-defending persona, creates those structures of literary theory and those works and critical readings that are needed to reinforce and justify that persona.

We are talking about what has been termed the "metaphysical pathos" behind the literary theory, the criticism that flows from it,

and the hierarchy of works which the criticism would appear to recommend. It is this metaphysical pathos[6] which predisposes the person to create the systems and personae that he creates, and these in
turn determine the style of his criticism and choose the works which
this criticism can most conveniently treat—more candidly, the works
it can use to establish and reinforce itself. Far from empirically
grounded, one's theory is thus seen as hardly literary in its source
within the person.

Is all theory, then—together with the choice and the criticism of
works which theory dictates—only the person's rationalization of his
metaphysical pathos? Examples such as Hegel's may make it tempt-
ing to say so. But of course such a claim suggests a solipsism so complete that it leads to an utter indifference to the objects of contemplation and to the problems they pose on their own grounds. For here
there are no grounds but the subject's. This hardly is very promising
for criticism as a progressive discipline, as one in which any dialogue
is possible. So there is good reason to resist limiting all that the
theorist and critic can say to mere rationalization.

Yet the evidence we glean from searching through the history of
successive and conflicting literary fashions is not reassuring to any
who wish to urge an alternative to critical subjectivism. It is also true
that an examination of the work of recent theorist-critics can lead us,
though in a less sweeping way, to the kind of charges we make against
Hegel, who is admittedly an extreme case since he is primarily and
almost exclusively a philosopher, and only derivatively a literary
theorist and critic. It has often been pointed out, for example, that
criticism and literary theory in the wake of Eliot—the old New Criticism—was in large part guided by its attitude toward religion, man,
and authority as it created a method that chose and served the Metaphysical poets. Whether it was dealing with poems for which its
method seemed to have been created, downgrading poems unsuited
to it, or reinterpreting them radically in order to make them proper
objects for it, the bias of this criticism and the other-than-literary
reasons for it could be (as it has been) demonstrated.

When, as an antidote for such antiromantic and at times theological
assumptions as underlie this criticism, Northrop Frye introduced to
another critical generation a new set of terms and methods, they were
automatically accompanied by a new set of heroes and rejects, of
favored and less favored texts, and of some violently reinterpreted
ones. Literature was to circulate about a new center, and its name was
William Blake, Eliot's Antichrist now canonized. And behind Frye's

vast structure in *The Anatomy of Criticism* we sense the profound commitment, personal and professional, that propelled his faithful study of Blake, *Fearful Symmetry*. The further we go from Frye's system's center in Blake—to Shakespeare or to Milton, for example—the more we sense the imprint of Frye's vision at the expense of our previous sense of the poet himself.

The same sort of difference appears when we move from Georges Poulet on Mallarmé to Poulet on, say, Balzac.[7] Poulet and his associates, the so-called "critics of consciousness," provide another Romantic alternative to the New Critics. If we feel comfortable with Poulet on Mallarmé (as we did with Frye on Blake), it is because he is at home there, his person—as he tells us—becoming one with his object. So he is being faithful to this poet because he can do so by being faithful to himself. It is when he moves off to objects less natural to him, less obviously a reflection of himself, that we feel the need to forgo our former sense of the author if we are to accept the critic who has usurped his place. Thus Balzac appears to us, via Poulet, as too much the soaring lyric poet. In such airiness what has become of the prosaic chronicler of a solid world whose heavy furnishings so impressively weigh down his work with their bulky reality? If Poulet is also one with his object here, it is because he has transformed his object to himself. Few contemporary critics seem to make freer with their authors than does Poulet, as he reduces them to his reading self, making many different works seem like only slight variations of the same work.[8] This is but a stronger version of the charge I have been suggesting against critics generally.

In another essay I have tried to suggest and to probe the existentialist consciousness that lies behind that development out of the later New Criticism which I have termed "contextualism."[9] This essay traced the relationship I saw between the theoretical interest in literary complexity and the philosophical distrust of universals. The critic's search for a unique system of interrelations among the elements of a literary work turns out to reflect his conviction that existence presents a series of irreducibly particular persons engaged in problematic moral experiences. Irony, paradox, tension become effective literary devices for those who believe that existence is equally enigmatic, beyond the reach of philosophic propositions, and needs an enigmatic literature to illuminate it. Poetic discourse, accordingly, comes to be treated as a series of special and autonomous systems (one per poem); it is seen to be distinguished from normal discourse by the nonreferential particularities which multiply themselves, thanks to the poem's internal relations. It may be, then, that, because the person of the critic needs to create a literature which will justify his existentialist commitment, he proclaims and propagates a contextualist aesthetic. He arranges his collection of valued works accordingly, whether convenient to his critical (and existential) needs or rendered convenient by his strenuous operations upon them.

It is true that I earlier claimed to find a traditional and theological set of prejudices behind criticism in the wake of Eliot, while I now find an anti-authoritarian, even subversively antisystematic tendency as a motivating force for this later development of it, which I call contextualism. Aside from changes that occurred along this developing line, we must take into account the extent to which, from T. E. Hulme and Ezra Pound onward, Bergsonian dynamics and its consequent organicism accompany and modify—even if they contradict—the drive to freeze literature into serving static universals.[10] Perhaps this is a useful way to remind us that we earlier looked, at some length, at ways in which the critic's person disrupted the system of the critical persona by introducing contradictory, or at least antagonistic, elements. Then we turned this process on its head, by finding ways in which the person had originally justified his attachment to existential commitments by initially creating that literary system for his persona. The first process saw an existing systematic attachment for the persona which was subverted by the person; the second saw the system which was to be represented by the persona as having been created to begin with as a rationalization of the person's existential needs. We can trace elements of both processes, both operations—systematic and antisystematic—of what I have been calling the critic's person, in the confusions of at least the older New Critical formulations.

As contextualist theory developed and more systematically emerged —at least as I have seen it and worked with it these last dozen or so years—the conservative and static elements appear to have been dropped in favor of the greater and more consistent emphasis on those dynamic elements that represented the existentialist impulse from the time of the earliest New Critics, well before they were aware of, or would care to claim, any such influence or allegiance. Thus, as a more recent contextualist, I must openly face the likelihood, strongly pressed by W. K. Wimsatt,[11] that my theoretical claims rest on motives which are other than literary and that the works I have chosen to treat have been either too carefully selected or too persistently adapted to my vision, so that a variety of authors have been converted into unwitting fellow existentialists. Some readers may well feel more strain in my treatment of Alexander Pope than in my treatment, say, of Joseph Conrad.

Like the other critics discussed here, however, I must hope that I am searching for truth (a truth that will hold for more than myself), that my generic claims about literature *really* tell us something about it that is so, that the works *really* are as I say they are—and are not just my reckless and subjective manipulation of them. But my person, with his interests, stands somewhat behind my efforts, reminding me how many of my pretentious claims to normative and objective reality are only a reflection of his demands—reminding me of all this and sneering just a little. Of course, if the critic allows the person to reveal himself behind the mask of the system—as I seem to be doing here—we must not trust him, since, once the person goes public, he becomes a persona—and another mask—of himself. So, as I expose the existential pressures to which my theoretical claims either happily and coincidentally conform or just dutifully respond, I am confessing the role of the person; and I invite both trust and distrust—both of these for both the system *and* the person—while I apologize for the partial, parochial, or even sectarian nature of my theory, its foundation in other-than-literary issues. As I have tried to show, rival critical positions are subject to similar exposures. The critic's role *is* a complex one, as is his struggle for balance among his several selves that face the selves revealed in the work before him.

IV

This entire discussion treats the critic as a paradoxically dramatic figure. This is to treat him and his strategies as Kenneth Burke would, or as Stanley Edgar Hyman treated his thinkers—as self-conscious makers of metaphor—in *The Tangled Bank*. How and why they conceive discloses their creativity and vision more than does what they say. But such a view of criticism returns us to the extreme skepticism of my starting point, where we saw Faulkner's Hightower, in turning from Tennyson to *Henry IV*, create for literature the function of feeding his existential needs. For all their fancier literary notions of what they are doing, the persons of critics might be seen as preventing them from doing much more than he did. If our poetics is only a pragmatic structure to help us justify who we are, then the works themselves must equally be victims of that rationalization. And all we see is what the constitutive forms of neo-Kantian psychology permit us to conceive to be our reality, so that our existential insularity is epistemologically—and then ontologically—sanctified.

If we assume that criticism as a collective endeavor has the obligation to transcend these subjective traps, that it must preserve the corrigibility of individual judgment as a hoped-for possibility, then we may be tempted to work toward neutralizing what is individual in our response in order to preserve and elevate what is common in it. In a manner like that of eighteenth-century common-sense universalism, our Realistic instinct leads us to ask for the purging of the personal as eccentric and even idiosyncratic, and to expect, as a result of multiple cancellations of the private, that what is left will be meaningful to the common core of humanity. This instinct suggests that we throw the many hermeneutic circles at one another; even if, where they fall, there may be only the slightest portion of them that overlap, we can eliminate all but that overlapping and preserve *it* as the precious residue of the meaning and the judgment which criticism must preserve. The objective work, available to us all (if we too are stripped of our idiosyncrasies), would be what was left when all that was personal (imposed on it by persons or personae) was deducted.

But such cheery empirical universalism did not work in the eighteenth century, and it will not work now. Experience, as filtered through consciousness, just does not happen that way. All our subtractions of eccentricities are only subtractions of the human from human experience, and not the sum of human experience. The common residue of such subtractions tell us how little a work can mean in its commonness, not how much it can mean in its uniqueness. Once we reject the naive Realism that posits a universal core at the center of rings of peripheral particulars, we recognize that collective criticism cannot provide more than a series of partial, unyielding, and often incompatible responses. But these responses are, each of them, the product of fully human consciousness, and hence indivisible. So we must work with the totality of the criticism, saturated as it is with persona and person, for finally there are no separable elements in the vision and the version of the work and its world which that criticism gives us. And yet, even when we accept the hermeneutic gap that separates every critique from the work, we need not deny the reality of that work, or deny our need to confront that reality along with the

critical transpositions of it by others. For, as readers of literature and
its criticism, we never, in our own persons, turn away from the fact
that the work *is* beckoningly out there; and it's the same work that all
these other fellows are talking about, some more faithfully than
others, though none altogether faithfully. At some level, in spite of
persuasive epistemological skepticism, all of us share Dr. Johnson's
hardheaded, rock-kicking impatience with the unbridgeable private
worlds of solipsism.

For most of us there has always been the tension between our vision
of the world—the world as we would have it—and the unyielding contingent reality that we fear is out there on its own, indifferent to us
and our visions. We may share the "dream of man" which is the
product of Northrop Frye's conception of human imagination, em-
bodied in our "order of words"; but we are also aware of that external, inhuman reality which makes up what he terms the "order of
nature." Or to put it as Wallace Stevens did, we may live within and
celebrate the human construct as our necessary fiction, but not without remembering that it is, after all, a fiction, with a nagging reality
beyond, that remains stubbornly unadaptable. We all remember the
wondrous, if humorous, metaphorical worlds that create the eccentric reality in which the characters of *Tristram Shandy* live. They are
all up on their hobby-horses, riding off in their many solipsistic directions. But there is another reality that will not be hobby-horsed away,
the reality of chronological and biological facts that finally have their
way, in spite of all human inventiveness. All of Tristram's metaphors
are undone—Tristram the supreme hobby-horse rider—as he is pursued on horseback by Death, in a metaphor that signals the end of
metaphor, that threatens to empty all metaphor into the common
refuse-heap of factual, time-ridden history.

But the internal forms of private imagination can take a perma-
nently visible form in the materials of public reality, the artist's
medium. So the literary object, though a product of inner reality, is
yet an object; as such it is so fixed in its final form that—despite its
wondrous humanity—it becomes a chunk of that (usually inhuman)
external reality too. Though a human metaphor that serves our hobby-
horse mythologies, it exists, finitely and measurably, in the world of
time as well. Fiction may defy history's reality, but as an object it
takes its place in history. And it would be a mistake for us, enam-
ored by the subjective necessities of the critical act, to refuse to grant
the literary work its special status as object, though an object
freighted by all the subjectivities of consciousness that normally

resist object-ness. Not even critical persons, whether they are creating or undoing their personae, should keep us from taking advantage of this unique doubleness in the literature they treat: its function as a metaphor that transforms reality into human hobby-horsical shape, and its function as a completed entity that becomes part of that extrahuman reality, changing that reality as it takes its place in it.

I put this matter (of the resistant reality of the object despite our subjective remakings of it) perhaps more cogently in an earlier statement of it.

> Whatever our decision about the ontological status of the literary object, its existence, meaning, and value before we collide with it, we know that we can speak of it only out of the dust of that collision. We pick ourselves up, no longer quite the same selves, and try to speak with precision about what has struck us and the force of its impact. And we probably will give the usual one-sided version of what has transpired and what sort of antagonist we have encountered. Who is to correct us except others who have suffered similar encounters and whose descriptions will be as partial and as self-serving? None may deny the encounter, none deny how profoundly he has been changed by it; yet each will have his own version, each levy his own assessment. Since each is changed, the alienating quality of the force—and its forcefulness—are beyond question. . . . The force which is the work itself lives only in those singular visions and in their mutual modifications by men honestly trying to look, and to move, beyond their own limitations, though it is these limitations that define who they are. Yet it is the force that helps define who they are to become.[12]

For the critic, the crucial part of that stubborn reality out there, which resists being dissolved into our idealisms, consists in those approachable, but hardly knowable, aesthetic objects around which his and his fellows' arguments try to—and often seem to—revolve. And the wholly purposive form of such an object may make it a valuable model that tells him about the less purposive parts of that reality— which is why it is, for the critic, the crucial part.

It is this notion, that the work hangs out there in reality, as a normative object after all, that I believe gives the contextualist poetic an advantage over others. We have granted that even the most modest critic attempts to reduce the object to himself, and in so doing cannot help but impose his own language upon the language of the work. But the contextualist begins by maintaining that the work has its own intramural system that can be reduced to no forms or language beyond its own. He can claim that all prior languages, including the critic's, are inadequate to the peculiar set of contextual interrelations that define the full language system of the work, so that for the critic to impose any definition from the outside is for him to violate the principle of formal integrity that gives life to the work. He would thereby deaden it by adapting it to an alien set of transcendent meanings, those which existed prior to and independently of the special symbolic cluster that makes up its total meaning. All this the contextualist can claim in theory, although of course in practice he is subject to all the hermeneutic traps that beset his colleagues. But his initial theoretical stance at least prepares him for the humility that looks for an ought-ness in the object by putting the soliciting power out there in it and no more than a responsive potentiality in him. Still, his response, once he tries to put it in his language, is guaranteed to be inadequate to its object, the unique poetic context. His language must be one that preexisted this poem: it is necessarily generic insofar as it is drawn from other experiences of other poems, while the language of this poem should be an original synthesis that violates and reconstitutes forms and meanings that came before.

If, then, as we have seen, the critic is doomed to the self-deception that imposes subjective structures and calls them the object, is there not an advantage to the theory that proclaims his failure as a necessary one and suggests that he *can* be corrected by the object? Whatever configuration he finds that he proclaims to be the form of the poetic context may indeed be his rather than the poem's, despite the "data" in the text that his critic's ingenuity parades as his "evidence."

We can renew our suspicion that his hope for impersonal findings is a fond and delusive one by recalling the charges I have mentioned that contextualist critics have shown excessive zeal in "discovering" irrationalist, antipropositional dramatic structures. Nevertheless it would seem that, if the critic must be dominated by the primal (and more than literary) interests of his subjectivity, his best chance to move beyond the vanity of his task lies in a criticism that has an other-directed, ergocentric impulse—even if, at its strongest, this impulse is doomed to be thwarted. And if this criticism requires its practitioner to assume also that the poem is a completed language complex which resists definition by all other languages, including his own, then his delusion will at least be that much lessened. If he cannot eliminate his personality in the face of the work, at least he need not cultivate it in order to outface the work.

Contextualism may, then, be representative of that mood in us which holds onto our imagined reality, while retaining an awareness (I almost said "a wariness") of that other reality outside—and struggles with the maddening incompatibility of the two. It encourages us at once to hold and to reject the metaphor that is the literary work, that sweep of subjectivity which is also a fixed thing in the external world. We can—and do—open ourselves to the work's system in spite of our attempt to reduce it to our own. We may seek automatically to control reality by forcing it into our categories, thus hobby-horsing it away. But we also respond to that alien reality, occasionally even reshaping our categories and altering personality. And no piece of reality can grasp us and change us more profoundly than can the work of art, because—though a fixed object—it is not *only* alien, but is humanly responsive to our humanity. Like all extrahuman reality, *King Lear* will always be *King Lear*, extending and ending itself in the same way, with the same words and actions, whatever we do with it and whoever the *we* are who do it. As we accept that fact, no matter how many ways we seek to remake the work, we come also to allow it to remake us. In short, we learn from it. And it must exist independently from us for it to educate us and enlarge us.

So the critic's personality (however compounded of person and persona) is the powerful, primitive moving force behind all he can do for the rest of us, giving us his reality as the container for the literary works that make it up. But the work also has its own reality for us, outside even the most powerful critical personality and the shapings of the work which that personality gives us. Finally, beyond the critique, then, the work remains, unabsorbed, as unshakably there as Peele Castle described by Wordsworth in "Elegiac Stanzas." Like Peele Castle, it is a grand reality unshaken even by the fact of death. For the world of objects, the fact-ridden world beyond man, beyond man's control by his hobby-horses, will in the end be responded to directly, or will preclude man's response: it will, alas, overwhelm both the person and persona of the critic with its reality that persists—as these do not. But if, in this outside reality that persists, there is an objective embodiment of human consciousness within a humanly created form, then it will be humanity itself that persists.

Notes

---

1. It should by now be hardly necessary to repeat that this conflict may be no more than the opposition between two personae, one the apparent persona

and the other the apparent person underneath. When, after all, does the sophisticated public writer let us through to see the real person, if indeed there is one beneath the succession of antithetical roles he plays? An inventive student of mine, Miss Pat Finnerty, has written movingly, in an unpublished manuscript, of these alternative possibilities of man as either the artichoke, whose layers surround a heart, or the onion, composed of successive layers only.

2. I discuss this striking ambivalence at length in "Fiction, Nature, and Literary Kinds in Johnson's Criticism of Shakespeare," *Eighteenth-Century Studies* 4:184–198 (1970–71), and in "Samuel Johnson: The 'Extensive View' of Mankind and the Cost of Acceptance," *The Classic Vision: The Retreat from Extremity in Modern Literature* (Baltimore, 1971), pp. 125–145.

3. In *A Defense of Poetry* Shelley refers to the "peculiar order" which relates sound and thought in the words of a poem: "Hence the vanity of translation; it were as wise to cast a violet into a crucible that you might discover the formal principle of its colour and odour, as seek to transfuse from one language into another the creations of a poet. The plant must spring again from its seed, or it will bear no flower—and this is the burthen of the curse of Babel."

4. See Chapters I–IV, in contrast with Chapters XIII and XV of Croce's *Aesthetic.*

5. See Arnold's arguments concerning the "creative power" versus the "critical power" and "the power of the man" versus "the power of the moment" in the early pages of his essay "The Function of Criticism at the Present Time."

6. This phrase, as used here, means no more than one's conceptual assumptions (conscious or unconscious, but probably unexamined) about the nature of reality, assumptions which his primary existential stance requires him to make.

7. See Chapter 5 and Chapter 9, the concluding chapter, of *La Distance Intérieure.*

8. In fairness to Poulet we must recall that he does not think of himself as a critic in the usual sense, but as a writer of "literature about literature."

9. "The Existential Basis of Contextual Criticism," *The Play and Place of Criticism* (Baltimore, 1967), pp. 239–251.

10. The influence of Bergson, it should be mentioned, is shared by this group I have represented by Poulet. This common influence should make the opposition between the two groups less extreme than the history of recent theory would suggest. It is this uncertainty about the exclusively anti-Romantic sources of contextualism, and about its anti-Romantic nature, that I am suggesting here. But I could hardly turn around and suggest an equal modification of the antiformalism of the Poulet group.

11. I have included his extended criticism of my position in *The Play and Place of Criticism* ("Platonism, Manichaeism, and the Resolution of Tension: A Dialogue"), pp. 195–218.

12. In the concluding paragraph of "Literary Analysis and Evaluation—and the Ambidextrous Critic," *Criticism: Speculative and Analytical Essays,* ed. L. S. Dembo (Madison, Wisc., 1968), pp. 16–36.

Paul Ramsey

ABSOLUTISM AND JUDGMENT

IN THIS PAPER I WISH TO TRY TO MAKE SOME SENSE OUT OF A CONFUSED
and confusing subject. To do so I shall expound, defend, and clarify
the following statements:

1. Aesthetic absolutism, as defined below, is true; aesthetic subjectivism is false; no third position is possible.
2. Relativism is not a position, but a muddle. Insofar as what it says
is true it is covertly absolutistic; insofar as it is subjectivistic, it is
false.
3. Literary judgment is possible and fallible. The final act of literary
judgment is singular, and no theory, however refined or elaborate,
can take its place.
4. Most analyses have truth in them; most analyses distort. Some
analyses are better than others. No analysis is exhaustive of its
object.

The term "absolutism" conveys some range of meaning; its meanings do not bear equal defense. What I mean by "absolutism" in the
basic sense is that there is real value in literature, or other kinds of
art, and at times my arguments shall be more generic than that. Aesthetic value is real, not a delusion, and our statements about it can
make sense and be true. That may seem a small claim, and one which
most subjectivists or relativists would at least in practice agree with.
But not so: the claim is important precisely because it is fundamental to literary discussion and understanding, and both relativism
and subjectivism imply that it is not true. The fact that relativists and
subjectivists in practice act and speak in ways which imply that absolutism is true contradicts rather than strengthens their fundamental
position. Relativism and subjectivism are a complex sisterhood of
notions, but insofar as their positions have a common substance or
near-substance, it is in their denial of the reality of aesthetic value, in

their insistence that, while a statement such as "some cows have legs" can be just plain true, a statement such as "Shakespeare is a great poet" cannot be just plain true. My insistence is that such statements can be just-plain-true, a "true" that is so fundamental it is probably at least indefinable (it can be best defined by metaphors such as "corresponding to reality" or "fits reality exactly," which are less precise than the meaning of the term itself). That is the quarrel, an important and fundamental one. Nor is it only a literary quarrel.

Is the quarrel, at least with many relativists, a quarrel of words rather than things? Yes and no; no because yes. Maybe it would be better to give up all the words concerned—absolutism, relativism, objectivism, subjectivism, perspectivism, historicism, and such—and start over. But new terms would doubtless breed new troubles. So I shall keep the term "absolutism" and shall try to make clear what I mean and do not mean by it.

Further, some statements subjectivists and relativists make are true, or partially true, or true with qualification. None of such statements contradict absolutism in the basic sense, and a large number of them entail it. Truths can be accommodated, and real agreements can appear from behind verbal barriers or smokescreens. It is splendid that they should do so; one of my aims (if hardly hopes) in this essay is to quieten some noises that disguise agreements. But a relativist who is an implicit and inconsistent absolutist should at least know so. The verbal confusions are many. Real quarrels remain.

AN ARGUMENT FOR AESTHETIC ABSOLUTISM

My fundamental argument is a transparently simple one. It is this: if the *Iliad* is a poem of some poetic merit, then aesthetic absolutism is true; but the *Iliad* is a poem of some poetic merit; therefore aesthetic absolutism is true. The premise is almost comically mild. Its mildness is its strength. For the premises would still be true if the *Iliad* were a preposterously bad poem with occasional and incidental poetic virtues. All one needs to maintain is that at least that much is true, that the *Iliad* does have at least some incidental poetic virtues. But, in truth, the *Iliad* is an overwhelmingly great poem of massive, sublime, and frequent excellences and what is more, we know it: we have powerful and converging evidence for the greatness of the poem. Consequently the mild statement of the premise is about as certain as a statement can get, of the order of certainty (this side of absolute rational certainty) of such statements as "some people have fingers." The premise makes sense, is true, and unmistakably makes a judgment which is an evaluative judgment of a work of literature. The conclusion manifestly follows. Hence the argument does prove that aesthetic value is real, not a delusion, and that statements about it can make sense and be true. I realize that the phrase "literary merit" can be quibbled with. But the meaning is plain English and an ordinary educated reader knows what it means. Aesthetic absolutism is, then, true. But if aesthetic absolutism is true, then aesthetic subjectivism—in its most fundamental sense—is false. For the positions are really inconsistent.

It may be objected that the argument is circular, since the premise "the *Iliad* is a poem of some literary merit" presumes the truth of the conclusion "aesthetic absolutism is true." In asserting the notion "literary merit" I have asserted the idea I want to prove. True enough, but that doesn't make the argument circular in some sense whereby the circularity vitiates the argument. For if we know a statement to be true, we can infer statements entailed by the statement (including its presumptions) to be true. But we really do know (in a plain and ordinary sense of "know") that the *Iliad* is a poem of some literary merit. Therefore we can and must know (in a plain and ordinary sense of "know") that aesthetic absolutism is true.

Other positions or claims often called absolutistic or objectivistic are related to, but separable from, this basic absolutism. Among them are the positions (1) that one can know with certainty, or absolute certainty, aesthetic truths; (2) that aesthetic value inheres in the object rather than the subject; (3) that some aesthetic principles are universal and admit to no exceptions. I shall discuss all three, in order, the first briefly, the other two at more length. What I most wish to insist is that the truth or falsity of basic absolutism does not depend on the truth or falsity of any one of those three positions. They could all be false and the fundamental position could still be true. I have a hunch that a good many people doubt or reject one or more of these three positions or other, related positions, and feel that therefore they should doubt or reject absolutism as such. That is a serious and persistent confusion and the very vagueness with which the relations are perceived makes it difficult to overcome. Clarity is important.

CERTAINTY

Certainty is (certainly!) an intricate and confusing subject about which I shall say only a few things. First, and most important, the aesthetic absolutist does not need to maintain or to prove that we can know aesthetic truth with certainty or absolute certainty; what he needs to maintain is that there is better and worse aesthetic judgment. For if there is better and worse aesthetic judgment, aesthetic absolutism is true.

Nonetheless it does seem to me that there are genuine senses in which we can say that we "know with certainty" aesthetic truths (some of them), as well as other kinds of truth. If we mean that we have a firm conviction, good reason to believe, and no real reason to doubt, that we often have psychological certainty which we have a moral right to have, then we frequently know things with certainty. I am certain that I have enjoyed reading *Lycidas*; that I have fingers; that San Francisco is in California; that Robert Frost wrote some good poems; that some cows have more than two legs; that lying is something wicked; and I am certain (so are we all) of a very great many other things. I can even say that I am absolutely certain of them, at least in some sense that makes "absolutely" pleonastic. I really am sure; I have good reasons for being sure; I surely have a moral right to be sure; and to say that I am less than really sure would be to violate honesty. If on the other hand "know with certainty" means to know with absolute rational certainty, certainty perfectly sustained by demonstrative argument based on premises themselves rationally certain, then I seriously doubt whether we know anything at all with that kind of certainty. In a very severe Platonic sense of "knowledge," I fear that we have no knowledge, only opinion. We are not angels but men. But that is another discussion.

VALUE "IN" THE OBJECT

In such statements as "aesthetic value is in the object," "in" is a metaphor, and confusion flourishes when metaphors are leaned upon with more weight than they can bear. A beautiful waterfall is in space and is beautiful. It seems odd to say that its beauty is in space, odder yet to say that some part of the object is not in space. An odd dilemma. But to flee it by saying that the beauty is "in" the observer(s) is to flee to another and less clear metaphor. We divide the undivided to analyze, then use our analyses to deny the reality of the experience we had to assume to begin the analysis. A strange and comfortless procedure. In some senses beauty is "in" objects, waterfalls or poems; in other senses it makes only a confusing sort of meaning to call them "in" or "out." We stumble into some of the same puzzles with Berkeley, glaring at tables. Are they there or here? How do we know? Where and what is the seam between he who sees and what is seen? We hesitate, and suspect that the trouble lies in the first step out of common experience into the special terms of the analysis. Secondary qualities, then primary qualities vanish before the philosophical glasses. We remove the glasses and the qualities move back in place. It should be the glasses we distrust, even if we cannot give an adequate analysis of the experience. Either we trust, within some reason, our experience or we don't; if we don't trust in the first place, we have no business to dismiss the experience by analyses that presume it. It is not, finally, "naive realism" that is naive. Criticism stands on and in our experience, and our experience has more than one thing to say.

First, there are senses in which value is "in" the literary object. A dull reader misses beauties that are there; a more astute reader sees those beauties; a dull or astute reader is apt to misread and consequently have experiences of beauties or flaws not in the work. To deny that is to deny what is patently obvious in experience; it is also to deny the possibility of understanding or teaching literature. But if those statements are true, beauty is in objects.

Second, there is a plain and probably tautologous sense in which nothing whatever can be talked of "apart from" human perception and experience. If we talk of, we talk of. If we see, we see. But it remains true (and we all know it as firmly as we know anything) that trees exist in space when no human being is looking at them, and it remains true that the *Iliad* would be a great poem even if it had not survived. We wouldn't know of it or know that it is great, but it would nonetheless be great. It is certainly true that there have been good poems that no living human being knows of at present; some of them will be discovered in the future (manuscripts do show up, as they have in the past), many of them will not. The statement "some poems are better than others" is not just an elaborate shorthand for an obscure something else. It is a statement about poems, just as much as "the leaf is green" is a statement about a leaf, even though we cannot know leaves without experiencing them. That is, beauty is, in very real ways, in objects. More timidly, adjectives such as "beautiful" or "good" can be predicated about literary work and do tell us something about the work itself, a very important something. In fact the most natural question to ask about a literary work (and probably the most frequently asked after "Who wrote it?") is "Is it good?"

But of course ordinary experience does not push us to the extremes of dichotomy either. Literary works are made by people for people;

human response is deeply involved, as means to knowledge and as the final cause of the intent. In some sense every reading of a poem realizes, makes real, what existed as potentiality before. But if the poem is potentiality which is made real by human experiencing, then its reality is defective until it is performed, experienced, felt. At the same time, many readings of a poem are imperfect—do not realize what is in the poem to realize or add what is not there. The work exists to be realized; it exists as a real entity that no experiencing quite perfectly catches; it is and is not "in" minds. To the complex reality of literature and its experience, the analytical dichotomy of pure subject as against pure object simply does not do justice. Analysis strains what we know and can clearly say about individual poems. There is value in the poem and value in the experiencing, the values being neither equivalent nor independent. Most important, the truth of aesthetic absolutism does not depend on the precise analysis of subject-object puzzles and confusions.

UNIVERSAL AESTHETIC PRINCIPLES

The term "absolutism" is also used to cover the position that there are universal aesthetic principles which admit to no exceptions. Are there such principles? In a modest way, yes; but they are less important to the discussion than members of both camps often make them appear. They are less important because judgment does not derivatively and simply depend on principles. Literary principles are tools, not tyrants. The master workman is judgment, not theory.

If absolutism were the position that literary judgment consists exclusively of accurate and logically precise application of general principles to particular cases, then absolutism would be false. Such an extreme position is never held in practice, though critics on either side sometimes sound as though it were. Likewise, the position that "all literary principles are universal and admit to no exceptions" is false. The milder and more defensible form is simply "some literary principles or judgments are universal and admit to no exceptions."

Such principles (in ethics or aesthetics) are hard to come by. Many stout and widely applicable principles admit to at least a few exceptions, and principles stand in complex relation to judgment. To explore some, perhaps not much, of the uneven ground, I shall first take a couple of examples from ethics.

Take two statements: "Lying is frequently morally wrong." "Lying is always wrong." Most people would agree (at least when not carrying philosophical banners) without argument that the first statement is true. One has to judge to which instances of lying the statement applies, but it is a widely accepted, valuable, fallible guide to action. Most people would say, very likely, that the second statement is false, though quite a few would feel that a serious moral stance requires that one never lie. The latter position is frequently scorned as inflexible or "absolutistic" or such. The moral fierceness with which advocates hold limited moral views does some damage to the credit of absolutism, but no logical damage. In fact, if such "absolutists" are wrong or overfierce, then moral absolutism is true. And it is only fair to add that moral fierceness is not confined to one party.

Relativists or subjectivists are apt to argue against absolutism on the ground that such generalizations as the one about lying do admit to exceptions, that it is sometimes morally right and even a moral duty to tell a deliberate falsehood. But that statement entails absolutism in the more basic sense. If it is on some occasions a moral duty to lie, then moral absolutism is true: that is, there is at least one statement making a moral judgment which is meaningful and true.

Or, to take a well-known literary example, it has been held that neoclassicism, with a narrow absolutism of rules, denied the excellence of Shakespeare's plays, and that *consequently* that narrow absolutism is false. That view is a parody of neoclassicism (Dryden loved Shakespeare, on neoclassical principles), but it serves my purpose here. For, in holding neoclassical "absolutism" wrong, the argument implies absolutism in the basic sense, by holding that there is truth about literary value (that Shakespeare's plays are good), that such truth can be known and can be used for argument across literary periods.

Similar and powerful confusions exist in political terms. Relativists frequently, by polemical sidewardness or open declaration, line up relativism and democracy as companions. Political absolutism is pernicious; democracy opposes it. Hence by an accident of language and less than faint logic, moral absolutism becomes objectionable and somehow antidemocratic. But the statement "political absolutism is pernicious" or even the statement "democracy is for some societies a better system of government than absolutism" entails absolutism, that is, it assumes the reality of value (a value which "moral" must extend somewhat to cover, but the generic kinship is plain).

Also it is felt that absolutists take extreme positions and hence block the path to the rational compromises needed in politics and international dealings. The root error remains: if moderation and compromise are better in international dealings than extreme positions (say, surrender or nuclear war), then they are *better* and once again a fundamental absolutism is entailed. If they are not better, why defend them as better? Extreme positions are often wrong: they insist on some values or commitments at the expense of others, ignore the evil in what they defend and the good in what they attack. To say that they are wrong, to see what they miss, is to be an absolutist. Obviously, men work for democratic values because they really believe in those values and really believe that those values are better than antidemocratic values. Men work against the mistreatment of Negroes because they really believe that it is wrong to mistreat Negroes. To obscure those truths is to do a considerable disservice. Relativism obscures and denies those truths.

The peculiar difficulty of the relativist and subjectivist can be put generally. All moral discussion presumes the reality of value, and the relativist or subjectivist is perpetually in the strange case of undercutting the ground he stands on. Those views might, in some strange silence, be true, but they cannot be consistently defended.

Nor is even the narrower case finally tenable. Some moral and aesthetic principles do admit to exceptions when it is falsely claimed that they do not. But that does not show that there are *no* statements of aesthetic or moral principle which admit to no exception. The very proposition "All generalizations of moral or aesthetic principle admit to exceptions" itself entails moral absolutism and, as a generalization, dances perilously near the edge of self-inconsistency. Maybe over the edge.

In a real sense, the moral principle "lying is wrong" admits to exceptions. But only in a sense. It seems extravagant to affirm that we should avoid any act whatever which involves lying, no matter what other good or evil may be lost or won in the bargain. Nonetheless there is something fundamentally wrong in lying. To-say-the-thing-which-is-not insults God, the author of being. One might put the matter roughly thus: all actions which involve lying are imperfect actions morally. That is, lying is always wrong as an ingredient of an act. But our actions are often necessarily imperfect, and we have a duty to choose the better, the least imperfect, of two imperfect acts (when there is no third option). To walk about the world is to get one's feet dirty. In one sense, then, lying is always wrong. In another sense it is not always wrong and may be a duty. Neither sense countenances a fundamental subjectivism or relativism; in fact, each sense entails absolutism. This moral example closely parallels aesthetic ones. For instance, unconsciously awkward language is always, in itself, an aesthetic flaw in a literary work, but does not automatically make the work in question a poor one. Virtually every work is guilty of some inept phrasing; some important works may have a good deal of it. Still it is a flaw whenever it occurs, and unless a work is extraordinary in other ways, a large amount is fatal.

Another kind of principle appears in such statements as "Murder is always wrong" and "Literary impropriety is always wrong." Both statements are true and partially true by definition. Self-defence is not really murder; mock-epic is not really improper. All murder is wrong because murder has come to mean only those examples of homicide which are morally (or legally) wrong. Literary impropriety implies wrong (i.e., improper) relations between subject and style, etc. The statements are true and, in a frustrating way, universal because they have built into them, hidden in them, a means of rejecting exceptions. But, though they are in some respect tautologous, they also have real meaning. The assertion that murder is always wrong includes the very important notion that some examples of homicide are morally wrong. The statement about literary impropriety includes the notion that proper or improper relations can obtain between work and subject and style and author and audience, one of the most central of literary ideas. Generalizations such as these are principles involving value and in form universal. But they are not very triumphant examples; there is something patched about them; their ungeneral character is tucked away in their phrasing. Other generalizations are more satisfactory, or at least avoid that difficulty, though none is adequate to the theorist who wishes to discover a theory that will, by simple inference from universals, yield all the correct particular judgments we need. Such a theory does not exist.

The demand placed on universals has been too great, and the consequent rejection of them is more thorough than need be. Swellings much resemble hollows. But principles of literary judgment do exist; they are patently valuable; and some of them are universal in form (or can be made universal in form by rephrasing), however metaphysically potent or overrated that form may be. "All" is not magic, nor does thinking just deal with or from "all." Many aesthetic statements beginning with "all" are false ("All protagonists should be named Henry"); but one can, by the right sort of qualifying or, if you will, finagling, produce an indefinite number of true ones. Some follow. The low voltage is deliberate.

All good novels should show some skill in the handling of plot or character or theme.

All good lyric poems should express feeling.

All good political novels are something more than crudely melodramatic propaganda.

All good traditional epics are longer than ten verses.

All of the best seventeenth-century metaphysical lyrics are ingenious and expressive.

All good comic short stories should be funny.

All sections of *Gulliver's Travels* have considerable literary merit.

All good literary works should delight or instruct, or do both.

All good serious epics have a serious style.

One could obviously go on indefinitely. None of the statements are richly exciting or sufficient to turn ordinary men into infallible critics, but they do share some features: (1) they are all true; (2) they are virtually undebatable; (3) none of them is merely tautologous, though some come closer than others; (4) all involve both aesthetic judgment and matter of "fact"; (5) all of them are universal in form. That is, they are general literary principles which admit of no exceptions, and hence, however timid they may appear, constitute a proof that such propositions exist.

They are in one way not completely general. They do not apply to all works of literature without exception. To ask that of a principle is to ask a great deal. Yet there are principles that meet even that test:

No good work of literature is consistently boring to all good readers.

All good literary works show some power of expression and achieve some formal order.

All good literary works express some proper attitudes.

All good literary works imply or suggest some important truths about human experience.

All good literary works are in some sense representations of life.

All good literary works are in some degree expressions of the authors' individuality.

All good literary works are, so to speak, just and lively images of reality.

These principles are not new or surprising, and do not take us very far toward sound literary judgment, though they have value. But they are universal, evaluative, factual, and true, and they do apply to every work of literary art without exception (even to bad and indifferent ones in their implications). They do prove the point, that absolutism in this special sense is true. There are some universal literary principles. They surely disappoint a certain kind of demand. To see why they disappoint, one needs to reflect about principles and singulars and judgment.

JUDGMENT

Here are some statements not entirely singular or entirely universal, statements about literature which I consider valuable and true. Some are debatable. Some are not very debatable. Some are cribbed. Some could rather naturally be called principles; to some we would deny that name or would hesitate to assign it. At least they will raise the question whether we have a very clear idea of what we mean by, or expect from, literary principles. We should not mean or expect too much, or too little.

1. Richardson tends to be too gushy, Austen too cool, though both are admirable novelists.
2. William Carlos Williams's theories about poetry are confused, valuable in helping us understand his own excellent poetry; and an encouragement to laxity of style and rhythm in some of his followers.
3. Many modern poets are too self-effacingly and self-ironically cute.
4. Certain comic works, notably *Volpone* and Faulkner's "Spotted Horses," reach a depth of metaphysical horror in portraying the perversions and confusions in human justice.
5. The will cannot do the work of the imagination; but neither can the imagination do the work of the will.
6. Art perfects nature.
7. Sometimes artistry of style becomes too visible.
8. The chief temptation of free verse is to slide into medley, or prose.
9. Swift is a master of plain style, Browne of highly figured style.
10. *Tristram Shandy* is imperfectly ordered, but in many ways brilliantly ordered, and for all its good fun and sentimental benevolence is at times so morally perceptive as to be terrifying.
11. The concept of "tragic flaw" as developed by later criticism, whatever Aristotle may have meant by *hamartia*, is a valuable notion, but it can be seriously misleading when applied to certain plays, *Macbeth* for one.

The list can go on and on and on. Such statements *are* literary criticism; they are not universal in form; they do not apply themselves; they are neither infallible nor capricious; they do help us compare and judge; they are reached neither by simple intuition nor pure reasoning; to understand them or apply them one must be able to respond to, and to think about, literature. They stand or fall as judgment. Informed and responsible and imaginative judgment is, in varying degrees, possible.

But one cannot waive theory aside, or pitch all weight on the particular case. In each of the above statements, what is particular, singular, and general fit each other in ways more complex than one is apt to pound into nice logical paradigms. Judgment is prior to epistemological pigeonholes. We need to thing about singulars, even though we never exhaust them by thinking about them. Good judgment needs good theory, at least implicitly. Theory can strengthen literary understanding; it can lead away from or distort literary understanding when it sets up as a separate kingdom or as the final cause of literature. The relations between theory and judgment are themselves, as are the relations between general and individual, dense and individual. Perhaps the most fundamental relation is that good judgment uses theory; it is not theory's creature or theory's servant. One corollary of high rank is that good criticism should lean heavily on particular criticism. Principles should be tested against poems, poems against principles.

Here an opponent (a, let me hope, stronger-than-straw man) may say, "Ah! By making judgment prior to theory, you maintain an anti-theoretical theory and such theories are inevitably self-inconsistent." Perhaps; but I am not persuaded. A theory which maintains the fundamental invalidity of theory undercuts itself, but to claim that theory is a valid but limited instrument is not, so far as I can see, self-inconsistent. That theory is itself true, and limited. It will not take the place of judgment in judging literary works. It is arrived at by judgment.

But judgment, it may be urged, must have some *basis*, and that basis must be solid theoretical principle. That argument is impressive, but not, finally, satisfactory. For "basis" is a metaphor, albeit a good one, and in some ways crucially misrepresents the issues. Why should principles "stand under" aesthetic and moral discussions? Those discussions are not parrots on perches. Further, a defense of even a fairly strict rationalism is self-inconsistent if it has nothing stronger to offer than a metaphorical argument. Metaphors are not demonstrative; they are useful and must be used with good judgment.

But, comes the obvious retort, if a judgment isn't soundly based on good theory, it is arbitrary and capricious, and literary discussion must cease to make any sense. If one refutes the rationalist, one is left with silence. Again, not so. The disjunction is false, a variant or neighbor of the notion that we must have either absolute rational certainty (or demonstrative probability) or a scepticism in which all moves lead equally nowhere. There just is—and we all experience it—a middle ground. Good literary judgment is not simply an inference from clear principles, nor merely a heaping-up of facts, nor an undiscussable intuition. There is something informed and thoughtful, and something undiscussable, about it, and the epistemology which will corral and tame the relations is not yet to be had.

Or we can say (after all, the metaphor "basis" is a powerful and natural one) that of course good literary judgment is soundly based, but that the basis is not merely or even necessarily abstract theory. Good literary judgment is "based" on feeling, thought, experience, comparison, inference, listening, information, responding, analyzing, good luck, hard work. Why single out one of the real bases as somehow the only real one?

But surely, the plausible moan returns, we can't validly believe what we don't have good reason to believe, and that sends us back to principle. The premise is true to the edge of tautology, the conclusion false. For a reason, even a very good reason, need not be a principle. A man goes to market to buy a pig. The pig is the reason, but hardly a principle. There are lots of good reasons for doing and believing. These reasons do imply or suggest principles (not necessarily universal ones), but the reasons are not simply principles and it is not an act of principled inference which brings reasons and principles and singulars to coordination. What does that, then, if it is done? Judgment.

Or, to put it another way, a good cabinet-maker needs good tools. He makes the cabinet with the tools. He does not ask the tools which one to use at what time. *He* uses the tools. How did he learn to use the tools? By being told some truths, by getting the "feel" of the operations, by practicing. The tools are in the analogy the literary principles and reasons. My analogy is of course just an analogy, but it has one powerful advantage over the "basis" metaphor. Literary judgment, like cabinet making, is a human activity. To analyze the active purely in terms of the passive or static is precisely to deny what is active. (Several important and invalid arguments for determinism depend on just such a confusion.)

Or, if the cabinet metaphor seems too ordinary, there is the organic metaphor, a much-lauded metaphor and of course a valuable one. A flower garden requires good soil and good seed and good knowledge and good skill. Beauty requires the mysterious and the known. One cannot raise flowers, without soil or seed, by rational fiat. The artifact and organic metaphors are both great and traditional metaphors. So is the metaphor of the base. But no such metaphors apply themselves. That requires judgment.

THE LIMITS OF ANALYSIS

Judgments about singulars are apt to be firmer (better based, as it were) than the reasons and analyses adduced to support them. There is more disagreement over whether the *Iliad* is a well-unified poem than over whether it is a great poem. Our trained response is apt to be more, not less, precise than our analyzing. We often analyze to show what we have already, before the analysis, seen. The following couplet of Pope's is brilliant and discussable: "Yes, I am proud; I must be proud to see/Men not afraid of God, afraid of me." It can be discussed biographically (Pope's cunning and moral verve collide, and sustain each other), or rhetorically (the parallel of "God" and "me" is impudent and sharp), or metrically ("proud" and "proud" receive like stressing; so do "afraid" and "afraid"; the pairing of the two pairs, with their dance of relationships, is somewhere near the heart—or heartlessness—of his meaning). The analysis is, at least I mean it to be, true; but it is other than and necessarily less than the couplet. In reading the couplet one experiences the reality of the couplet in its meaning and its quality. In talking about it, we can point out and point up, but we cannot render. Analysis of verse is by nature partial; the verses are their own event. I belabor a commonplace; it is a true common place which sets a limit beyond which theory and analysis in real senses cannot pass, and should not try to pass.

Insofar as analysis is, as its name suggests, a breaking-down into parts, it is self-inconsistent as well as empirically false to talk about exhaustive analysis. For a survey of the parts of an object, even if that survey, *per impossible*, could cover every single part and all the mutual relations of the parts, would still be a multiplicity, not a whole. Or if one wishes to say that the survey is one, the summing-up of all the parts, that whole is a different whole from the object. Wholes and parts have paradoxical relationships which analyzers and theorists had better respect, even if it takes some tempering of zeal. *We don't, after all, know very much.* Further it is plainly true that no analysis does in fact cover all the parts and relationships within an object. Cowboys know some things about cows that zoologists don't, zoologists some things that cowboys don't, and they should respect each others' knowledge and ignorance. If my analogy tends to class literary critics with veterinarians, neither cowboys nor zoologists but a bit of both, the veterinarians I know are courteous and will not mind.

I beg indulgence for one more, queerish analogy. Literary analysis is not picking up lumps out of a box; nor is it pointing to the pedestal (basis) a poem sits on; nor is it even cutting where the joints are. It is more like using an X-ray machine. What we see (1) is elsewhere; (2) is miscolored; (3) is misshapen; (4) needs interpretation; (5) gives clues to but does not change the reality of the object examined (with the fascinating exception—let the theorist heed—that if one is X-rayed too often, one dies); (6) is, properly understood, true; and (7) can be very important in understanding the object. Most of all, an X-ray machine needs a skilled interpreter, with good eyes and strong and practiced judgment. Human activity is what we do.

SOME THINGS MORE

I have argued and asserted, and stand on what I say, but feel frustrated. Subjectivism, in the strict sense, is either right or wrong: I think it wrong. But relativism is a marsh, and cleaning up a marsh is a complicated and tedious engineering feat. There is so much that relativists say, so much that poses as relativism, so much true and false and confused that an essay cannot cover the subject. I shall save most of the rest for another day; but I would like in closing to deal with, however summarily or inadequately, a few relevant issues.

Two notions in my fundamental argument were that the *Iliad* is a poem of some poetic merit and that we know that it is. I do not really think that either statement should need defense, since they are about as patently true as anything in our experience, so much so that it requires a special and peculiar cast of theorizing to doubt them or even to raise the possibility that they might be doubted. Still there are theories that would cast those statements into doubt, or deny them. They can be doubted or denied by general scepticism, by epistemological twists and turns, by the magic work "culture," by various attempts at psychological dissolution. Much of the scepticism and epistemologizing falls into the same trap: in undoing other beliefs, they undo themselves. Universal acids do not last long; they dissolve themselves. Furthermore, the usual forms of attack entail absolutism, since many of the objections are fundamentally moral and often carry a high charge of moral indignation. To assert that one should not hold a position without clear proofs of special kinds is to make a moral assertion, which entails absolutism and undercuts itself. "What right," it is frequently and firmly asserted in these or similar words, "does one have to make moral judgments of other people, or other cultures?" The word "right" is the beautifully damaging word. Relativism is likewise recommended because of its presumed beneficial effect in producing tolerance. But if tolerance is good, then moral absolutism is true. And if tolerance is not good, if it is just another culturally imposed moral opinion with no hook into reality, then there is no reason to recommend it.

It is often hinted or asserted that the trouble with literary judgment is that there is no "evidence" for it. That view is not only false, but fantastic. There is excellent and widely known evidence for believing that the *Iliad* is a good poem. The fact that much of it is evidence that can be assessed only by a person capable of imaginative response does not damage its claim to be good evidence: that is a rule for handling such evidence. To gather astronomical data with a telescope, one needs eyes. To see how powerful a poet Homer is, one needs to be able to respond to poetry. It is the crudest sort of epistemological mistake (which will cripple every form of knowledge, including the physical sciences) to put epistemological demands on a subject that do not grow out of a particular and thoughtful exploration of the subject itself. Feeling is a necessary condition of genuine literary knowledge—a statement for which the *evidence* is huge.

But, it is objected, there is such disagreement among literary critics. The dissidence of dissent is, I grant, a loud noise. But, on the subject at hand (Homer's value) there is almost universal agreement. There is disagreement in a huge variety of disciplines: politics, economics, sociology, theology, ethics, history, philosophy, others. If disagreement is a proof of falsity or meaninglessness, then a good bit perishes with aesthetic absolutism, including, naturally, aesthetic relativism and subjectivism. Moreover, there is often more disagreement about matters of fact than about matters of value. A classic example is Shakespeare's sonnets: there is far more agreement about their value in general and even about which groups of poems and particular poems are the better ones (though there is a fair amount of disagreement there) than about what people, if any, the sonnets concern. But that is a question of fact. The value of the *Iliad* is agreed on; its unity of authorship is not. The value of *Peri Hupsous* ("On the Sublime") is asserted by romanticist and neoclassicist alike. Who "Longinus" was, when and where he lived, and even his name, are uncertain. In general, it is an illusion based on a highly selective choice of examples that Facts are solid and agreed on, Values vague and problematic. The position this paper takes is that, so to speak, value is a fact. It takes a complex process of abstraction *from* our experience to separate fact and value; it is only after establishing, by logical violence, a value-free world as reality, that one can wonder how to get from a world of fact to a world of value. We are already there, in our world and its truths.

Beyond this, moral disagreement or aesthetic disagreement entails that both parties to the disagreement imply an acceptance of absolutism. Otherwise they aren't disagreeing. If two men disagree about a poem, one saying it is good, the other saying it is bad, the disagreement vanishes if it turns out that what their statements mean is merely that one is pleased by the poem and the other displeased, two perfectly consistent truths. But they surely think they are disagreeing; therefore they surely do not mean merely some psychological statement when they say "Poem J is bad"; "No; poem J is good."

But, the rejoinder rejoins, taste is dependent on "culture." We think Homer is good because we are part of our culture. A different culture, different standards. In such statements "culture" may be so general as to include everything except genetic structure. In that case its meaning includes everything, including valid value judgments if any, and hence cannot be used to reject value judgments or anything else. If the word does not have such a broad meaning, such statements are manifestly false. Homer's world is enormously different from ours, as well as much like ours. It is the likeness or the difference which determines the invalidity of the taste? Neither makes much sense, on serious reflection. Or such statements may mean that readers like Homer merely because they have been told to in advance, because it is a cultural belief imposed on them that Homer is a powerful poet. But many readers do respond powerfully to Homer, readers who do not always respond as they are told to.

But, it is further said, our responses depend on our nervous system. So our literary experiences and pleasures aren't "absolute," but relative to our experience. It is very hard to see what is meant by "absolute" in such a statement. Our experience is our experience, and in a sense (though not in every sense) we know nothing apart from it. But that objection applies as strongly to other subjects, *all* other subjects, as to literary experience, and hence undercuts all positions with equal force (including, once again, relativism and subjectivism). If we can't fundamentally trust our experience, we are truly out of luck. All of us.

In some very important sense indeed, our knowledge stands on faith in experience. If that is so, then absolute rational certainty would seem impossible (except perhaps on a very few matters, and even then I have my doubts), for I do not see how one can prove the veracity of experience without assuming it. To attempt the proof, one has to assume the conclusion. Of course one has to assume the conclusion to carry on any argument; but necessity is not as such proof. At the same time, arguments offered against that faith in experience tend to undercut themselves in a very special way; they have to assume the veracity of experience in order to cast doubt on it (this is one of several reasons why I believe that theism is more *rational* than opposing views). But this matter is intricate, and I shall not attempt here a thorough handling of it. Here I shall merely assert that there is a middle ground between strict rationalism and strict scepticism—namely, all of human experience and existence. It is a ground with limits and confusions and shadows, some of them dark. But we can and do stand on it, and we do and should make the act of faith it perpetually requires. That act of faith itself, and all the discussion we engage in depends on it, is absolutistic. And relativists and subjectivists *do* engage in the discussion.

Adele Austin Rickett

THE PERSONALITY OF THE
CHINESE CRITIC

POETIC CRITICISM IN CHINA COULD PERHAPS BE SAID TO HAVE STARTED
·with Confucius's pronouncement on the *Book of Poetry*.[1] Though
Confucius did not seem to have too much concern for the aesthetic
qualities of the 305 poems in the anthology, he did comment on the
social and political advantages to be gained by a mastery of the
terms for birds, beasts, flowers, fish, etc., mentioned in its lines, and
the moral advantages to be gained from the fact that the poems contained "no depraved thoughts." His utilitarian approach to the art of
poetry set a precedent that was to continue right up to the twentieth
century.

A somewhat more subjective interpretation of the poems, i.e., that
poetry is an expression of one's will (intent, or innermost thoughts)
is found in various texts prior to the Christian era, and this concept
too persisted in the writings of critics through subsequent ages. But
it was not until the second century A.D. that literature was for the
first time contemplated as literature in itself and that critical powers
were brought to bear on the aesthetic quality of writing. Ts'ao P'i's
(187–226) essay on literature, "Lun wen," followed by Lu Chi's
(261–303) "Wen fu" [Prosepoem on Literature], followed in turn
by the monumental and unique work of Liu Hsieh (c.465–522), the
Wen-hsin tiao-lung [The Literary Mind and Carving of Dragons],
moved the development of literary criticism along, albeit at a snail's
pace.

In the T'ang dynasty (618–906) criticism, particularly in the area
of prose, became more common, but as the twentieth-century scholar
of Chinese literature Kuo Shao-yü has pointed out, the T'ang was

essentially a creative period in which new forms of both poetry and prose were appearing. The creative efforts of men of letters were concentrated on actively practicing these new forms and they displayed less interest in discussions of techniques or philosophy of expression. In strong contrast to the T'ang, the Sung dynasty (960–1279) could be characterized as a "contemplative age."[2] The forms of literature had solidified and interest turned then to a consideration of the style, technique, content, and value of poetry and prose.[3] The role of the critic became more pronounced in this age, and since then criticism of poetry and prose has continued to hold a prominent place in the world of letters.[4]

In this paper I shall attempt to define who the critic is in China, what he is criticizing, and why he undertakes to do so. I shall explore the limits society places upon his personality, and in contrast, what the possibilities are for the critic in the Chinese intellectual world.

THE ROLE OF THE CRITIC

It is a commonplace in the West to view the creative artist and the critic as two separate entities, either diametrically opposed to each other or in the relationship of host and parasite. That the two could coexist in the same person and often did (Coleridge, Wordsworth, Eliot, to mention only a few) does not seem to have impressed the Western mind and the dual picture of the two roles has persisted. In China, however, there has never been any question that the poet is at the same time a critic and the critic a poet. Naturally there have been exceptions. Liu Hsieh, mentioned above, wrote the first and only book of criticism organized into full-length essays prior to the twentieth century, and we never thing of him as a poet. Although a few of Yen Yü's (fl. c. A.D. 1200) poems are to be found in anthologies of Sung dynasty poetry, he is known primarily for his *Ts'ang-lang shih-hua*, a work which applies Ch'an Buddhist concepts to the evaluation of poetry. And in contrast, it is possible to find greatly esteemed and loved poets such as Li Yü (937–978), last ruler of the Southern T'ang, or Wen T'ing-yün (fl. c. A.D. 859), one of the earliest masters of the lyrical *tz'u* form of poetry, who have left us no pronouncements on literature.

There is, it seems to me, a very logical explanation for the existence of the poet-critic or critic-poet in China. First of all, men did not function in traditional Chinese society as professional poets. One must again cite exceptions, the most notable being Li Po (701–762), who was appointed to the Han-lin Academy but who held no official post in the T'ang government; but generally speaking the poets of China have all been, first of all, officials. They were brought up in strict Confucian orthodoxy, and their goal was to pass the examinations which would assure them a post in the government. In these examinations proficiency in the writing of poetry and essays counted heavily. Thus each aspiring official was at the same time an aspiring poet or essayist. Since they were all traveling the same road to advancement, the body of knowledge being mastered was common to them all. They therefore formed, by the very nature of their position, an elite body of educated men, capable of talking intelligently to each other on scholarly and literary subjects. It was very natural for them to want to criticize and encourage each other and to use letters, prefaces, and colophons among others as vehicles for critical judgments and evaluations.

The nature of this elite group also influenced in no small way the form and rhetoric of criticism. I am fond of quoting what may seem a rather facetious statement by the late scholar, T. A. Hsia, who commented that in general Chinese critical essays are written for sharp-witted men to read: one point and all is immediately clear with no need to waste words. Western critical essays, he maintains, are written for dull-witted men to read; thus they must explain clearly the principles involved.[5] He is saying in sharper words what Yü P'ing-po had said some years earlier in describing the small work of poetic criticism by the scholar Wang Kuo-wei (1877–1927), *Jen-chien tz'u-hua* [Talks on *Tz'u* in the Human World]:

> Actually if the clues hinted at in this book were drawn out and explained it would become a gigantic tome, but the strength of its interest would be lessened. Bright pearls, kingfisher feathers, they are easily picked up, yet there are none which are not rare gems. But to build them into a "seven-jewelled tower" would be like adding feet to a snake.[6]

Thus when Wang Kuo-wei wrote: "The line 'A pair of golden partridges on a painted screen,' written by Wen T'ing-yün, typifies the quality of his *tz'u*," he was confident that his readers would understand the purport of this particular "bright pearl."[7] But present-day Chinese students and many Western scholars who have never read Wen T'ing-yün's poetry or have no idea of the poet's background feel lost, as do my students when I ask them if they can hazard a guess about Wang's intent here. He is taking (if I understand him correctly) the image of exquisitely embroidered birds to represent the beauty of Wen T'ing-yün's poetry but at the same time the "manu-factured" nature of it. His poems are not real birds but likenesses of birds, and not painted likenesses but rather ones which require a special technical skill to achieve. His classical-scholar reader need simply call to mind some of Wen T'ing-yün's poems, which he can recite from memory, and then nod in agreement, "Ah, yes, Wang Kuo-wei has really caught the spirit," or shake his head and write a comment of disagreement in the margin which he may later incorpo-rate into one of his own slight works of criticism.

I do not want to give the impression that because the style of writ-ing in literary criticism has traditionally been terse and scattered, the amount of printed material is somewhat scanty. This is far from the case. Scholars seemed to feel the need to comment on other people's poetry almost as much as they did to create poetry of their own. This, then, brings us to the consideration of why scholars became so in-terested in the practice of criticism. It seems to me that we must view the activity of the critic from his dual position as poet and official. He could be a good poet relegated by the tide of fortune or high inci-dence of factionalism in the court to a minor office in a provincial town; or he could be a mediocre poet enjoying a position of authority in the government. He could be a bad poet in a minor post (in which case we probably don't know much about him), or a good poet in a high post. He could hold a position with little change for a number of years, or be demoted, banished, exiled, reinstated, even executed for reasons over which he had no control. His personality might be such that he would grow weary of court strife and retire to the mountains to live the life of a recluse. But in any case, he maintained a strong interest in scholarly matters which was as much a part of him as breathing. Except for the recluse who shut his doors to the tumul-tuous world of men, this scholarly interest included a strong sense of responsibility to others in the closed little circle in which he operated. Thus scores and scores of letters were written and conversations re-corded in which a master would criticize, encourage, and instruct his friends and disciples in the writing of poetry.

One of the most conscientious in the area of critical responsibility was Huang T'ing-chien (1045–1105), who lived in a by no means untypical era torn by dissension and factionalism in the court. Many of his contemporaries, in particular his friend and master Su Shih (1037–1101), considered poetry a proper vehicle for criticizing the government and giving vent to one's anger over inequities in society. Many, because of this, found themselves banished from the court.

Huang disagreed completely with this point of view and felt that poetry should keep clear of politics. But even at that he too failed to escape the effects of factionalism. Because of his sympathy for unpopular policies he was sent far from the court in the later years of his life. In the realm of poetry he felt that a man should concentrate his efforts on perfecting his style and attaining a measure of skill that would push him over into the realm of naturalness transcending mechanical art. He has been looked upon through the ages as the man who gave formal expression to the concept of imitation in the writing process, and he pointed to the stylistic genius of the T'ang poet Tu Fu (712–770) and the metaphysical genius of T'ao Ch'ien (365–427) as most worthy of emulation. Tu Fu's poetry through much of his life was concerned with revealing the ills of society and mildly criticizing policies of government, but in his later years when it had become quite clear that he would never be called to an influential post, and as his health began to fail, he wrote poetry reflective of a more introspective and melancholy nature. It was the poetry of this period that Huang T'ing-chien particularly admired. In writing to friends and disciples, therefore, he closed his eyes to much of the earlier content of Tu Fu and used the later poems as examples to be studied. Tu Fu's attitude toward study, his statement that he had "read to tatters 10,000 volumes" before he felt ready to write poetry himself, was also an important element in Huang's advice to aspiring poets. In one letter he wrote:

> . . . I have read and reread the poems and essays you have sent. The ideas (*yi*) expressed approach those of the ancients but they still cannot compare with them in versatility and proliferation of style. Your ideas also show that in your reading of the works of the Chien-an poets (A.D. 196–220) and of T'ao Ch'ien and Tu Fu you have not yet entered the spiritual (*ju shen*). . . .[8]

And in another letter he said:

> . . . In the poems you have sent there are many excellent lines. I only regret that you have expended so much effort on cutting and polishing. Anyone who reads the poetry of Tu Fu after he went to K'uei-chou will gain [a sense of] simplicity in method of expression and his skill will be perfected. [His verse] is an open plain, calm and clear, and yet its full measure is no more to be reached than the top of the highest mountain, the depths of the deepest water. Successful compositions show no traces of axe or chisel. . . .[9]

Criticism of this sort, then, was of a practical nature in that its purpose was to help young poets. Yet in addition to specific references to techniques of creative writing one can find discussions on the theory of literature and the history of literature. Since, however, the purpose of the criticism is to help the reader or pupil improve his style so that he can make a better show in the official world, the theoretical and historical elements are brought in primarily to bolster the points being made for practical purposes. (This will be made more clear in the discussion of Ssu-k'ung T'u, below.) In the same way, the critic is not so interested in analyzing the strong and weak points of former masters for their own sakes as he is in *using* them as examples. Criticism in this respect is a means to an end, and the critic employs it quite consciously in this way.

The critic also writes for a broader audience than the single friend or disciple, of course. As a staunch Confucian he may write for all the poets and essayists of his age when he feels that the vehicle of literature has become so corrupted that it can no longer impart the true and moral Way of the ancients. He takes himself very seriously as a self-appointed whip lashing out at the decadent elements of his society. In such cases, the theory that he expounds has a practical application. He is not interested in rhetoric or diction from an aesthetic viewpoint but rather in what that rhetoric does to the content of the piece. If it is so ornate that the Way cannot be imparted, it is time for someone to set people straight. The critic speaks out and often fierce verbal battles ensue between him and those who accept the current styles. It is interesting that of the hundreds of writers whose names appear in works of criticism, the most eminent among them seem rather consistently to have been those who showed themselves to be reacting *against* the current of the time. Dissatisfied with the popular styles accepted by their peers, they sought to effect a change, but over and over the approach they used was to urge a return to styles of former days. Liu Hsieh, writing in an age marked by excessive ornateness of diction and a precise parallelism in style, pointed out that a man's best chance of achieving fame was through writing, but that since writing in his age had deteriorated to such a low level, he felt called upon to remind men that emphasis should be put on the essential and not the superficial and eccentric.[10] Similarly, the Ku-wen Masters of the late T'ang and Sung dynasties deplored the styles of their times and called upon writers to look back to the works of the Chou and the Han dynasties, to the ancient styles, as the title "ku-wen" implies, for inspiration.[11] Even Taoist and Buddhist critics such as Yen Yü felt constrained to use the example of earlier writers in contrast to those of their own time whose ornate style they could not abide.

Not all critics were as pedagogically minded as Huang T'ing-chien, nor were they all as concerned about the general state of society and the function of literature in it. Men also commented on literature as a way of expressing their very personal feelings about the beauty of nature, human relations, and the state of the world, or their concept of the creative art in general. The casual nature of these comments can be seen in the form adopted. *Shih-hua* or "Talks on Poetry" consist of small paragraphs written at various times, sometimes over a period of years, and eventually gathered together into a series of chapters to make a book. In them the critic expresses his views on poetic theory, technique, style, genres, etc.[12] The titles of these works of criticism often reflect their nature: *Night Talks in the Cold Studio* (*Leng chai yeh-hua*) by the monk Hui-hung (1071–1128), or *Rambling Thoughts from Pi-chi* (*Pi-chi man-chih*) by Wang Cho (fl. c. A.D. 1162). Most often they appear without a preface, but when they do, the mind of the writer is revealed quite clearly. Wang Cho in his preface to *Pi-chi man-chih* tells us:

> . . . Every time I returned home from a drinking party I did not dare go straight to bed. Since there was no one to talk to I relied on the sights and sounds which the songs had called forth that day, once more to examine the customs of the ages, and let my thoughts recall the discussions of ordinary times. I wrote them all down and collected 110 pages which I mixed in with all my books and did not keep in order. This past autumn when I opened my book boxes I found the scattered fragments. Only seventeen pages were left, so I put them in proper order and made additions to form a book of five *chüan*. I called it *Pi-chi man-chih*. Now that I am growing older I regret that as a youth I lacked a calm, dispassionate heart. Having completed this, what use is it? Yet I cannot bear to burn or throw away these drunken jottings of the moment.[13]

The book is divided into five *chüan* or chapters. The first contains comments on concepts of the ancients about poetry and song, starting with the question, "How did songs arise?" In *chüan* two Wang Cho discusses various poets from the T'ang to Sung dynasties, while *chüan* three is devoted to discussion of particular songs. *Chüan* four contains anecdotes from history books about poetry and music in the court, and *chüan* five is devoted to various *tz'u* patterns.

These critics wrote, then, for three reasons: (1) to help present and future writers improve their style, (2) to correct decadent tendencies in literature, and (3) to satisfy their subjective need to express their thoughts on past and present writers and writing.

THE CRITIC'S LIMITATIONS

Since he so often found himself swimming against the tide in reaction against the general trend, the critic often developed a pessimistic and negative attitude toward life. The tradition of the "frustrated scholar" is usually traced back to the poet-official Ch'ü Yüan (4th cen. B.C.), who is pictured as a man truly out of joint with his times. "The world is dirty, I alone am pure." [14] When the critic applied this attitude to poetry, his concern over the licentiousness and impropriety of certain types of verse grew so strong that he refused to accept them as they appeared. Instead he would try to interpret them as political allegory. Wang Kuo-wei in his *Jen-chien tz'u-hua* was particularly critical of this ultradidactic approach, and he singled out Chang Hui-yen (1761–1802) as a prime example. To illustrate his point he cited Chang's explanation of a poem by Ou-yang Hsiu (1007–1072).[15] The poem is a slight, lyrical, self-pitying poem in two stanzas, a *tz'u* to the tune of "Tieh lien hua":

> Deep, deep the courtyard far within
> Where mist enfolds the willows.
> While over there among the screens and curtains too numerous
>   to count,
> Fine young men make gay in luscious company,
> I, high in my tower, cannot see the Chang-t'ai Road.[16]

> The rain drives fierce, wind blows wild at end of spring,
> The gate stands closed at dusk.
> Can spring be held no longer?
> With tear-filled eyes I ask the flowers, but they do not speak.
> Swirling red petals fly past the swing away.[17]

Chang Hui-yen attaches political significances to this *tz'u*. He interprets the first line to mean that the inner apartments of the palace are far distant from where the poet is, and thus that the ruler is inaccessible to those desiring to see him. The last line of the first stanza means that the wise kings slumber on, remote from the streets of pleasure-seekers and petty men, that is to say, the Chang-t'ai Road. He goes on to say that the fierce rain and wild wind in the next stanza signify that the government's orders are extremely urgent. In the last line, the petals flying past the swing mean that many men have been thrown out of the government or banished to remote posts.

As Professor Chia-ying Yeh Chao has pointed out in her study of the Ch'ang-chou School,[18] Chang Hui-yen and his brother compiled the anthology of *tz'u* poems to provide fitting examples in the education of the young men they were tutoring at the time. They felt that to take the love poems at their face value would not coincide with propriety. At the same time, they could not close their eyes to the interest displayed in lyrical poetry in the *tz'u* form. Their solution to the problem lay in using the Confucian blanket of morality, i.e., political allegory, to cover over the sensual vibrancy of the original poem.

In studying the process of anthologizing as a form of literary criticism, I have been struck by the inconsistencies displayed in the inclusion or exclusion of certain poems. Often a scholar of Confucian background will include in his anthology of, say, *tz'u* from the Sung dynasty a number of poems that are admittedly quite sensual. If he is like Chang Hui-yen, the anthologist will try to rationalize his selection by imparting a hidden meaning to them. But other anthologists seem to feel that the name of the poet, often a man of unquestioned stature in both the scholarly and political world, such as Ou-yang Hsiu, is enough to give sanction to the selection. Since most of the anthologists do not give a detailed account of their reasons for selection, we can only proffer some tentative assumptions.

It seems to me that the anthologist could quite possibly be of two different minds on the matter. He may be so completely imbued with Confucian standards of morality that it would be inconceivable to him that a man like Ou-yang Hsiu could spend any time in the frivolous art of love poetry. Therefore such poems cannot under any condition be taken as they appear, and it is up to the anthologist, as a commentator, as a critic, to point out to other, less pure, readers what is obvious to him. The other mind may see the poems as expressions of love and therefore as potentially "dangerous" for young minds. But at the same time he may realize that they have gained acceptance over the ages and that he would be in error not to include them. In fact, he himself might be very fond of them. To salve his own conscience, therefore, he attempts to offset the emotional impact by giving the images a political depth. But whether he is being honest or not, the limitations set by this type of criticism are obvious. The critic is constrained by the limits of his own vision as prescribed for him by the morals of his traditional upbringing to view the poems in a way that most of us would find deplorable. That a great deal of criticism in China, starting from the earliest commentaries on the

Book of Poetry, was concerned with the application of political significance to simple love poems is a phenomenon that has not been equaled in the West.

I think it is possible to see related to this attitude toward poetry another aspect of the Chinese critic which is an outgrowth of his society. The New Critics in the West would certainly consider it a limitation; I am not so sure. The aspect of which I am speaking is the tendency to spend a great deal of time as a critic or commentator on establishing the time, place, and reason for the writing of a poem. Now the poet himself (and here the line between poet and critic is very close) is often concerned about making clear the details surrounding the composition of a poem. He tells the reader in the title or subtitle where, when, and under what conditions he has written it. Thus we find a title like Hsieh T'iao's (464–494) "On Receiving a Temporary Commission to Go to the Capital I Set out at Night from Hsin-lin and on Arriving at the Capital Wrote This Poem to Send to My Colleagues back in the Western Prefecture." Actually the Chinese title is only sixteen characters long, but still it seems rather topheavy for a poem of twenty five-word lines. If you want to examine the content of such a poem simply from the point of view of the poem itself you will have difficulty. The poet does not want the reader to see his poem in isolation. He wants the reader to know that it was at that particular time and in that particular place that conditions inspired him to take up his brush. No other place or time would have produced that response. Although we certainly have our counterpart in Western poetry, this type of verse seems to have an extraordinarily prominent place in Chinese literature. The critic, therefore, conditioned by his own approach to this type of poetry, tends to feel that a reader can understand a poem only if he knows its background. A great deal of commentary is devoted to establishing the date of a poem and a great deal of scholarly squabbling has filled pages in an attempt to pinpoint the date or location of a poem's writing.

Now I do not think that in some cases this is such a bad idea. In China many poets, because they were officials (or should I say many officials because they were poets), used poetry as a vehicle to comment on the times. Most outstanding is the example of Tu Fu, who has been called a historian-poet; a great number of his poems are, indeed, tied to specific incidents in the history of his time. Through his poems we can gain a fair picture of the contrast between the opulent life in the court and the grim plight of the common people, or the effects of war on young and old, rich and poor. It could be argued, I suppose, that a description of the anguish felt by a bride and groom on their wedding night which was at the same time the eve before the departure of the young man for war, could stir the hearts of readers in any age, any society. And this is true, for certainly his "Parting of a Newly Wedded Couple" cannot fail to move an American in the twentieth century. But the Chinese have tended to look on such poems as significant because of the time in which they were written.

So strong was this tendency that a form of literary criticism developed in the T'ang dynasty called *pen-shih shih,* usually translated as "background facts about poetry." [19] These consisted of anecdotes recounting the occasion on which a particular poem was written. Sometimes the details involve ghosts and spirits and are so far-fetched they defy credibility. In such cases they approach the realm of fictional short stories and one can only assume that they were written to amuse rather than enlighten. However, the tradition had become firmly established by the Sung dynasty, and we find short pieces describing the setting in which poems were composed scattered liberally through the pages of *shih-hua* and *tz'u-hua.* One example may suffice to illustrate the form:

> Mei Yao-ch'en was sitting with Ou-yang Hsiu one day and said he considered Lin Pu's *tz'u* on spring grasses quite beautiful. Before leaving, Mei composed a *tz'u* to the tune of "Su mu che" [on the same theme]. Ou-yang Hsiu clapped his hands in delight and composed one of his own to the tune of "Shao-nien yu ling." Not only was it far better than the other two but if placed in the collections of Wen T'ing-yün and Li Hou-chu it could pass for one of theirs. What a pity it is missing from his present collection. [20]

If the critic is not content unless he can see the poem in its proper setting, what does this do to his understanding of the meaning of the poem as an aesthetic experience? Is he so limited by the practical considerations of time and place that he loses sight of the other possibilities of the poem? In this respect we can refer back again to the place of the critic-poet in his society. The critic who feels that he is writing for a select circle who share his knowledge of Chinese literature may very well feel that it is not important to talk about what a poem *means* in metaphysical or abstract terms. If he can set the stage for the composition of the poem, his reader will then react immediately, "Oh yes, that was how it was. Of course so-and-so would have written such a poem at that time. I would have felt the same myself under those circumstances." Or if not quite in those terms, the reader would at least feel that he understood the reason for writing the poem.

Such attention to detail is seen in a slightly different way in the penchant many critics have for categorizing and classifying. In the general field of literature this took the form of establishing genres and then setting standards through example for each one. Hsiao T'ung in the sixth century A.D. compiled the *Wen hsüan*, an anthology of literature arranged by genre, and stated in his preface to the work that he had gathered together the best pieces of literature he could find to delight readers of present and future ages and to serve as examples for their own creative effort. The significance of this anthologizing activity has been described above. Of much more limited scope was a slightly different form of categorization, i.e., the grouping, classification, comparing, and pairing of poets. The first major effort in this direction was Chung Yung's (fl. c. A.D. 500) *Shih p'in* [Classification of Poets], in which he grouped 109 writers of five-word-line verse into superior, next to superior, and not so superior. (The inclusion of a poet to begin with meant that he was worth considering.) It was as if a Western critic had taken all the major writers of sonnet form and arranged them into three classes. Like the critics who come at the end of an age, Chung Yung was concerned about what he considered the decline in poetic values from simple, straightforward expression of emotions and virtuous sentiments and sought for a return to standards of earlier ages, namely the *Book of Poetry* and the *Ch'u tz'u.* His classification was, on the negative side, an attack on current ornateness and floweriness, and on the positive, an attempt to lead the literary world back to purity of diction and content. His efforts placed him far from his contemporaries and his judgments have been criticized over the centuries,[21] but his method was uncontested and became extremely popular among later critics.

I do not mean to suggest that there were any more books written exactly like the *Shih p'in*, but a great deal of space in *shih-hua* and *tz'u-hua* is taken up by such statements as "I would rank So-and-so above Mr. X but below Mr. Y." Sometimes the critic will attempt to elucidate his remark with a few lines of evaluation so that the reader will have some faint clue to the basis of his judgment, but most of the time we are left in the dark. He undoubtedly feels that his readers know so much about the poetry of the men involved that he does not need to elaborate. But to me this is representative of a most unsatisfactory form of criticism with little value beyond telling us something

about the state of mind of the critic himself. In some of these comments we can see a strong Confucian bias, a frustration with the man's
current age, and a desire to straighten people out; in others we can
sense a personal prejudice against the poet being categorized, which
reveals a smallness of mind on the part of the critic. When a number
of comments by one man are brought together it is quite possible to
gain an understanding of him simply from the way he ranks the various poets. His very subjectivism, while a limitation as far as literary
criticism is concerned, becomes valuable in terms of coming to know
him as a man.

Related to the process of categorizing is another activity of the
Chinese literary critic: commenting on comments made by other
critics. Even though fires, wars, pestilence, and floods took their toll
of thousands of books and libraries through the ages, the number of
books that were preserved has been staggering. Scholars took immense pride in amassing libraries even though they moved so frequently from post to post, and there seemed to be an almost irresistible
urge among them to add to the existing store of critical judgment by
commenting on that judgment. For example, we find Wang Kuo-wei
saying:

> Chou Chi said: "The most excellent examples of Wu Wen-ying's *tz'u*
> are like sunlight[22] and shadows dancing on the green waves, caress-
> ing, playing without tiring; yet when we pursue them, they are already
> far in the distance."[23] In reading through Wu Wen-ying's collected
> verse I have found nothing that merits such a comment. If we were
> to attempt to point out any, would it be perhaps the two lines:
>
> Across the river stands a man, raindrops dripping, dripping,
> The evening breeze through the reeds rouses autumn sadness.[24]

THE CRITIC'S POSSIBILITIES

The same form of criticism which operates as a limiting factor can
also be considered in positive terms. As mentioned above, in the nature of Chinese criticism sustained works of book length are a rarity.
The works which were published as books were mainly *shih-hua* and
tz'u-hua, some several hundred pages long, it is true, but all comprised
of short, choppy comments, usually less than a page each and some
only two or three lines. The comment by Wang Kuo-wei quoted
above is a good example. We must piece together the literary theory
of a man from these random comments together with the bits of wisdom scattered through his letters to friends, prefaces and colophons

to various works, and his own poetry. In order to get his point across in these restricted areas of expression, he will usually rely on vivid images and metaphorical terms. What a Westerner would take a chapter to develop and explain, the Chinese could present in a paragraph or less. Naturally, the fact that the critic was writing for a select circle of men with similar educational backgrounds must have had a great deal to do with this phenomenon, and the terse nature of the Chinese language itself must also be considered; but I feel that the critic who was so sure of his audience that he did not need to spell out his ideas in great detail must have sensed a freedom quite exhilarating.

This reliance on vivid images, metaphorical terms, and obscure, half-stated observations was the result of a blending of Confucian and Buddhist/Taoist training. The Confucian aspect of a man's training pushed him to do something about the state of the world in which he was living. He could not *not* speak out. That most of these critics looked to past ages for the models and precedents that would lead men on to the future is also of Confucian origin. And we can perhaps also credit Confucius with the fact that the critic expected a great deal of the reader. Confucius said, "When I give a man one corner of a subject, if he cannot get the other three corners himself, I will not repeat it." (*Lun-yü*, 7:8). The critic says, "Here is my theory. If you don't grasp my intent, that is your responsibility." Such is the "this-worldly" aspect of criticism, to borrow Feng Yu-lan's phrase.[25]

On the other hand, many, many critics came into contact with Taoism and/or Buddhism at some point in their lives and were influenced to a greater or lesser extent by this "other-worldly" philosophy, which led them to look for a meaning to man's existence beyond the bounds of the mundane world. Under the influence of such a philosophy the critic would be inclined to distrust the power of words per se and would expect his reader to see beyond the printed page to grasp the truth unexpressed. The possibilities for creative understanding on the part of the reader under such conditions are untold. The minds of critic and reader can blend in the world beyond words and achieve a harmony that would be impossible if they had been bound by excessive explanations. And yet, of course, many readers *do* sometimes need some explanation, and thus the critic will attempt to elucidate the key phrase or word that forms the basis of his poetic theory and sets him apart from other critics. But more often than not his elucidation will again be a series of images that require a high level of training on the part of the reader. It is no wonder that at this stage in the study of Chinese literary criticism in the West, so much energy is devoted to an analysis of terms of criticism. The terms are the key; if they can be made clear, the theory will be much easier to understand.[26]

In order to illustrate how a blending of Confucian and Buddhist/ Taoist ideas influenced the personality of a critic and, in turn, his work, I would like to present here a translation of a letter written by a critic of the T'ang dynasty, Ssu-k'ung T'u (837–907) to a friend, Mr. Li:[27]

> Prose is difficult but poetry is even more difficult. There have been numerous illustrations of this through the ages but I feel that [through the example of] differentiation of flavors we can come to an understanding of poetry. All those people who live south of the Yangtze [all the way to Kwangtung (i.e., the less civilized part of China)] are content to eat whatever is palatable. For example, pickled [vegetables] are acceptable so long as they have a sour taste, and salted [vegetables] are acceptable so long as they have a briny taste. The people of China proper, however, whether quick or slow in satisfying their hunger, know that beyond those briny and sour tastes there is something of a refined and delicate nature yet untasted. But those people from the south have become so accustomed to their food that they are no longer discriminating. Is it any wonder?
>
> The six tropes of poetry contain within them satire, praise and blame, breadth of learning, profundity, and refinement. However, the works of former generations have not shown extraordinary skill in mastering this to produce a unique style. And need we mention those that fill the lesser ranks? Wang Wei [701–761] and Wei Ying-wu [736–830] were clear as fresh water, fine as soft-textured cloth. Style in their hands, could it be anything but of superior vigor? Chia Tao [779?–843?] truly wrote some extraordinary lines, but when we look at his work in toto his ideas are somewhat impoverished. He probably felt that only through harsh and bitter struggle could he realize his talent to the fullest, but he lacked the proper basic pattern. And need we mention those who were lesser men than he? Alas! [To comprehend] what is close by yet not floating on the surface, what is far distant yet not to the end—then one can speak of the transmission of something beyond words.
>
> In my youth I was rather self-important but as the years have gone by I have felt my limitations more and more. However as I encountered different experiences in life I felt inspired to write verse. In early spring I wrote:
>
>> Tender shoots of young grass take over the sand,
>> Thin layers of ice melt against the rain;[28]
>
> and:
>
>> People's homes at the Festival of Cold Food[29] under the moon,
>> Flowers' shadows at midday under the sky;

and again:

Rain, fine, my song holds thoughts of love full-brimming,
Flowers, falling, my dreams are sad, of purpose lost.

When in the mountains I wrote:

Mountain slope warm, in winter bamboo shoots appear,
Pines cool, in summer a man feels invigorated;

and again:

The river so clear a rainbow reflects the rain,
Trees so dense the birds make brush with humans.

When in Chiang-nan [the area just south of the Yangtze] I wrote:

The frontier drums sound in harmony with the water's motion,
    dark,
Boat lamps shine upon the island, desolate;[30]

and:

Jagged-edged lake at end of spring in rain,
Fang-hsiang[31] in depth of night on the boat;

and again:

When nights are short, apes' mournful cry is less,
When wind is soft, magpies' joyous being fulfills its prophecy.[32]

When I was up in the passes I wrote:

Horses' spirits through cold of winter droop dejected,
Eagles' cry carries sound of hunger pushed too long.

In a time of disaster I wrote:

The famous steed[33] recalls its old home,
The parrot has lost its beautiful mistress;

and:

The huge fish stranded in the ocean of men,
The forest goblin perched high in the thorny jujube trees.[34]

In the Taoist monastery I wrote:

The sound of chess pieces behind the flowered courtyard, closed,
Shadows cast by streamers on the stone altar high.

And in the summer I wrote:

The cool ground makes tranquil the crane's dream,
The quiet forest makes solemn the monk's ritual.

And in a Buddhist temple I wrote:

Sun through the trees brightens the golden image,
In the moss-covered shrine the wooden fish [clapper] resounds;

and:

Knowing how to sing a priest is also a layman,
Fond of dance the crane becomes cheapened.[35]

In the outskirts of the city I wrote:

> On the far slope the spring grasses look like drops of water,
> And the water birds are flying.

In the houses of entertainment I wrote:

> Evening makeup left on pays homage to the moon,
> Spring sleep enhances fragrant beauty.

In loneliness I wrote:

> A solitary firefly emerges from the desolate pond,
> Falling leaves blow through the old house.

Written in a time of relaxation:

> Guest comes just when I feel relaxed,
> Flowers open just as my song is finished.

Even though they do not necessarily verge on the vulgar and superficial, they still cannot escape my criticism. Using seven-word line verse I wrote:

> When in flight from disaster, men divide up wastelands,
> When set free the deer go forth from the cold forest;

and again:

> Grasp a sword and suddenly you have added a sturdy retainer,
> Lose a book for long and one seems to think back on a good
>   friend;

and again:

> Solitary islet, pond riplets, in spring water overflowing,
> Little balustrade, flowers' beauty at noon's clearing burst
>   forth;

and again:

> Toward dawn with melancholy heart I toss and turn on my
>   solitary pillow,
> The light of the dying lamp shines on the fallen blossoms;

and again:

> Full of zeal the first day of the year,
> Everything in confusion, again another year.

These are not at all limited to one form.[36] Now concerning the writing of quatrains, this entirely depends on a high level of study. In addition through 1,000 changes and 10,000 shapes, one does not know what makes the spirit, but the spirit of itself is there. Can this be a simple matter?

Now our contemporaries find your poetry of inferior quality. If you will apply yourself assiduously to perfection of every aspect of the art you will come to understand the meaning of the taste beyond taste.

Work hard! My respects to you.

Ssu-k'ung T'u was born in one of the most turbulent periods in Chinese history. Imperial power had become so ineffective that various generals were carving up the country and fighting among themselves to keep the emperor from regaining any possible authority. The life of an official was fraught with danger, and although Ssu-k'ung T'u held various posts in the earliest part of his life, he eventually came to feel that he could offer little to the bureaucracy. In 887 he withdrew from official life and retired to an estate in the mountains of Shansi, his native home. During the next twenty years he was appointed to several different posts at court but he managed to avoid taking any of them. In 905 he actually had to appear in court, but he acted the part of a man with no regard for proper etiquette and the minister who had summoned him, realizing that it was pointless to try to involve him in governmental affairs, allowed him to return home. Upon hearing that Emperor Ai had been put to death in 907, Ssu-k'ung T'u stopped eating and died.

Even this short summary should be enough to show the contradictions in Ssu-k'ung T'u's life. Educated as a Confucian scholar, he assumed as a matter of course that he would serve his ruler in official capacity. As affairs worsened, however, he became disillusioned and lost the will to continue. His interest in Taoism and Buddhism led him quite naturally to the life of a recluse, and he passed his time, apparently, in the company of like-minded men, both priests and laymen. However, the loyalty to the throne which had been instilled in him from an early age was never obliterated.

The letter to Mr. Li illustrates all of this very well. First, the very reason for writing it shows that he felt a responsibility to use literature as a way to instruct and help friends. Although no date is given for the letter, it must have been written after 887 when Ssu-k'ung T'u retired from public office since some of the couplets are taken from poems written after that date. This means that the writer had already become disillusioned with the role a scholar-official could play in the corrupt government of his time. He had already become imbued with Taoist and Buddhist philosophy and felt at ease in using metaphors such as "salty" and "sour taste" to describe poetic discrimination. Chu Tung-jun pointed out in his discussion of Ssu-k'ung T'u that a story in the Taoist work *Lieh-tzu* makes a similar point in using the metaphor of horses.[37] Duke Mu of Ch'in asked Chiu-fang Kao, who had been pointed out to him as a connoisseur of horses, to find him some exceptional steeds. Chiu-fang Kao came back after a few months and said he had found a fine horse, a yellow mare;

but when the duke's men went to fetch it, it turned out to be a black stallion. The duke was naturally displeased and asked Po-lo, the man who had recommended Kao, what had happened. Po-lo sighed in wonder and said: ". . .What such a man as Kao observes is the innermost native impulse behind the horse's movements. He grasps the essence and forgets the dross, goes right inside it and forgets the outside. He looks for and sees what he needs to see, ignores what he does not need to see. In the judgment of horses of a man like Kao, there is something more important than horses." And sure enough the horse turned out to be truly great.[38]

In Buddhism we can find a related concept, as illustrated in discourses of monks who were contemporaneous with Ssu-k'ung T'u. The monk Yi-ts'un of Hsüeh-feng (822–908) said to his disciples: "When I speak of this thing or that thing you put all your efforts in the pursuit of my words, in a chase after my phrases. But if I were like the antelope that hangs by its horns, where could you grab hold of me?"[39] And the monk Tao-ying (d. 902) likewise said: "You are like the well-trained hunting dog who understands only how to follow traces on the ground. If he were suddenly to meet an antelope hanging by its horns, not only would there be no question of traces in this case, but he would not even recognize the scent!"[40]

Here the Buddhists are using the image of the antelope to describe the process of sudden enlightenment which can only come intuitively and cannot be grasped by any tangible means. Yen Yü in the thirteenth century applied this image to poetry with the idea that one does not learn to write good poetry by grubbing along, adhering strictly to form and the rules laid down by previous versifiers. There is no trace in a good poem of conscious craftsmanship yet the idea in the poet's mind shines out through the words. The reader sees it but he does not know how it is achieved. There is no indication in any of the records that Ssu-k'ung T'u had ever come in contact with the two Buddhist masters, but his statement toward the end of the letter about the spirit of a poem undoubtedly shows the influence of Buddhist and Taoist philosophy.

However, having made his point about "taste" he then goes on to talk about the six tropes of poetry and includes among them the arts of satire and praise and blame, two functions of poetry that lead us right back into Confucian didacticism. The other qualities too, are mentioned over and over with reference to Confucian learning. And yet, to return to Taoist thinking, it might be argued that what I have translated as breadth of learning, *t'ing-hsü*, could be the same as one of the twenty-four modes in his *Shih-p'in, han-hsü,* which the Yangs translate "Pregnant Mode" and which begins:

> Not a word said outright
> Yet the whole beauty revealed;
> No mention of self,
> Yet passion too deep to be borne (p. 68)

And could "profundity and refinement" (*yüan-ya*) be described by the sixth mode, "Polished Mode"? The Yangs translate it:

> A jade wine-pot brimming with spring,
> A thatched hut to enjoy the rain,
> And there sits a worthy scholar
> With tall bamboos upon his left and right.
> White clouds are scattering after rain,
> Birds race past in the deep stillness;
> Then pillowed on his lute in the green shade,
> A waterfall cascading overhead,
> As petals fall without a sound,
> The man, serene as the chrysanthemum,
> Sets down the season's glorie—
> Here is something well worth reading! (p. 68)

Ssu-k'ung T'u's choice of poets to illustrate the passage in the letter shows clearly his alienation from official life. Wang Wei, after some years in government service, retired to the mountains to become a recluse. He has been called the Buddhist poet by later ages. Wei Ying-wu also preferred the artistic life to the official one, although he did hold important posts in the government. And Chia Tao, having started out as a monk, floated on the edge of officialdom for much of his life.

Curiously enough, Ssu-k'ung T'u does not quote any lines from other poets to continue his discourse. He must have felt that his own poems were strong enough to impress his friend. Others have not been so impressed, however. Chu Tung-jun felt that most of the couplets were not really good enough to serve as examples of the Grand Mode (*Hsiung-hun*), Vigorous Mode (*Ching-chien*), Untrammeled Mode (*Hao-fang*), or Poignant Mode (*Pei-k'ai*).[41] Perhaps they do not live up to Ssu-k'ung T'u's own theory of poetry but they do, it seems to me, have one point in common. All those for which he has supplied a time or place paint a picture that gives life and color to that specific moment or spot; they create an atmosphere in which the reader can contemplate something beyond the mere words. The fact that he has used very few allusions and, generally speaking, has maintained a fairly simple rhetoric also fits in well with his theory of poetry. Mr. Li must have had to read and reread that letter many times to comprehend the message, but Ssu-k'ung T'u certainly must have felt that he had spelled it out clearly for anyone with imagination and creative sense.

We can also gain some insight into Ssu-k'ung T'u's reasoning in the choice of the couplets from the point of view of form. Of the fifteen couplets out of the twenty-four that are to be found in extant poems in his collected poetry (SPTK), one is an ancient-style poem, one a quatrain, and the rest are all five- or seven-word-line regulated verse. All are either the second or third couplet in the poem and all show strict adherence to the rules of prosody for regulated verse, particularly parallelism. In other words, he has chosen perfectly regular, orthodox lines.[42] It seems apparent, therefore, that he is not encouraging Mr. Li to strike out in new directions, to try new forms. The old forms are adequate for expression of any sentiment or occasion, be it happy, sad, reflective, or active.

Finally, the couplets lead logically into the comment on the spirit of a poem. Although he does not say so explicitly, one senses that Ssu-k'ung T'u is criticizing Mr. Li for paying too much attention to the external character of the word, to fancy rhetoric. "You see," he seems to be saying, "how much I can express without having to resort to allusions or ornate expressions. The spirit is there because I have not smothered it." Mr. Li should write so that the reader's mind can wander freely beyond the limits set by words to enjoy the taste beyond taste. Ssu-k'ung T'u knew that salty and sour flavors were familiar to everyone and that the reader could relate to that image immediately. Add to this the comparison between the lack of discrimination evinced by the uncultured people of the south and the delicate powers of the refined gentlemen in the north, and his audience, who undoubtedly came from the ranks of the latter, would rise to the occasion and strive to live up to the characterization. How he received the last part is open to conjecture, but Ssu-k'ung T'u has given him much food (or taste?) for thought, and at the same time set a precedent for later critics to follow in the use of similar images.

In summary, the Chinese critic may at times seem pedantic and overly concerned with the practical aspects of criticism. Even when he is grappling with questions concerning the essence and meaning of poetry, he is motivated by the desire to answer them in terms of clarifying points to help others. But at the same time he comes to criticism as a poet and he has the ability, if not the genius, to present his ideas in poetic terms that excite and stimulate the imagination far beyond what a prosaic Westerner could do.

Notes

Abbreviations used:
SPPY: *Ssu-pu pei-yao* edition.
SPTK: *Ssu-pu ts'ung-k'an* edition.
TSCC: *Ts'ung-shu chi-ch'eng* edition.
THTP: T'ang Kuei-chang, ed., *Tz'u-hua ts'ung-pien*. Pref. dated 1934.

1. Donald Holzman's "Confucius and Ancient Chinese Literary Criticism," read at the St. Croix Conference on Literary Criticism, Dec. 1970, has some cogent observations on Confucius in this respect.
2. Kuo, *Chung-kuo wen-hsüeh p'i-p'ing shih* [History of Chinese Literary Criticism] Taipei, 1934; repr. 1969), I, 372. This is not to say that there was not a great deal of discussion centered around the Ku-wen Movement (return to the ancient classical prose form in contrast to the ornate parallel prose style common during the T'ang), but the area of discussion was still rather limited in comparison with the critical writing of later ages.
3. Ibid.
4. Criticism of fiction and drama came rather late in China since these forms of literature held an inferior position in the eyes of scholars. Scholars wrote novels and plays for amusement but this vulgar form was considered too trivial to merit scholarly criticism. It is only in the twentieth century that a marked change in attitude has occurred.
5. Hsia Tsi-an, "Liang shou huai shih" [Two Bad Poems], *Wen-hsüeh tsa-chih* 3(3):18, 1957.
6. See Yü's preface to (*Chiao-chu*) *Jen-chien tz'u-hua*, ed. Hsü T'iao-fu (K'ai-ming shu-tien, 1939). For a translation of this work see Rickett, *Wang Kuo-wei's Jen-chien tz'u-hua: A Study in Chinese Literary Criticism* (Hong Kong, 1973), forthcoming.
7. Hsü, ed., *Jen-chien tz'u-hua*, p. 6.
8. "Yü Wang Hsiang Chou-yen shu" [Letter to Wang Hsiang], in *Yü-chang Huang hsien-sheng wen-chi*, 19/15a–b (*SPTK*).
9. "Yü Wang Chü-fu shu" [Letter to Wang Chü-fu], in *Yü-chang Huang hsien-sheng wen-chi*, 19/15a–b (SPTK).
10. See Liu's Preface to his *Wen-hsin tiao-lung*, X, 50/18a–21a (SPPY); for translation see Vincent Shih, *The Literary Mind and Carving of Dragons* (New York, 1959), pp. 3–8.
11. See Mason Gentzler, "Liu Tsung-yüan on Literature," read at the St. Croix Conference on Literary Criticism, Dec. 1970; also Diana Yu-shih Mei, "Han Yü as a *Ku-Wen* Stylist," *Tsing Hua Journal of Chinese Studies* 7(1):143–208, 1968 (n.s.).
12. See Rickett, *Study in Chinese Literary Criticism*.
13. In *THTP*, ts'e 1.

14. Ch'ü Yüan, having sided with the wrong faction in the government of the state of Ch'u and having been slandered in front of the king, was banished from the court. One of the pieces in the *Ch'u tz'u* or "Songs of Ch'u," which describes his state of mind as he wandered sadly along river banks, is "The Fisherman." A fisherman with Taoist leanings asks him why he is in such a state and he answers with this line. See *Ch'u tz'u*, 7/1b (*SPTK*) and David Hawkes, *Ch'u tz'u, The Songs of the South* (Oxford, 1959), pp. 90–91.

15. See Yü's preface to *Jen-chien tz'u-hua*, p. 58.

16. Chang-t'ai Road was a place in the capital where entertainers and prostitutes lived; thus it came to signify a place for pleasure-seekers. It was also the main road leading out of the capital. It was the custom to see a loved one off along that road and at parting to break off a willow to give to the departing one.

17. See Chang Hui-yen, *Tz'u hsüan*, 1/12a–b (*SPPY*).

18. Yeh, "The Ch'ang-chou School of *Tz'u* Criticism," read at the St. Croix Conference on Literary Criticism, Dec. 1970.

19. The first of these collections of anecdotes was compiled by Meng Ch'i and has been translated by Howard Levy, "The Original Incidents of Poems," *Sinologica* 10 (1):1–54, 1968.

20. As recorded in Wu Tseng's (A.D. 12th cen.) *Neng-kai chai man-lu* [Rambling Record from Neng-kai's (Mr. Can-change) Studio], 17/431 (*TSCC*).

21. For example, he placed the poet T'ao Ch'ien in category B when most critics felt that he belonged in the A group.

22. Reading 天光 instead of 水光 in accordance with the *THTP* edition of this work.

23. This comment is to be found in Chou Chi, *Chieh-ts'un chai lun-tz'u tsa-chu* [Miscellaneous Discussions of *Tz'u* from Chieh-ts'un's Studio] (*THTP* ed.).

24. Hsü, ed., *Jen-chien tz'u-hua*, p. 32.

25. Feng, *A Short History of Chinese Philosophy* (New York, 1948), pp. 7–8.

26. See my article "Technical Tterms in Chinese Literary Criticism," *Literature East and West* 12 (2,3,4):141–147, 1968.

27. Ssu-k'ung T'u is most famous as a literary critic for his *Erh-shih ssu shih-p'in* [Twenty-four Modes of Poetry]. There have been various translations into Western languages, but the one I like best is by Hsien-yi and Gladys Yang in *Chinese Literature* 7:65–67, 1963.

28. I have tried in this and the following translations to be as literal as possible in order to preserve a sense of the original, particularly the parallelism. I am indebted to Prof. Isabelle Liu-yi Yuh of the University of Pennsylvania for her advice and suggestions on the translation of the couplets.

29. This festival occurs around the beginning of April, one day before the Ch'ing-ming Festival when people go out to sweep the graves of their ancestors.

30. The words "dark (*an*) and "desolate" (*yu*) have a double meaning here that is difficult to convey in English. *An* refers to the darkness of the water and at the same time the "dark" or muffled sound of the drums. *Yu* refers to the desolate state of the island, but also describes the lonely effect produced by the boat lamps shining dimly.

31. A musical instrument of sixteen metal plates arranged in two rows on a frame and struck with a small wooden hammer to produce a sound something like the celesta.

32. The wind is soft in springtime. The magpie is traditionally thought of as a harbinger of good news, an auspicious bird.

33. Hua-liu was one of the eight fine horses belonging to King Mu of the Chou dynasty, and has since become simply a metaphor for a good horse.

34. The "huge fish" is a fierce predator that eats other fish. The "forest goblin"

was a creature that was supposed to harm people. Both images indicate evil people who are finding life difficult in troubled times.

35. Both the priest and the crane are looked on as living aloof from worldly pleasures.

36. That is, there are ancient-style poems and five- and seven-word regulated verse and quatrains.

37. Chu, *Chung-kuo wen-hsüeh p'i-p'ing lun-chi* [Essays on Chinese Literary Criticism] (Hong Kong, 1941; repr. 1962), p. 16.

38. *Lieh-tzu*, 8/8b–9b (*SPPY*). Tr. from A. C. Graham, *The Book of Lieh-tzu* (London, 1960), p. 170.

39. *Ch'uan teng lu* [Record of the Transmission of the Lamp] (*Taishō Tripitaka*, No. 2076), 16/328b.

40. Ibid., 17/335b.

41. Translations of these terms are from the Yangs.

42. Actually of the five *chüan* of his extant collected poetry three are devoted to quatrains.

Hans H. Rudnick

KANT AND THE PERSONALITY
OF THE CRITIC

KANT'S THIRD CRITIQUE, THE CRITIQUE OF JUDGMENT (1790)[1] WAS NOT
intended by its author to make any direct statement on questions of
aesthetic relevance. The *Critique of Judgment* was rather to close the
gap left open by the preceding critiques of pure reason (1781, revised 1787) and of practical reason (1788). The *Critique of Judgment*
addresses itself to the border area between cognition and will, between nature and freedom. Understanding (*Verstand*) recognizes
what nature offers to the perceiving senses, it recognizes what *is*.
Practical reason (*praktische Vernunft*), on the other hand, determines what *should* be done. In order to mediate between these two
basic faculties of cognition (*Erkennen*) and desire (*Begehren*),
Kant resorts like Tetens to the faculty of judgment (*Urteilskraft*) as
a superior faculty of feeling which teaches not recognition, not
analysis, but judgment of nature according to notions of freedom.
The principle of such judgment is the notion of purpose. This notion
cannot be objectively derived from nature; the nature of purpose has
to be supplied by the interpretative power of the judging individual.
Such an individual performs the activity of a critic. The result of his
interpretative act is consequently based on the individual's critical
awareness and cognitive perception.

In order to characterize the role played by the critic in Kant's
system of thought, we will have to give a brief presentation of Kant's
major statements relating to aesthetics as given in the *Critique of
Judgment*. Then, rather careful attention will be given to a discussion
of the schematism of cognition and the interrelation between identity
and difference as developed by Kant in the *Critique of Pure Reason*.

I

Certain objects and processes in nature can only be perceived by the human being within the limits of partial recognition. Parts of organisms generate themselves in nature according to the form and existence of a whole. The human observer recognizes this phenomenon with a certain helplessness since he cannot clearly explain what this "whole" is which keeps everything together. Such a phenomenon in which the whole precedes the evidence of its supposed parts cannot be explained in accordance with the laws of mechanical analysis. The interpreting individual, therefore, will have to take refuge in the assumption of the "as if" (*als ob*), which posits that these presumed interrelations appear to be the result of some intelligence which cannot be objectively defined and explained by human faculties. The assumption of the "as if," however, will allow Kant to approach the objectively undefinable from the angle of subjective interpretation.

The heart of Kant's *Critique of Judgment* is, from the perspective of aesthetics, the development of the teleological judgment in the concluding two sections of the second book (Sec. 61–91) in which Kant reveals how he wishes to bridge the gap between the world of nature and the world of freedom. The principle of purposiveness (*Zweckmäßigkeit*) is the actual keystone which permits the connection between the objectivity of nature and the subjectivity of freedom.

Kant posits two kinds of purposiveness. There is the objective or real purposiveness in which the concerned object is identical with itself and defined by itself, by its nature, its notion, and its function. And there is subjective or formal purposiveness in which the concerned object has affected the observer's cognitive faculties (perception and thinking) in such a way that the observer's cognitive faculties have settled into a state of harmonious order. This state of harmonious order reflects the observer's individual solution of the objectively unbridgeable chasm between nature and freedom.

In the case of objective or real purposiveness the natural object is described as "perfect" (*vollkommen*) and consequently self-sufficient in its nature. In the case of subjective or formal purposiveness the object is described as "beautiful" (*schön*). The "aesthetic" judgment performed by the observing individual, on the grounds of his freedom of perceptive awareness and the categorizing faculty of freely ordering perceived sense impressions, deals with the principles which make possible the reduction of a multiplicity to a particular unity. This process of reduction involves the human faculties of perception—imagination and understanding—in an activity of pleasurable (*lustvoll*) quality which will be perceived as beautiful during the successful synthesizing process.

The beautiful thus becomes a notion of value which is solely based on the individual who has performed the judging process. The beautiful shares two of its qualities with the sensibly pleasurable and the morally good. The beautiful (1) is "without notion" (*ohne Begriff*), like the pleasurable, but the beautiful also (2) is "universal and necessary" (*allgemein und notwendig*) like the morally good. The first quality, "without notion," separates the beautiful from the good because the universal validity of the good rests on notions and, therefore, can be logically proven unlike the beautiful which rests entirely on the judging individual's faculty of perception and order. The second quality, "universal and necessary," separates the beautiful from the pleasurable—also "without notion" but not universal, since something that is felt to be pleasurable by one person need not be pleasurable to another. The beautiful asks for universal acclaim and universal recognition.

Another quality of the beautiful becomes apparent if the beautiful is contrasted to the useful (*das Nützliche*). In such a comparison it is evident that the observer will be interested in the practical usefulness, the sensible pleasurableness, and the moral good of the object; his interest in the beauty of the object is not perceptible. The third quality of the beautiful is therefore that it (3) evokes dis-interested (*uninteressiert*) pleasure in the existence of the object. This is a pleasure oriented toward no practical purpose; it is not an expression of joy about an object which arouses pleasure, nor an expression of approval and respect extended toward the morally good. It is rather an expression of a favorable inclination (*Gunst*) by the individual without direction toward a particular purpose or interest. This kind of pleasure which manifests itself in a "pure imaginative process" (*bloße Vorstellung*) might also be called contemplative or pure pleasure in the process of perception.

The fourth and final quality of the beautiful is that it (4) has "purity of form" (*bloße Form*), which says that its purposiveness is merely subjective and, consequently, purposeless on a broader scale.

Such a strict definition of the beautiful was based by Kant on what he called the "free" (*freie*) beauty which manifested itself in the arabesque style; in that style, the notion of a concrete object is eliminated in favor of a general feeling of pleasure which arises in the observer from looking at the pleasing proportions of stylized components. Different from the free beauty is the "adhering" (*adhärierende*) beauty of a building or a statue which shows not only a formal, decorative harmony caused by the horror vacu in the iconoclastic arabesques but also a congruence between the concrete form and the particular content, between the form and its importance, between the form and its notion, which helps define the object concerned. In adhering beauty the satisfaction aroused in the observing and judging person is no longer a merely aesthetic pleasure. It is a pleasure mixed with elements of intellectual satisfaction. The objectivity of nature and the subjectivity of freedom are two components which have merged into this satisfaction.

The mechanical composition of nature is interpreted by the individual's free and creative spirit on the individual's own terms. Kant has recognized the adhering beauty as richer and deeper in quality than the free beauty, ranking it higher because the faculty of "understanding" (*Verstand*) has been joined with the faculty of "sensible perception" (*Sinnlichkeit*) to create the feeling of a pleasing harmony within the observer.

The beautiful can manifest itself only within a limited form whereas the "sublime" (*das Erhabene*) transgresses the limits of a form. The sublime is without form and without limits; it is boundlessly large; it overcomes the observer by submitting the faculty of sensible perception to the faculty of "reason" (*Vernunft*). The effect of the sublime on the observer is such that the observing individual begins to see his own limits. The sublime seems to be a corrective which prevents the individual from overestimating his faculties. The sublime impresses the observer by its immense dimension (the ocean or the sky at night) or its tremendous power (thunderstorms or fire). The human faculties of perception and imagination cannot comprehend the mathematically sublime, nor can the dynamically sublime be checked by any human opposition.

Such a situation adds a certain degree of displeasure (*Unlust*) to the general disposition of pleasure in the observer. There is a definite though limited pleasure in the partial recognition of the overly large and overly powerful, but this pleasure is handicapped by the inability of human senses to adequately perceive the overly large and overly powerful. The pleasure is mixed with displeasure since the manifestations of the sublime are incommensurate with the faculties of sensible perception. On the other hand, human faculties are not completely inadequate for the perception of the sublime. The faculty which can abstractly perceive the large dimensions of the sublime is "reason." Reason cannot observe in concrete detail the largeness of the sublime. Yet, reason can perceive of the sublime through the abstract projection of the idea of the infinite. It gives the individual pleasure, even if it is only a limited pleasure, that he possesses a faculty of perception which can surpass in every respect the limits of sensible perception. In this insight lies the peculiar sublimity of the human nature. Reason and the moral determination of man, which is based on reason, make man superior to nature. Consequently, man enters the area of the sublime on the level of abstract perception. However, such an analytic access to the sublime is only open to the philosophically inclined individual who can perceive the general context between reason and moral determination. The average person who finds himself naively under the impression of the sublime confers his admiration for the idea of the infinite superficially to the object itself since the object seems to cause the idea of the sublime rather than the faculty of reason.

Kant wants to make it clear that the creative faculties of the perceiving individual are not only conditioned by objects which affect our senses. This condition would be merely a reproductive process which is empty of creative and dynamic activity. The notion of mimesis is dead since Kant, and genius (*Genie*), the faculty of original artistic creativity which is able to formulate "aesthetic ideas" (*ästhetische Ideen*), has taken its place. Aesthetic ideas are imaginary associations which add to a notion of reason a large number of related ideas which cannot be directly expressed within the confines of a concrete notion. Genial creativity is characterized by originality and unawareness of rules which the genius employs for the first time. The genius's work is supposed to be exemplary and inimitable. The gift of genius is a gift of nature, according to Kant, and this nature dictates the rules for the work of art ultimately through the medium of the creative artist who himself is unaware of his innovative activity. The exemplary works of art become specimens for other talented artists who are not invited to imitate the genius but rather are encouraged to follow the genius in their own creative way.

II

If we want to take Kant seriously in order to see his strong commitment to the creative freedom of the individual as artist and as
critic, and if we do not want to finish him off with a few fashionable
and irresponsible remarks focusing on the theoretical nature of his
critical idealism, we will have to enter in this context into a discussion of how, in principle, the critic as an individual can gather relevant information for his judging activity. First of all, the Kantian
critic will have to be considered as a personality with a critical mental
attitude, which means not only that he has to proceed in his critical
endeavors along the lines of judging *sine ira et studio* but also that he
will have to be aware, right from the beginning, that his findings will
be of a symbolic essence somewhere between what Carlyle called
the finite and the infinite. In all three critiques it was Kant's intention
to build a comprehensive system which would make a science of the
metaphysics possible. Nowadays we have only little concern for
metaphysics and the transcendental. The opposite notion of what we
consider as real and true is usually shrugged off with a superficial
condemnation. The metaphysical is practically of no concern.

Furthermore, psychologists have declared that the "metaphysical
denial" drives Werther into the arms of suicide.[2] The hero of Goethe's
novel is considered to be a person who lives Kant's ideas and perishes
because of the unbearable frustration he suffers from the incongruity
between the reality of nature and the ideal of the metaphysical. Similar disservice has also been done by some clinical psychologists to
Shakespeare's Hamlet character. The psychologizing critic himself
seems somewhat displaced; as if he had never heard of dramatic
effects in art, he takes the protagonist of a novel or a drama for a real
person. If art were as real as nature and as true as mathematics, the
person with an understanding of literature would not quarrel with
the psychologist's analysis. But on a more relevant philosophical level
there are the notions of "identity" and "difference" in Kant's system,
and there is a so-called *Schema* in Kant's system which should be
considered with regard to the critic's perception and understanding.
Therefore, it appears worth our while to investigate in some detail
what Kant says about the establishment of the schema in his *Critique
of Pure Reason*, since the critic reveals his power of order and judgment when he organizes his findings into a schematic structure.[3]

Just as the meaning of a metaphor, and other figures of speech, lies between two extremes—the tenor and the vehicle, if we want to use I. A. Richards' terms—so the meaning of the schema lies between perception (*Anschauung*) and category (*Kategorie*). The schema mediates, conditions, and also makes the synthesis of the judgment possible. If we ask what generates the schema, we will have to answer that the individual's power for such a "figurative synthesis" (*figürliche Synthesis*) is located in his faculty of imagination. The imagination makes possible the synthesis between perception and understanding along the lines of purposiveness which the judging individual was determined to follow. This means that the establishment of a schema is completely dependent on the judging individual's synthetic faculties. It has to be stressed that the *individual's* synthetic faculties are most important since this synthesis is not a normative synthesis which applies to all perceptions of the same kind. The establishment of the schema, dependent as it is on the imaginative powers, differs fundamentally and profoundly from its constituting components, perception and understanding. As the faculty which performs the synthesis, the imagination is dynamic in its nature. Its process is dependent on the objects with which it works, and its synthetic findings are a result of the synthesizing act which has been performed under the influence of a perceived purposiveness.

The schema functions as the generative power which brings the "synthesis of the imagination" about. It is an act of combining something which is given to perception (*Anschauung*) in a certain form with the principle of another form which already possesses the unity of apperception (*Apperzeption*) in our awareness. Such a process of ordering and combining is performed under the hypothetical pretense of establishing a method which has as its purpose the unity of definition. Departing from the multiple and driving toward the singular, the imagination of the observer is able to combine image and idea, via the act of synthesis, into the schema. The elements of sensible receptivity and individual spontaneity are already given as conditions for the synthetic process so that the schema can be developed by the critic in the purposive act of synthesis. Kant refers clearly to this concretizing process of the imagination as the schema since in this process "a notion is provided with its image" (*einem Begriff sein Bild . . . verschaffen*). The schema is, therefore, a synthetic and purposive faculty in the individual which provides "the principle of synthesis to imagination" (A 141; B 180).

The schema is not static and independent. It is rather a dynamic function of understanding which is methodically related in its notions to the given perception. Every schema is functionally related to the notion which generated it; it is a function of a particular notion. The schema establishes the indirect connection between category and perception, between understanding and sensibility, between the general and the particular. The schema of the imagination is the catalyst which allows the spontaneous and independent encounter between perception and understanding. The schema provides the notion which represents the pure and the formal condition for sensible perception and provides the purpose of the critic's judgment, because the schema itself is also the locus of the received form of perception.

Every notion is consequently tied to the schema of the process from which it has resulted. The schema of the notion of understanding, the potentiality of purposiveness of interpretation, is the formal and pure condition of sensibility. If insight is to come about, the category will have to leave the realm of pure thought and mingle with perception. Through this act of compromise the category submits to the process of the schematism which provides the notion with the means to search for a synthesis with the sense perception since the schema is not only "universal" and spontaneous but also dynamic and synthetic.

When Kant says that the schema "provides the idea with its image" (A 140; B 179/180), he does not mean that the schema establishes a material picture which actually represents an existing object in all its detail. Kant brings the schema close to the realistic process of perceiving but he does not identify the perceptive process with the schema. What he wants to illustrate by such a statement is the performance of a synthesis, the schematism, which unites perception and category. He refers on the level of perception to the image, which manifests itself as a particular content and a multifaceted object within the limiting category of time. "If I arrange five periods in a succession . . . . . , I have presented an image of the number five" (A 140; B 179). But such an image, which is an object of perception, does not contain any degree of universality. It is merely "a result of the empirical faculty of the productive power of imagination" (A 141; B 181) which has arranged the perceived sense impression into an image which can be recognized by the eye. However, the image of pure perception which transcends the particular and aims at the universal on the grounds of a transcendental purposiveness has to be reduced from the particularity of sensible perception to the perception of pure form. The purity of form which contains both, the pure perception and the pure image, is found in the category of space and, in addition, particularly in the category of time. "The pure image of all dimensions rests in space, not in the perceiving senses; and, above all, the pure image of the objects perceived by the senses rests in time" (A 142; B 182).

Therefore, if Kant speaks of giving a notion "its" image, he means that an image is the form of perception to which the category relates. But this is not yet sufficient. The category not only relates to the image, the category also defines the image on the grounds of perception. Again the dualistic character of the schema becomes evident. The schema has to be understood as a function of the category. A process of ordering and arranging has to take place in the judging individual's mind. It is not enough simply to observe one image, because it by itself can hardly be categorized according to a notion. The categorizing notion has first to be found and established in a process that reduces a number of concrete images to a certain notion which determines the purposiveness of the objects actually perceived. Understanding, as the faculty of pure thought, has no direct access to pure perception. Pure perception is the abstract image of time. Understanding must make use of the faculty of the schema in order to gain access to the concreteness of the image. Understanding has to employ the services of the schema in order to make the perception of concrete images possible. The schema is consequently a necessary faculty of the imagination, so to speak "a monogram of the pure imagination a priori" (A 142; B 181), which permits the building of a mutually necessary bridge between image and idea, between perception and reason.

The schema does not provide the observing individual with the material images. The perception performs this task. The schema, however, defines the concrete images with regard to form; and the form is defined by the category so that in the schematic procedure the concrete image of perception becomes the abstracted image of the category. The schema as a function gives meaning to the form of the established category; it relates the abstract content of the category to the concrete perception of the object as it exists. The active process of definition which is performed by the schema considers the time and the object, which could also be called the concrete image. The schema, therefore, primarily performs the act of defining the time (*Zeitbestimmung*) a priori—according to rules which have been established previously, rules which have been found and accepted to be valid categories (A 145; B 184). Kant's schema is, thusly, neither time-dependent as a form of perception, nor definition-related as a form of understanding. Kant's schema is rather a rule (*Regel*) used to define the particularity of time according to the order established by the categories. It must again be stated quickly that the categories themselves are neither independent in form nor independent in structure. The order which the categories reflect rests solely in the synthesis of the elements of synthetic judgment performed by the individual.

"The schema is always a product of the faculty of imagination," says Kant (A 140; B 179). The schema as the faculty of synthesis functions by relating itself to the perception as well as to the category. The synthetic power of the imagination manifests itself in the schema where the relation between schema and category, between imagination and understanding, is established spontaneously. Understanding and imagination, the structure of the category and its application to sentiment (*Sinnlichkeit*), are both subject to the notion of spontaneity. The understanding provides the forms of order; and the imagination transforms these forms into synthetic functions by relating them to concrete objects. The ordering function of the understanding and the concretizing function of the imagination are two different but necessarily related functions of a common and characteristic faculty shared by the understanding and by the imagination. The function of the schema contains the paradox of the figures of speech. The synthetic function of the schema provides homogeneity but does not dissolve the heterogeneous relationship that exists between the schema and the subject, and between the schema and the object. Indentity and difference coexist in the schema; both support each other.

Such a Janus-faced situation is always difficult to describe or explain. The central understanding of the schematism rests on the interpretation of the analytical and synthetic part of the *Critique of Pure Reason*. Heidegger has accused Kant of having destroyed the unity of the observing individual because of his analytical approach to the schematism. But Kant has intentionally tried not only to analyze but also to synthesize at the same time. Kant has considered the mysterious bond which can potentially unite the separated elements as something very real as long as the synthesizing power of the imagination can come up with a result. This bond is difficult to recognize but nevertheless it is something indispensable, carrying a constant challenge toward a synthesis performed by the spontaneous effects of the imagination.

Edition A of Kant's *Critique of Pure Reason* sees the imagination as an independent and transcendental faculty subject to the faculty of understanding in the process of the spontaneous synthesis. Edition B modifies this standpoint and clearly states the identity between imagination and understanding. Imagination as a figurative synthesis is a transcendental faculty, dependent on the understanding because it is a function of understanding. Kant revised the relation between imagination and understanding in edition B, but he left the chapter on the schematism unchanged. Consequently, Kant's final view of the borderline between imagination and understanding remains unclear with regard to the schema.

The schema has always been described by Kant as a product of imagination (A 140; B 179; A 141/2; B 181); and understanding has always been described as a faculty which has been unable to relate itself directly to perception (A 137/8; B 176/7). However, the way in which understanding would deal with these schemata has been explained as the "schematism of pure understanding" (A 140; B 179), so that understanding becomes the formal proving ground for the potential synthesis which the imagination cannot bring about by itself, since it does not contain the necessary form which creates the order. At this point the danger arises that the schema of understanding forces the understanding to become a functional principle of the understanding. Edition B attributes exactly this role to the imagination. Imagination is described as a function of understanding so that the understanding may manifest its existence. The actual function of the understanding expresses itself in the synthetic ordering process which is performed by the understanding on the basis of its faculty of spontaneity. In principle, schema and category are merely the function and form of an action which corresponds directly to the act of cognition. The potentiality of such an act is found in the imagination as the basis for the function of synthesis, and the potentiality of understanding contains the forms on which this synthesis is based. The potentiality of action rests exclusively on the spontaneity with which the synthesis between imagination and understanding can be brought about by the observer.

The forms of perception as deduced by Kant in the transcendental aesthetic are space and time. With regard to the schema, space and time not only permit and determine the perception of the multiple (*das Mannigfaltige*) and its interpretation, but also allow the perception of the pure form without the concrete particulars of the multiple. Kant equates the pure form with the pure image and says that the pure image of all quantities is found (still independent of the observer's senses) in space, while the pure image of all quantities when it affects the observer's senses is found in time (A 142; B 182). The concrete perception of the image by the observer contains the abstracted pure form of the sense perception. Thusly, "the *image* is a product of the empirical faculty. . . of the imagination" (A 141; B 181), and the schema becomes a process of pure imagination which makes the perception of images possible according to the established forms of understanding.

Consequently, imagination contains two separate faculties of synthesis. Imagination can provide in pure form the synthesis of judgment between notion (*Begriff*) and perception (*Anschauung*); imagination can also provide the synthesis of the image which has already occurred outside the observer in space and time. The synthesis of the image does not take place during the mere perception of the image, nor does it become an apprehension during the perceiving process; rather, it is performed by the activation of the unifying faculty of the imagination. Edition A is still speaking in this context of a synthesis of the apprehension in the perceptive process while the faculty of synthesis remains separate and subject to the spontaneity of the faculty of imagination. However, in edition B apprehension, which belonged before to the receptive process of objects (B 161, note), is now counted among the synthetic faculties, which are split into imagination and apperception (B 162, note). Thus the definition of the image which has been synthetically generated through the apprehension of perception or through the synthetic faculty of imagination cannot be clearly distinguished from the schema which has also been generated through synthetic—but also through pure—imagination. The exact limits of the faculty of the imagination cannot be defined in Kant's system, since the synthetic functions of the imagination reach down even to the sensibility of perception. Kant's separate treatment of perception and imagination should, however, not be interpreted as a split of the imagination into two separate faculties. The difference between these faculties is so minute that the ultimate unity of the imaginative process appears to remain untouched, even though Kant points with great sensitivity toward the complicated procedure of schematizing the concrete into the abstract.

The schema of the imagination, which supplies the idea with its image and which also provides judgment with the means for synthesis, becomes the ground for the possibility of synthetic judgment a priori, since the schema itself is the only means which is able to express the "similarity" (*Gleichartigkeit*) between image and idea (A 137; B 176). The schema as a dynamic and synthetic faculty of the imagination contains the important elasticity which is able to combine on equal grounds the pure and spontaneous categories of understanding with the purely receptive form of sense perception. The schema proves itself as a unifying faculty between image and idea; it permits judgment via equal treatment of concrete sense perception and of abstract categories of thought. The schema stands for the crystallizing process of judgment in the observer's mind. The unity of mental faculties is achieved by the schema's action so that reason, understanding, imagination, and perception support one another in the process of ordering the experience and its interpretation.

If we ask for the explanation of the synthetic power of the faculties, it will become rather obvious that the imagination is less a mediator between perception and understanding than expected. The faculty of understanding plays a more important part than the imagination. The synthesis between perception and imagination is dependent on apperception, which itself goes back to the particular forms of receptivity (*Rezeptivität*). The establishment of the synthesis is determined by the categories. This process also insures that the general structure of the categories is impressed, through the imagination, on the perception so that the perception is gradually conditioned by the categories. Among the conditions which permit the pure synthesis of judgment, the imagination is implicitly subordinated to the apperception of the understanding in the transcendental deduction of edition A, while in edition B the imagination is defined as a function (though transcendental) dependent on the understanding.

How can both sources of cognition merge in Kant's system? How can identity (*Gleichartigkeit*) be found between perception and understanding when the mediating perception has to be pure but also sensible? Kant finds the synthesizing third entity in the category of time. But such a mediating concept supplies only a schema of relations; it does not represent the actual synthesizing act. Time is something like a passageway in which the category relates itself to the particular matter. The transcendental-logical reflection recognizes time as a concept which determines the thought process. And it is the synthesizing process of thought which makes in its spontaneity all kinds of thought combinations possible. If spontaneity of thought is lost, and thinking continues along a detached course alone, we are leaving the premises of Kantian philosophy. Time itself is passive and functions as a medium; it has no synthesizing faculties. All meaning which has been established in considering sense impressions has been generated from the spontaneity of thinking, a purely human faculty. The formal influence of the categories, therefore, reaches beyond the synthetic function of the imagination right to the limits of receptivity, which has still maintained its independence from the spontaneity of thought.

Thusly, understanding emerges in Kant's system as a faculty which proves to be representative of subjectivity. This subjectivity is not absolute since the autonomy of the receptivity of perception is still present, but nevertheless, understanding has, relatively speaking, the strongest claim to subjectivity.

If sensible appearances are to be formally defined by an individual, a numerical identity with the apperception has to be established. All perceptions are assumed to be relating to a pure consciousness which interprets all perceptions as its own. Thus the foundation of subjectivity is laid and the consciousness of the Cartesian *ergo sum* arises. Such a consciousness (countering Descartes) is not yet cognition but it posits (following Descartes) the existence of the perceiving subject. The schema does not possess such defining qualities. The schema provides a service which makes the function of imagining and recognizing possible. But the imagining and the recognizing are faculties which spring from the spontaneous subjectivity of the observer's apperception. The schema should not be interpreted as the category of the imagination. Even if the imagination is realized and restrained (A 147; B 187) in the schema, the imagination still remains as a form of thought outside the schema, in the same way as the imagination's faculty, i.e., understanding, remains outside the schema. Understanding as such has removed itself from sense perception. Understanding is invisible; it is restricted to manifestation through application to sense impressions. Consequently, the schema has its place in the middle, between perception and understanding; "the schema becomes merely a phenomenon or the sensible notion of an object which corresponds to the category" (A 146; B 186).

Kant speaks of the schema as "merely" a phenomenon which removes the imagination as the faculty of the schema from its central position. The imagination as carrier of appearances (*Erscheinungen*) becomes subject to understanding. The imagination loses the position of being equal to understanding even if it retains its spontaneity. Imagination is closely attached to sensibility (*Sinnlichkeit*) so that the potentiality of the synthetic judgment a priori may be lost again because of the imagination's distance from the understanding and the implied inequality with understanding. The schema is in danger of losing its mediating position in Kant's system even if the imagination as a faculty of the schema had been defined before as a function of the understanding.

Kant has attributed to the schema a mediating role between perception and understanding. He has continuously insisted on the difference between the two basic faculties of perception and understanding. Kant has never been willing to present a full synthesis between the two basic faculties. He has instead emphasized the dualism between both faculties and has only suggested the potentiality of a synthesis through the schema. Judgment becomes possible along the lines of the schema as a synthesis of the similar, as a comparison between equal objects. Such comparative thinking does not negate the existence of the schema but it also does not propagate its creative powers since the possibility of placing the imagination into the center of subjectivity is not pursued by Kant. The identity between perception and understanding as it could be established by the individual is not focused upon in a formally exhaustive manner. Kant prefers the dualism between perception and understanding; he prefers a system of dichotomies which remain separate entities; he seems to feel that any further formalistic definition of the basic faculties would mean the end of the creative freedom which has to be allowed to any meaningful existence.

The dualism between perception and understanding is contrasted by Kant with the monism of Descartes. In Kant's cognitive process (*Erkenntnis*) "the *inner* experience, which was never doubted by Descartes, can only occur under the influence of the *outer* experience" (B 275). This means that truth and cognition will not be determined by any doubt-free thought process but rather in the synthetic judgment a priori in which inner and outer experience are so dependent on each other that cognition can only occur with reference to the interaction of both. The perception of outside objects which had been deduced by Descartes from the safely posited thinking "ego" (B 276) is in reality a "direct and immediate" (B 276) perception which does not need the positing of the Cartesian "I am" (B 277) for the definition of the "consciousness of our own existence." For Kant, the outer experience is the means and the condition for the inner experience which does know about itself directly. The inner experience can only recognize itself through the mediation of the outer experience. The perception (*Anschauung*) thusly sets the condition for the recognition of the "ego" in the observing individual.

The perception also secures the existence of the outer objects and, in addition, it sets the scene for the potential recognition of the self.

A meaningful existence of the self depends on the recognition of the necesary interrelation between perception and understanding. The potentiality of a synthesis has to be recognized and the conditions for such a synthesis should be explored by the searching individual. In theory, the synthesis is supplied in Kant's system by the schematism; in practice, however, the synthesis is furnished by the axioms (*Grundsätze*) which govern the observer's interpretation. But if the means for the synthesis of perception and understanding are given by the axioms, how then will self-recognition become possible at all? Kant relies on the synthetic judgment a priori as the basis for being scientifically apodictic (*apodiktisch*). He demands that the structure of nature, which can be recognized by man, be posited inside the searching individual. Thus the relation of the individual to his environment is defined in such a way that the individual can only recognize an object in accordance with the forms of pure perception (*reine Anschauung*) and that the object reveal itself to the observing subject alone. Since, however, human perception is only possible within the categories of time and space, the individual cannot make any final cognitive statements about the reason (*Ursache*) of the observed object itself (B 149). The object as a noumenon remains inescapably concealed before, in, and behind every experience.

If we follow Kant's explanation of the synthesis between perception and understanding further into the implications related to the individual as the recognizing self, we will realize that the "cogitating" individual stimulated his inner sensibility with the help of the pure schema. The resulting perception of the individual is not affected directly by the structure of the particular object, but rather, on the grounds of the a priori, by the spontaneity of the perception as it is contained in the schematism. The perception finds its form and definition through the ordering spontaneity of the understanding. This would mean that at the crossroads of perception and understanding, the understanding would have imposed its form on the perception, and the understanding would have manifested itself visibly, so to speak, as empirical perception and empirical cognition. But as we already know, understanding is in its purity an object as such (*Ding an sich*) which cannot manifest itself in a concrete form. This synthesis between perception and understanding would, however, lead to an identity between perception and understanding and consequently, Kant's primary concern, the purity of science as a metaphysics, would be jeopardized. The understanding cannot perceive directly, it has to make use of an alien and synthetically generated perception so that the identity of the self as an object as such can never be achieved. The tragedy of the understanding which cannot recognize the objects as such is dramatized and exemplified in the fact that it cannot even recognize itself in the act of the recognition of the self in Kant's system. The desire of the self for self-recognition is only superficially satisfied by the insight that the self seems to be empirically affected by itself, and as an appearance the self seems to be the condition of cognition. Such a recognition of the self (*Selbstaffektion*) is merely empirical and has nothing in common with pure recognition of the self. The self, purely perceived, as a thing as such can not be recognized in Kant's system; the observing critic can only function as a mediator within a preestablished set of conditions.

It is said of the schema that it is equal to understanding and perception in the act of pure self-recognition. And suppose we think of the faculty of the schema, which Kant had subjected to understanding, as the faculty which may, because of its equality, function as the common basic faculty of understanding and perception. Then it may be justified to proclaim the schema, as the embodiment of the self, to combine perception and understanding to such a degree that this faculty, the faculty of the schema, can think and perceive at the same time. Such a conclusion would secure the unity of the self and allow a pure and direct deduction of the cognition of the self. Kant, however, has hesitated to follow such conclusions. Such a complicated cognition of the self would divide the problem of cognition. The identity of the self has to maintain itself in the recognized subject, in two ways: (1) the self has to appear as a thing as such, as a "cogito"; and (2) the self has to show itself as a concrete and existing subject. Both aspects of the self as subject have to continue as a difference (*Differenz*). If it is the schema's task to combine pure perception and pure understanding in the act of self-recognition in the synthetic judgment a priori, the schema will doubtlessly shape the cognition and the cognitive process. If the same synthetic process is applied to the act of self-cognition so that the schema would combine the observed self of the perception and the conscious self of the understanding, the schema would combine noumenon and phenomenon in the act of self-cognition. The identity of the schema located in the pure and unrecognizable area of self-cognition changes immediately into a difference as soon as the self-cognition is attempted. The identity of pure perception and pure thinking in the act of pure self-cognition allows, through the schematism, the possibility of a metaphysics as science. But difference of apparition and object in the act of self-cognition becomes through the schematism the reason for the critical boundary between metaphysics as science and metaphysics as non-science. Schematism as the locus for the simultaneity of identity and difference contains the possibility of synthetic judgments a priori, as well as the critical boundary of transcendental analysis and transcendental dialectics. The schematism is characterized by such a contradiction in itself.

For Kant every synthesis has to build on two heterogeneous faculties: perception and understanding. Transcendental perception and transcendental thought search for the formal purity which makes necessity possible. Metaphysics as a science becomes possible in the difference between its heterogeneous poles, pure perception and pure understanding. In order to find beside its difference an identity of its own for metaphysics, the schema of imagination will provide the synthesis between perceiving and thinking in the act of pure self-cognition. Transcendental deduction and transcendental analysis of the axioms perform the very sensitive act in which synthesis cautiously hints at the identity of perceiving and thinking while the difference between appearance and object is still maintained. Kant's metaphysics as a science which is based on judgment stands and falls with the simultaneity of identity and difference. Kant has committed himself to this principle and he has submitted to the laborious task of proving the possibility of synthetic judgment a priori which also meant that metaphysics can be a science.

At certain points we have indicated how Janus-faced Kant's system is. It appears rather clear that a balance between identity and difference has to be maintained. A one-sided pursuit of identity on empirical grounds alone at the expense of difference would prove "destructive" to Kant's system. Kant has concentrated his philosophy of the metaphysics on the simultaneity of identity and difference; any other interpretation would develop a different approach to metaphysics and thereby change the role of the critic. Every attempt to deny a metaphysics as a science would lead us back into the uncritical field of the *metaphysica naturalis* which Kant intentionally wished to overcome by developing his criteria that allow metaphysics to be a science (B 22).

The critical path, which has been declared by Kant in the next-to-the-last sentence of the *Critique of Pure Reason* to be "the only one which is still open" (der *kritische* Weg ist allein noch offen), leads right into the dichotomy between identity and difference.[4] The observing individual has to make his way between the Scylla and Charybdis of identity and difference; he must reach his own conclusions in full awareness of the danger of being crushed to death, and the possibility of scraping through unharmed. The successful passage will depend on how well the critic has judged the operation of these two levels of reality which endanger the critic's personal existence. If the concrete and the abstract, if cognition and will, nature and freedom have been coordinated by the individual critic on a workable basis, which is determined by the individual's perception and his personal perceptive power, the passage will be deemed successful. Kant's *Kritizismus* as it reveals itself in all three critiques places all the responsibility of freedom in the hands of the individual critic. The critic has to earn his freedom of judgment over and over again in every critical process he undertakes. The freedom of the critic does not rest on the individual critic's perceptive and mental abilities alone, but is furthermore determined by the environment in which the individual finds himself. This environment is considered to be given and the individual will not be able to change it. However, the environment demands that its nature be interpreted and understood correctly so that the critic can demonstrate that he is aware of the bases from which he has to operate. Having understood the unchangeable bases of his thinking, the critic will then be able to undertake his own interpretative and creative ventures from there. The dichotomy between the finite and the infinite will remain, whatever the critic does. The critic can only affect the finite, whereas the infinite affects him.

Kant reveals his wisdom and analytical intellectual power by recognizing two levels of reality, so to speak. The first level is the outside level as manifested in the unchangeable environment in which man lives. The second level is the inside level as it reveals itself within the cognitive faculties of the observing and creative individual. The critic is only free on the second level, and this freedom is still conditioned by the first level. The critic stands between both dichotomies. The world which the critic builds is only his world, and it is only true as long as it corresponds to the world objectively given. The critic is free and unfree at the same time, which also reflects the prevailing dichotomy characteristic of Kant's *Kritizismus*. The critic has to be a scientifically operating individual who *sine ira et studio* will have to find his way into the full range of reality as it can possibly be perceived by a thinking human being. Any dogmatism conditioned by a limited perspective which denies the consideration of the facts *and* the potentialities ends the freedom of the critic and leaves the grounds of Kant's well-thought and responsible aesthetics.

Notes

1. Immanuel Kant, *Kritik der Urteilskraft*, Philosophische Bibliothek, vol. 39a, ed. Karl Vorländer, (Hamburg, 1963). All subsequent references are based on the German edition of this work. Translations of Kant's key terms are given by the author with the original German term in parentheses.
2. See Robert Kuhns, *Structures of Experience: Essays on the Affinity between Philosophy and Literature* (New York, 1970), p. 69.
3. Immanuel Kant, *Kritik der Reinen Vernunft* (from original ed. 1 and 2), Raymond Schmidt, Philosophische Bibliothek, vol. 37a (Hamburg, 1956). References to this edition are given in parentheses. The letter A followed by a page number refers to the first edition of 1781; the letter B followed by a number refers to the revised edition of 1787 as found in Schmidt's edition.
4. In a similar context, see Northrop Frye, *The Critical Path* (Bloomington, 1971), p. 13.

Annemarie Schimmel

LITERARY CRITICISM
IN THE FIELD OF ISLAMIC POETRY

We too have been in this world and have opened the eye of
understanding in this world; therefore trust in what we
say and reach such a way that every rose and thorn which
is visible in this rosegarden is plucked from what we have
cast from our eyes—

> When you look to the earth and towards the sky,
> it's through my seeing, but you don't see more:
> for all these things have gone through my view,
> I had already looked at what you see now!

THUS WRITES MIR DARD,[1] A MUSLIM MYSTICAL AUTHOR IN 18th CENTURY
Delhi, representative of the strictest Islamic fundamentalism (which
was, however, blended with tender mystical love and with a wonderful gift for poetry and music). It seems to me that he well describes
the peculiar position of any critical reader who approaches a new
artistic field: usually he sees the works of art—be they roses or thorns
—through the eyes of his predecessors (even if he should contradict
them), or of specialists; indeed, all

> the roses
> had the look of flowers that are looked at . . .

as T. S. Eiot says. Therefore it will be difficult, if not impossible, for
the reader to reach an unbiased understanding of any literary or aesthetic phenomenon. If even the way a poem is recited by its author

contributes to its interpretation, how much more is interpretation affected when later generations, deprived of the living experience of the artist himself, try to find the true meaning of his verses!

The literary critic is therefore by no means in an enviable position. This is all the more true for those specializing in an exotic field like Persian, Turkish, or Urdu poetry which seems, to the general reader, so outlandish and so different from his own tradition that he is willing to believe whichever learned specialist's work comes into his hands first; without further questioning, he sees both roses and thorns exclusively with his guide's eyes. But it is exactly here that the danger lies. In no other field of learning can the subjective judgment of a translator or a critic be more misleading than in the field of Oriental poetry and—an integral part of it—in Islamic mysticism.

The histories of Persian literature written by authors of the non-Muslim world reflect this difficulty excellently. The field of Persian is a model case: here the greatest number of books and translations are available to the nonspecialist, since Persian poetry has attracted scholars since the seventeenth century; further, most of the aesthetic judgments that are valid for classical Persian can be applied to classical Ottoman Turkish and Urdu poetry as well.

"The color of the water is determined by the color of the vessel," as the Sufis would say, or, as the Arabic proverb has it, "We can give only what we have received." Therefore, national, religious, political, and personal inclinations will always contribute to the image a critic produces from the given raw material. In the field of Islamology, J. O. J. Waardenburg's fine study: *L'Islam dans le miroir de l'Occident* (1961) well shows the different images of Islam produced by four scholars of different religious, cultural, and national backgrounds. In our field proper, a comparison between the two latest histories of Persian literature, A. J. Arberry's *Classical Persian Literature* (London, 1958) and J. Rypka's *History of Iranian Literatures* (Dordrecht, 1968), points exactly to this question. A relevant article, published in 1971 in the *Review of National Literatures*, quite lucidly elaborates the problem by showing the differences in approach between the British orientalist with artistic ambitions, who belongs to the humanistic tradition of E. G. Browne and R. A. Nicholson, and the sober, meticulous Czech scholar whose studies, like those of his collaborators, are tinged, of necessity, by the prevailing interest in the social and political role of the authors and their contributions to the enlightenment of the people. A. J. Arberry—though a careful editor of Arabic texts—took pride in his indefatigable translating activity,

adapting Persian and Arabic verses into soft-spoken though not always convincing English poetry; J. Rypka, on the other hand, never
ceased stressing the paramount importance of the study of the formal
aspects of Persian poetry, without the knowledge of which a true
understanding of Islamic literatures is almost impossible. If we add
to these two divergent but complementary approaches that of A.
Bausani, who with Mediterranean elegance discusses both aesthetic
and religious ideas in the history of Persian literature (1960), thus
opening an unexpected vista in the field of poetical expression without delving into the very depths of technical and artistic problems,
but also without denying his own religious (Bahai) background, the
reader will understand how difficult it must be, for a nonspecialist,
to bring the different bits of information into a coherent picture.

More than other philologists and historians—who can generally rely
upon a centuries-old tradition of interpretation—the Orientalist will
be prone to judge from his personal experiences and tradition the
literature with which he is confronted. The very choice of a special
field in the vast and mainly unexplored area of Islamic literatures is
already indicative of the critic's personality. Hellmut Ritter, the un-
disputed master of Oriental studies in Germany for many years
(1892–1971) and prolific editor of difficult texts, once remarked that
he almost assumed the form of the person about whom he wanted
to write (and thus became, indeed, the "persona," the mask through
which the original voice is resounding). He has, no doubt, expressed
an experience to which every truly great critic could subscribe. Ritter's major books on Persian literature show indeed a perfectly convincing approach to his subjects: so much so that one sees, after a
while, the Persian poet Fariduddin Attar (d. ca. 1220) or the mystic
Bayezid Bistami (d. 874) only through his eyes. Many books on Bayezid, the weird mystic of Iran, have been written, but the reader will
remember him best in the description by Ritter, who, following him
on his way towards higher levels of religious experience, in his disap-
pointment, and in his absolute quest for God, seems to reveal something of his own personality. And not less does he reveal some of his
personal sufferings in his masterful work on Attar, rightly regarded
as the most ingenious author of Persian epical mystical poetry. In
Attar's verses Ritter found problems of love and yearning, of suffering and questioning which he could echo and intensify by his own
experiences. It would be impossible to imagine that a book like Ritter's work on Attar, *Das Meer der Seele* (Leyden, 1955) could have
been produced by a scholar like J. Rypka, who, notwithstanding his

genuine admiration for Attar's work, saw him from a different angle. Attar will remain, henceforward, Ritter's mystical poet, recreated by him. Even the extensive learned apparatus of the voluminous book, which contains the most precious anthology of mystical stories and traces back most of Attar's motives to their sources, never hides the author's personal involvement.

The history of literary criticism in the field of Islamics is, to a large extent, a history of misunderstandings. This is all the more astonishing as one of the first to introduce Persian and related poetry to the West, Joseph von Hammer-Purgstall, had a remarkable insight into the working of Oriental artists and the character of Islamic art. Hammer, born in 1774 in Austria, belonged to those who took part in the education at Maria Theresa's *Sprachenaben-Schule*, a useful institute in Vienna where instruction in Turkish, Persian, Arabic, etc., was offered according to the future need for court-translators and diplomats of the Hapsburgian Empire. Not only the languages but also—contrary to modern methods of practical drill—the culture of the Islamic world must have been taught there to a certain extent. Hammer, the rather luckless diplomat and ambitious *Hofdolmetsch*, was to become the leading figure in the promotion of Islamic studies in Europe. He was certainly not a grammarian and true scholar like the French arabisant Silvestre de Sacy (d. 1838), with whom he had a long-standing friendship, but a man who loved and admired the Muslim world and tried to make his compatriots and the whole of Central Europe, acquainted with Islamic culture.

Hammer, who worked without any trace of fatigue until his death in 1856, was often attacked by the painstaking, meticulous philologists of his age and later times because he did not care too much for the rules of grammar; his translations from the three Islamic languages were criticized for their superficiality, his historical work for the Oriental flavor, viz., turgidity, by which their style was characterized and which covered the contents with a thick layer of baroque rhetoric. Nevertheless, the fact that Goethe was inspired by Hammer's translation of the *Divan* of Hafiz (1812–13) to compose his *West-Oestlicher Divan*, and that Friedrich Rückert was moved by reading Hammer's *Geschichte der schönen Redekünste Persiens* (1818) to write his most beautiful adaptations into German, e.g., the *ghazals* in the name of Jalaluddin Rumi, and the *Oestlichen Rosen* in the spirit of Hafiz, should be proof enough of Hammer's genuine greatness as interpreter of Persian poetry. For the Austrian diplomat —in spite of all the technical defects of his translations and compilation—had true feeling for the values of Islamic culture. The modern orientalist, carefully going through Hammer's free adaptations of Persian and Turkish poetry, is surprised to discover there a whole storehouse of information rarely found in modern studies on Islamic symbolism of Muslim thought. Of course, these lines or verses are not footnoted, nor are they explained by an extensive critical apparatus showing their exact sources—yet they convey a correct picture, as everybody who has lived in the East and knows the literary and popular tradition can easily prove. Thus Hammer's *Morgenländisches Kleeblatt* is a remarkable selection of Arabic, Persian, and Turkish wisdom and poetry, and the author's knowledge of the popular forms and beliefs of Islam—so often neglected by scholars—and the customs of the Islamic countries is amazing.

It was Hammer who, for the first time, introduced the symbolism of Islamic poetry. Goethe has gratefully acknowledged this attempt, and Rückert was well acquainted with Hammer's list of images, comparisons, and allegories as given in the *Geschichte der schönen Redekünste*. Here, we find the whole inventory of those images the knowledge of which is indispensable for the proper understanding and appreciation of Persian poetry. Likewise, Hammer's introduction to his translation of Hafiz—the fountainhead of Goethe's inspiration—contains, in a few pages, a beautiful sketch of the imagery of Persian poetry (p. xxxvi f.) which every admirer of Hafiz should read; it is as valid today as it was 150 years ago. We may criticize Hammer because he wants to see only the "natural" meaning of Hafiz's poetry, and follows the commentary of Sudi, the most sober of the numerous Turkish commentators who wrote about classical Persian poetry; but we will certainly agree with him that not every Persian verse should be interpreted by the—rather insipid—"mystical" method, as later writers tended to do. The Austrian orientalist tried to imitate the original form as closely as possible, that is, as closely as a person without great poetic talent can (without, however, attempting to write exact *ghazals*); in any case, he was right to underscore the fact that he preferred the use of short verses, contrary to the predilection of the English translators for longish paraphrases:

> Hierdurch unterscheidet sich diese Uebersetzung gar sehr von den neusten englischen, die im eigentlichsten Verstand nichts als Paraphrasen sind, wo zwey Zeilen des Originals nicht selten in einem Strophenschwall von acht und zehn Reimen ersäuft sind (p. vi).

These comparatively short verses are indeed one of the positive aspects of Hammer's translation; though sometimes rather unpoetical, his lines are often closer to the original than many later versifications published in the name of Hafiz. He likewise kept to the verbal sense, even if it might look at times repellent to Western taste. Thus he did not change the pronouns the gender of which is not visible in Persian and Turkish, from the—intended—masculine to the more moral feminine. He boasts

> dasser an Stellen, die sich unmöglich auf weibliche Schönheit deuten lassen, sich keine Veränderung erlaubte, was er hätte tun müssen, wenn er nicht in Ungereimtheiten verfallen und z.B. Mädchen wegen ihres grünenden Bartes hätte loben wollen (p. vii).

—certainly a very wise remark when we think of the later interpretation of the Beloved as feminine, so often illustrated in most tasteless pictures which surround Hafiz with buxom handmaids.

Hammer's praise of Hafiz (p. xxxix) is poetry in itself; not being able to produce high poetry himself, he was yet a master of rhythmical prose. His love becomes eloquent when he sings of the beauty of Hafiz's poetry, and here his understanding reaches, not the artificial "mystical" interpretation of Persian poetry, but the "religion of beauty" of which Hafiz's verses are the purest and most radiant mirror. And who else has described the overwhelming mystical fire of Jalaluddin Rumi better than Hammer in the soaring sentences of the *Geschichte der schönen Redekünste?*

Among all the critics of Persian, Turkish, and to a lesser extent Arabic poetry in those decades, Hammer was probably the one who understood this art best, because he had lived in the East, and had always had Oriental friends. That was, in his time, exceptional: most other Oriental scholars knew the Islamic languages only from their grammar books (and would regard, as legend tells, the word *Aisha* only as a participium active femininis of an irregular verb without realizing that it was the name of Muhammed's most beloved wife); and many of those historians of literatures who wrote about Oriental poetry, copying the writings of earlier critics, had never seen a Persian poem in its original form.

The "masculine pronoun" which Hammer accepted as a natural feature of Persian poetry, was one of the aspects of Hafiz which first interested Graf Platen in the Persian poet; he thought to find a kindred soul in him. This was shown, with many details, by F. Veit in his thesis on *Graf Platen's Nachbildungen aus dem Divan des Hafiz und ihr persisches Original* (1907), in which he pointed out that "the knowledge of Persian language and poetry is not as highly developed as the author's interest in sexual psychology. . . ,"[2] so that the homosexual component of Persian poetry is grossly exaggerated and coarsened, since it is seen without its mystical backround, i.e., the "chaste looking at the beautiful Beloved." And a man like Daumer could pour into the verses he wrote in the name of Hafiz all his hatred against the Protestant theologians with whom he had just broken, because he took at face value the traditional juxtaposition of the orthodox ascetic and the carefree lover. The garb of Oriental poetry was a fitting cover for all those who dreamed of sensual paradises and did not dare express their fantasies in a nineteenth-century German environment. Poor Hafiz had to lend his name to their more or less frivolous expectations.

Compared to these distortions of Hafiz, Hammer's work is a solid and healthy source. For, understanding the imagery of Persian poetry, he maintained that this poetry can be appreciated only when the reader disentangles the intricately interlaced words, recognizes their refined internal equilibrium, and perceives the peculiar, but strikingly logical system in which they are combined. It is not enough to know that wherever a rose is mentioned a nightingale must appear in the same verse; the whole precious fabric of allusions, rhetorical forms, and wordplays can be fully understood only after an intense study of its elements and—not to be forgotten—with a solid knowledge of the Quran and the Prophetic tradition. F. Rückert, in his *Grammatik, Rhetorik and Poetik der Perser*—an interpretation of the contemporary Indo-Persian work *Haft Qulzum* which he undertook in 1827 on Hammer's behalf—has given the best and most congenial introduction into the "witty" character of Persian poetry. And when Goethe recognized *das Geistreiche* as the essential character of Persian poetry, he was certainly indebted to Hammer's emphasis on the formal elements of Oriental poetry for his correct statement (Goethe's *Noten und Abhandlungen zum West-Oestlichen Divan* remains one of the best studies known into the spirit of Persian poetry).

In many cases, a practical knowledge of the spoken language in which this imagery was invented is required of the interpreter. One would be quite surprised to read that a poet in the twelfth century speaks of his "coming out of a certain situation like a hair out of the dough"—unless one knows the Turkish idiom *tereyağdan kıl çıkar gibi*, "to come out like a hair from the butter," that is, very smoothly and gently. Examples of this kind occur frequently in poetry; Hammer, tongue in cheek, apparently indulged in picking up such strange-sounding expressions and sometimes combined them in a rather absurd fashion so that the uninitiated general reader is, now and then, slightly shocked. Yet Hammer had a sense of humor which enabled him to understand (sometimes also to misunderstand) certain humorous plays of words in Oriental poetry. He was able to apply his practical knowledge of the languages to his understanding of poetry. That is why his work in Persian and Turkish literature is so superior to that in Arabic, a language which he had never practised to the extent of the other two, and which offers almost unsurmountable difficulties to someone who is not very fond of spending too much time on grammar.

Further, one should not forget that the language of Persian poetry is largely colored by mysticism. The tendency of the mystics to speak in subtle allusions, in cryptic ciphers, and sometimes in uncouth yet fascinating symbols, found its most perfect expression in Persian poetry. It is the oscillation between the mystical and the profane meaning that constitutes the true charm of this art which, in its best examples, reaches a perfect equilibrium between the sensual and the spiritual components. Rückert, still dependent upon Hammer's translation (later superceded by his own wonderful verse-translation) has described this quality of Persian lyric in lines worthy of Hafiz:

> Hafis, wo er scheinet Uebersinnliches
> nur zu reden, redet über Sinnliches.
> Oder redet er, wo über Sinnliches
> er zu redenscheint, nur Uebersinnliches?
> Sein Geheimnis ist unübersinnlich,
> denn sein Sinnliches ist übersinnlich.

No other verses interpret Persian classical poetry better than these. Hammer and, following him, Goethe and Rückert understood that "the word is a fan," which at the same time hides and reveals the deeper meaning behind it. But many later critics and translators lacked, and still lack, this understanding, an understanding that is absolutely necesary for an appreciation of Islamic poetry: Is Islam not the religion where God is revealed in the Word, i.e., in the Quran, which is His own uncreated and coeternal word? The importance of the word as means of revelation is, therefore, one of the cornerstones of Islamic *Weltanschauung* and has to be taken into consideration, especially when one deals with poetry.

A blatant example of an interpretation which misses this character of Islamic poetry is the beautifully produced *History of Urdu Literature* (Oxford, 1966) by M. Sadiq. It seems grotesque that an Oriental scholar should be accused of having overlooked the deeper layers of his own literary tradition, but being a professor of English literature, the author judges the whole tradition of Urdu—which in its classical

period is largely dependent upon Persian models and rules of aesthetics—from the viewpoint of British literary criticism. To be sure,
none of the few extant histories of Urdu literature can satisfy our
need for a valid critical evaluation: neither Garcin de Tassy's useful
enumeration of all available writers in his *Histoire de la littérature
Hindou et Hindoustani* (1870–72), nor W. G. Bailey's short, dry, but
informative booklet (1932), nor the rather verbose study by R. B.
Saksena (1927), who, as a Hindu, was not particularly conversant
with the Islamic background of Persian and Urdu imagery, although
his approach is sympathetic.

In our day, the difference between the Western approach to Persian poetry and that of an Oriental scholar trained in Europe or in the
United States seems to be that the Westerner tries to understand the
foreign material by entering deeper and deeper into the historical,
literary, and religious sources which contributed to the growth of a
certain literary phenomenon. G. F. de Fouchécour's book *La description de la nature dans la poésie persant du IIème siècle* (Paris, 1969),
is an excellent model for such most useful inventories of literary expressions. The Oriental scholar, on the other hand, becomes more
critical of his own literature, and aims to prove his modern progressive attitude and his breaking away from his old-fashioned, non-
Western, feudalist, religion-bound, etc., tradition by judging it merci-
lessly according to those Western values fashionable at the moment.
This attitude can be observed in the writings of modern Turkish and
Arab critics as well; in fact, the differences between the French and
the British school of literary criticism can be easily detected in the
various currents of Arabic, Persian, and Turkish prose and poetry
which emerged since the end of the last century. In the thirties, T. S.
Eliot became the hero of literary critics almost everywhere in the
Muslim world; today the concepts of various sociological currents,
Freudian psychology, Marxism, concrete poetry, etc., are applied by
the Islamic writers to their own tradition. The results are sometimes
rather surprising.

To return to M. Sadiq's interpretation of classical Urdu poetry: a
typical example is his discussion of Mir Dard (1721–1785), the mystic of Delhi whose saying opened this article. Dard was one of the
leading mystics of eighteenth-century India; his role as one of the
"Four Pillars of Urdu Poetry"—a literature which developed during
his lifetime and partly under his auspices—was always unquestioned;
but his voluminous mystical work, mainly in Persian, has rarely been
studied in full, although these writings convey highly interesting de-

tails of later Sufi theories and practices. M. Sadiq interprets large parts of Dard's small Urdu divan as purely erotic poetry. Thus the lines:

Lament and sigh, and drink the blood of your liver—
the time of youth is the season of *nā ū nūsh* [banqueting],

are translated as:

Go, cry and sigh and eat out your heart—
it is well said that youth should be given to wine and revelry.

The verse, however, speaks of the constant weeping and sighing of the lover, a topic often used in mystical poetry. The expression *nā ū nūsh*, lit. "flute and drink," connects the lover's sigh in the first hemistich with the sound of the *nā* or *nāy*, the reedflute, for the reedflute is the traditional symbol of the soul, yearning for God from which she is separated like the reed that is cut off from its reedbed; this is a typical allusion to the first lines of Jalaluddin Rumi's *Mathnawi*, the vade mecum of every Persian-speaking mystic, which supplied later poetry with countless symbols and images. The "drinking," then, goes back to the "drinking of one's blood," i.e., the permanent suffering by which the liver becomes emaciated so that "revelry" is, in fact, the "feast of lamenting and suffering." Dard himself has explained a number of his Persian verses in highly technical mystical language; but even without reading his own explanations, no one who has studied the ascetic life of this man, and has read his books filled with theological discussion, replete with prayers and heartfelt admonitions, would agree with Sadiq that "he was a man first and then a theologian" and that "his mind was delighting in physical beauty for its own sake, and not treating it as a mere stepstone to the supersensible" (p. 103).

Trained according to European literary standards and unaware of the values of his own tradition, uninitiated into the twofold or threefold meaning of each word, many a modern Oriental critic will commit similar mistakes: no longer at home in the colorful world of inherited forms and *topoi*, these critics tend to understand classical poets, like Ghalib (d. 1869), at face value and to interpret him in a modern way, turning him or any other eighteenth- or nineteenth-century poet into a socialist, an advocate of ecumenical thought, or a defender of women's lib. Undoubtedly a great poet can and must be understood in various ways; but certain rules of interpretation, mainly the correct use of the imagery, and a careful study of the whole religious and social background out of which this imagery can be explained, must be observed.

To return once more, after these digressions, to the figure of Hammer-Purgstall: it can be argued that his translations were not as correct as they ought to be (although it can be proved, at least in the case of the translation of Hafiz, that quite a number of verses which seem to make little sense or to contradict the original wording, have been distorted by small though decisive printing mistakes which the busy, but flighty, translator overlooked). Yet, Hammer had at least a feeling for the living values of the Islamic culture, a culture which he loved. He certainly did not assume the "person" of this or that poet, but he tried to introduce him as he saw him, and with as few distortions as possible, to the European reader. F. Rückert's role was, then, to adopt the forms as well and to orientalize himself to such an extent that his translations from Arabic, Persian, Sanskrit, and other languages are in part more artistic and Oriental than the original. Hammer could not have done this, for he was not primarily a poet but a poetically minded amateur in the best sense of the word. Rückert, for all his unsurpassable poetical ingenuity, was—unfortunately for the history of Persian literature—not a critic; he never wrote anything about the principles of interpretation, although he was the best authority in this field. His reaction to poetry was almost feminine: i.e., receiving inspiration and producing spiritual "children" without elucidating this process theoretically. Hammer, moveable and active, could bring every aspect of Islamic literatures and culture to Europe. At least in this respect his diplomatic mission was successful: he was the perfect cultural ambassador. He made his florilegia attractive by nicely painting their background, but never took the trouble of discussing any literary problem at length theoretically. His method of untiringly collecting whatever seemed important and valuable to him is similar to that of the indefatigable scholars of yore in Bagdad, Damascus, or Istanbul, who amassed material to write their huge works, which are generally lacking in architectural structure but put an immense wealth of details before the patient reader; they resemble rather carpets made of small pieces of wool, and filled with colorful arabesques and flowerwork. Hammer did the same with the material required for his numerous studies on literary history and criticism. We may even say that his books in themselves should be considered adaptations in a Western language of the Islamic spirit—carpet-like, florid, extending over large areas, covering the ground of an Oriental domicile where he felt at home and where he invited his guests from the German-speaking world to entertain them.

During Hammer's lifetime, when Islamic studies in Germany began to flourish, the first attempts to understand Islamic mysticism were made as well. The Protestant theologian H. G. F. Tholuck published his valuable booklet *Ssufismus sive theosophia Persarum pantheistica* in 1821, two years after Rückert's adaptions of Jalaluddin Rumi's *ghazals* had been written. Rückert, faithfully following Hammer's raw translations in the *Geschichte der schönen Redekünste*, but adding some verses from his own knowledge of Persian mystical poetry, produced that image of Rumi in which the great Persian mystical poet was to become known and loved wherever German was understood—once more a proof that Hammer's unartistic versions had something in themselves to inspire great and congenial poetry. Hammer himself translated some of the most important mystical works from Persian and Arabic, though without much success, but his stray interpretations in his various books show a fine understanding of at least some salient features of Sufism. Tholuck, on the other hand, tried, for the first time, to interpret mystical texts which he had brought together according to the facilities of the libraries in Berlin and other places. He judged Sufism from the viewpoint of a Protestant theologian—that means, of necessity, with considerable criticism and a feeling of unhappiness at the sight of these verses, legends, and thoughts which seemed to contradict the pure teaching of Protestantism and might lead the reader in the abysses of pantheism.

Such an uneasy feeling in the presence of even the finest mystical poems of Islam is even more evident in the writings of another German theologian and orientalist, Ernst Trumpp (1828–1885). Trumpp, as a missionary of the Anglican Church, stayed in Sind and the Northwestern Frontier of British India, and edited, for the first time, the famous Sindhi mystical poetry of Shah Abdul Latif (d. 1752). His remarks about Sufism and Sindhi Sufi poetry show such a negative attitude towards mystical Islam that one can scarcely understand how a scholar—a first-rate philologist—could devote long years of his life to the study of texts, the contents of which he intensely despised and which he regarded, at best, as interesting sources of grammatical forms. The fact that Trumpp, with all his learnedness, did not know the Quran well enough to recognize many of the allusions in the mystical verses before him added, of course, to his conviction that this kind of literature did not make much sense. Trumpp's views exactly oppose the irenic and all-embracing approach of the Austrian diplomat-orientalist. Such comparisons of Hammer-Purgstall with his contemporaries show quite well the important role of the scholar's personal background (sometimes even tinged by the province of birth and the family roots) and his religious and social orientation in his judgment of literary products, especially if these literary products grow from a soil permeated by religious tradition and mystical thought. This theory can be further supported by the fact that the best studies into the history of Islamic mysticism during the last decades have been carried out by Catholic scholars—mainly of French origin—like L. Massignon, L. Gardet, G. Anawati O.P., S. Laugier de Beaureceuil O.P., A. Gramlich S.J., and late P. Nwyia S.J.; all of them possessing both an innate and a tradition-bound understanding of the mystical side of religion.

Reading literary histories of Oriental literatures in the various European languages—from Russian and Czech to Italian, French, German, and English—gives a good picture of the political, religious, and social tendencies of the authors, and even the most carefully selected bibliography cannot veil the personal engagement, or the special predilections and antipathies of the scholar. We may compare the critic to a prism which singles out only the rays of a certain wavelength from the fullness of the spectrum: the personal (material and spiritual) make-up of the scholar as well as environmental influences contribute to the selection of colors which are then often presented as "the" true light. But only all of the colors can give a true impression of the radiant beauty of a work of art.

To the interpretation and criticism of a poetical work a line can be applied which the Sufis used to say about God Who is beautiful and loves Beauty:

Your Beauty is one, but our ways of worship are different.

Notes

1. Mir Dard, *Chahār risāla*, Bhopal 1310 h., Nāla-yi Dard Nr. 15.
2. H. H. Schaeder, *Goethe's Erlebnis des Ostens* (Leipzig, 1938), p. 174, note 13.

René Wellek

WALTER BENJAMIN'S LITERARY
CRITICISM IN HIS MARXIST PHASE

IN A PAPER, "THE EARLY LITERARY CRITICISM OF WALTER BENJAMIN" (IN
Rice University Studies, 1972), I showed that one cannot speak of
Benjamin's Marxism before 1925. Also his book *Ursprung des deut-
schen Trauerspiels*, written in 1925 though published as late as 1928,
is unaffected by Marxism.

One must speak, however, of a conversion to Marxism, of an ardent
engagement in the cause of Comunism after 1925, even though Benjamin never joined the party and was far from uncritical of the sights
and atmosphere he encountered in the winter of 1926–1927 on his one
visit to Moscow. His travel report, published in *Die Kreatur 2* (1927,
reprinted in A, 103ff), while proclaiming that "only a person who has
decided [in favor of Communism] can see in Russia" (A, 103) makes
no bones about the housing shortage, the lack of privacy, the transformation of the Russian intellectual into a bureaucrat, the low level
of taste, the xenophobia, the grotesque ignorance of the West. An
article "Die Politische Gruppierung der russischen Schriftsteller"
(Mar. 11, 1927, A, 190–4), while mainly informative, does not con-
ceal that "Russian literature is today—quite rightly—a bigger topic
for statisticians than for aestheticians." The new authors "drill according to political commands and the ABC is their ammunition" (A,
194). Benjamin's experiences with an article on Goethe he contributed
to the *Bolshaya Sovetskaya Entsiklopediya* did not enhance his respect for either the knowledge or the courage of the Russian scholars.
It was mangled, cut, and conflated with other contributions as it
seemed too "radical" to the Russians. In the private letters we can
trace his increasing disillusionment: his unease at the trials of the

thirties, to which he professed to have "no key" (Jan. 31, 1937, Br, 728) and finally his despair at the "Machiavellism" of the Russians and the "Mammonism" of the French leadership (Mar. 27, 1938, Br, 747) in the spring preceding the Munich agreement.

Still, it is impossible to ignore Benjamin's commitment to Marxism and Communism, to consider it merely an effort at self-deception, or to ascribe it to the "baneful, and in some respects, disastrous influence of Bertolt Brecht" as his friend Gershom Scholem did (see *Über Walter Benjamin*, p. 152, 1968). Benjamin not only had political sympathies for Communism, comprehensible in the years of the rise and triumph of Nazism, but he definitely adopted the central doctrines of dialectical materialism, proclaimed them, and applied them as a critical standard to friend and foe. He constantly repeated his allegiance to some basic Marxist views: the precedence of Being before Consciousness, the derivation of the superstructure from the substructure, the concept of triadic evolution, the rejection of relativistic historicism in favor of a contemporary judgment of the past, and particularly the view of the class struggle as the key to history and the diagnosis of capitalism as a world of alienation which led to the "reification" (*Verdinglichung*) of all human relations and the fetishism of things. Also on a concrete issue Benjamin agreed with Communist literary politics. In a lecture in Paris (Apr. 27, 1934, printed in *Versuche über Brecht*) he proclaims the duty of the writer to side with the proletariat and produce work with a purpose (*Tendenz*). He argues that correct political tendency includes literary quality. Literary quality is guaranteed by the invention of new techniques for which Benjamin cites Sergey Tretyakov's reportage *Vyzov* (*The Challenge*, called in the German translation *Feld-Herren; Der Kampf um eine Kollektivwirtschaft*, Berlin, 1931), which describes his experiences and his active share in the total collectivization of Russian agriculture. A new relationship of author and reader is envisaged: the author should become a producer, a worker. Benjamin recommends the "factography," "the social command" of the first Five-Year Plan with assigned tasks for writing. The commitment could not be clearer. (Ironically, Tretyakov became a victim of the purges.)

In his article on Eduard Fuchs, the well-known author of histories of manners, of erotic art, and of caricature, Benjamin endorses Engels's view (in a letter to Mehring, July 14, 1893) that there is no "independent history of art and thought" and in a complete reversal of his previous position, quoted in my earlier paper, Benjamin recommends the study of the reception, the post-history of writer (A, 303). Dialectical historiography sacrifices contemplation, the epic element in history. "It pries the age loose from the factual continuity of history: it depicts the experience of history for us now, not the eternal image of the past and puts this experience of history to work today" (A, 304). Benjamin also endorses "the manly recognition that art can have its rebirth only after the economic and political victory of the proletariat" (A, 315).

The same ideas recur in earlier and later pronouncements. Thus in a review of Werner Hegemann's *Das steinerne Berlin* (1930) Hegemann is chided for being merely "critical" of the conditions of the city. He does not properly "unmask the concrete constellations of a historical moment" as only "the dialectical insight (*Blick*) penetrates into the interior of history" (A, 447). Similarly, in a harsh review of Theodor Haecker's *Vergil: Vater des Abendlandes* (1932) Haecker is taken to task for asking the dilettantish question "What is Virgil to us?" instead of giving a "history of the reception and interpretation of Virgil's poetry" (A, 472–3). Haecker, Benjamin argues, believes wrongly in man in general and does not question the barbarous conditions to which present-day humanism is tied (A, 473). Benjamin also rejects a moralistic interpretation of history which he finds incompatible with materialism (A, 325). In a discussion of French surrealism (1929) Benjamin commends the surrealists for their effort to procure the "forces of intoxication (*Rausch*)" for the revolution. He praises the role of the revolutionary intelligentsia in breaking the intellectual dominance of the bourgeoisie but chides them for failing to establish contact with the revolutionary masses (A, 214). This is a task which cannot be accomplished "contemplatively": the writer must become a revolutionary: an essential part of his function might even be the interruption of his "artist's career" (A, 214).

Much of this has little to do with literary criticism: it is ideology and, in the context of the times, a commitment to a struggle with pen and ink against Nazism. It should, however, be recapitulated, as it has been doubted and as, in the correspondence with his friend Gershom Scholem in Jerusalem, Benjamin often sounds apologetic. In a letter (May 6, 1934) he speaks of Communism as "the lesser evil," a "much lesser evil [in comparison to Nazism] that it has to be approved in every practical, fruitful form" (Br. 605). Earlier, before Hitler's seizure of power, he pleaded with Scholem not to "restrain him from displaying the red flag" in the west of Berlin; even though he knows that his writings are "counterrevolutionary" from a party point of view he wants at least "to make them completely unpalatable to the Right" (Apr. 17, 1931, Br, 531). In a letter to the Swiss critic Max Rychner (Mar. 7, 1931, Br, 523–4) Benjamin pleads for an understanding of his turn to materialism by his distaste for the scholarship of the George circle, for Gundolf and Ernst Bertram, which is only less than his distaste for conventional idealistic literary scholarship of the type represented by Emil Ermatinger and Oskar Walzel. A review of *Philosophie der Literaturwissenschaft* (1930), edited by Ermatinger, expressly declares his distaste for the sacred slogans: "creativity, empathy, *Zeitentbundenheit*, *Nachschöpfung*, *Miterleben*, illusion, and *Kunstgenuss*" (A, 433), for the whole eclecticism and Alexandrianism of official German literary scholarship. The attitude of the materialist seems more fruitful in human terms and in scholarship (Br, 524).

To turn now to Benjamin's actual literary criticism one could say that the central topic of all his later writings was an attempt to construe a scheme of the history of art in the nineteenth century: the paper "Das Kunstwerk im Zeitalter seiner Reproduzierbarkeit" (1934) puts it in the most general terms with emphasis on the role of photography and the film. As an avowed Marxist Benjamin welcomes the spread of works of art to all manner and conditions of men, the ease of their reproduction, and the rise of the new media; he seems, almost like Marshall McLuhan, to predict the end of the Gutenberg era, the end of contemplative reading and viewing, "the liquidation of the traditional value in the cultural heritage" (I, 153). He welcomes the new possibilities of an imaginary museum, the museum without walls, later celebrated in Malraux's *Voices of Silence*. Clearly, however, Benjamin's attitude is ambivalent: he also deplores the destruction of what he calls the "aura," the halo around a work of art, the detachment of art from cult and myth. It is an elegy to the past of art and of his own former concept of art which had centered on myth and the mythical as the acme of art and truth.

The central idea of this paper informs also the other projects, fragments, and essays. "Paris, the Capital of the 19th Century" offers Baudelaire as the exemplary poet in revolt against bourgeois society, as the poet who abandoned the aura, lost the halo in the mud, and did not bother to pick it up: a sketch in *spleen* which is central to Benjamin's interpretation. Baudelaire is seen as the first poet of the city who experiences it as an outsider, an alienated man who goes through the crowd indifferently as a stroller (*flaneur*). Baudelaire's main poetic method is that of allegory, which according to Benjamin means "reification," a reduction to thing, a dispersion in time, a destruction of the world into fragments and ruins. Unlike baroque allegory Baudelaire's shows "traces of resentment in order to destroy the harmonious forms of this world" (I, 256). It also means empathy for the inorganic, the dead, the unnatural, for minerals and jewels (B, 59). What in the book on German tragedy was viewed with sympathy has now become a symptom of capitalist "reification," of man's surrender to things, to commodity economy. Baudelaire stands at the point when the bourgeoisie withdrew its mandate from the poet: when he became not only a Bohemian but an outcast, a Cain, a conspirator and mystifier and somehow also a defiant hero of Modernism, which Benjamin contrasts with the resignation of Romanticism (B, 80). Baudelaire's poetry exemplifies the process of the decay of "experience" (*Erfahrung*), of a genuine relationship which, in Baudelaire, is replaced by the experience of shock in the crowd. Time disintegrates in Baudelaire; the poet seeks prehistory, reminiscence, but fails: even Spring has lost its odor. He succumbs to "spleen" in which there is no "aura." The world ceases to respond: eyes do not answer any more as in the early poem *Correspondances* where the forest of symbols returned "familiar looks."

All this and much more amounts to a fine characterization of Baudelaire as a poet and type in his time, but one wonders how the laboriously accumulated information on social conditions and details gleaned from hundreds of books can do more than give picturesque concretization to the Paris of Baudelaire's time, while attempts to make this knowledge bear directly on an interpretation of Baudelaire's text often become strained, far-fetched, and even definitely mistaken. Much is made, for instance, of Baudelaire's mystifying habits, his sudden reversals which are said to parallel the shiftiness of Napoleon III, who "almost overnight changed from protectionism to free trade" (B, 10–11). Nor can one see how Baudelaire can be called a "conspirator" whose strategy was the sudden shock, the flash, the *putsch*, in order to draw a parallel to Blanqui. "Blanqui's deed was the sister of Baudelaire's dream" (B, 110) seems to me a conclusion in no way justified by Baudelaire's overt or even latent attitudes. Nor can I see why the shock experience of the stroller in the crowd has anything to do with the shock of the worker handling an object on the conveyor belt (B, 141) or why this experience is, in turn, parallel to the jerky movements of the gambler who is in servitude to chance (B, 142). Baudelaire, Benjamin admits, was no gambler. Nor can I see that the decay of the aura is, otherwise than chronologically, connected with the rise of photography which, in

Benjamin's account, brought something inhuman, reified into art. Benjamin argues that "to experience the aura of any appearance means to lend it the ability to return your glance" (B, 157). This is possible only in poetry and painting; photography prevents such a return. Still, Benjamin can consider the "destruction of the aura" a merit of photography; the work of art becomes impersonal, the result of a moment of the click of the camera, a "collective formation" (Gebilde) (see "Kleine Geschichte der Photographie," A, 245). But it is hard to see why Baudelaire figures so centrally in such a story. Actually if one studies his writings on aesthetics he will appear as a good romantic who believes in "constructive imagination," a term ultimately derived from Coleridge. In spite of many vacillations Baudelaire hoped for the reconciliation between man and nature. He said, like a good romantic: "Art is to create a suggestive magic containing at one and the same time the object and the subject, the external world and the artist himself" (Art Romantique, p. 119; see my History of Modern Criticism, 4:441).

Benjamin's interpretation, while often illuminating of the poet's attitude and social situation, seems to me mistaken if one analyzes his thought and position in the tradition of poetry. Adorno in a letter (Nov. 10, 1938, Br, 785) objected to the manuscript submitted by Benjamin that his "dialectics lack mediation." "The tendency predominates," he argued, "to relate the pragmatic contents of Baudelaire immediately to neighboring traits of the social history of the time." Adorno concluded that the work is "situated at the crossroads of magic and positivism" and rejected it for publication in the Zeitschrift für Sozialforschung. Benjamin, who as a refugee in Paris was financially dependent on Adorno's support, rewrote the piece without, however, substantially changing its tenor. The new version was published under the title "Über einige Motive bei Baudelaire" (1938).

Proust was an early love of Benjamin and Benjamin was one of Proust's first translators into German. In the Baudelaire essay Proust is seen as the man who tried synthetically to reconstruct the original experience available to the poet. The involuntary memory of Proust is, however, left to chance: to the tasting of the madeleine (B, 117). It is thus, as an earlier essay on Proust (1934) suggests, nearer to forgetting than remembering. In Proust's involuntary memory only that is available which had not been experienced (erlebt). The experience of eternity in Proust, Benjamin argues, is neither Platonic nor Utopian but "ecstatic" (I, 364), an "eternal restoration of the original, the first happiness" (I, 358). But Benjamin misses in Proust the heroic defiance he found in Baudelaire (I, 369), though he ad-mires his merciless criticism of French high society (A, 280) and approves his defense of sexual inversion (A, 280).

Proust is worked into the general scheme of the decay of the aura. I cannot see that Benjamin even tried to fit Kafka into it. Brecht, as Benjamin reports, complained that his essays had isolated Kafka's work and had even "encouraged Jewish fascism" (Brecht, 121). Ben-jamin rejects both the psychoanalytical and the theological interpre-tation of Kafka, particularly Max Brod's view of Kafka as a saint or a man on the way to sainthood. He also objects to a theological read-ing of *The Castle* which ignores the repulsive and terrifying aspects of the upper world, the alleged "realm of grace" (Br, 758). He sees no grounds for claims of Kafka as a prophet or even the keeper of some special wisdom. Kafka, Benjamin argues, fails to change fiction into doctrine (A, 258). Kafka is rather an inventor of parables who combines the "greatest mysteriousness with the greatest simplicity" (*Schriften 2*, 208). Benjamin admires Kafka's serenity and purity but sees his work as a personal and artistic shipwreck. Kafka's world is not mythic, and not prophetic. It rather harks back to the oldest pre-historic world, to that of fairy tales, of German folklore where chil-dren, fools, and animals, the lamb-cat, Odradek, the flat, starry-shaped, spool-like creature, and Gregor Samsa, the beetle, escape from the swamp world. Benjamin concludes by quoting a poem about a hunchbacked hobgoblin: "Pray for the little hunchback too." It is Kafka's prayer for himself, the spiritual cripple in the world of fathers and officials; a prayer for all the lowly and innocent, the childlike and the foolish (A, 263).

Both Proust and Kafka come late in the history of fiction. They do not tell stories, according to Benjamin. In an essay on the Russian novelist and short-story writer Nikolay Leskov (1936) Benjamin sketched a history of fiction which fits in with his overall scheme of the atrophy of experience and the decline of wisdom illustrated by Proust's and Kafka's desperate attempts to recapture them (see B, 117). The teller of a story, Benjamin explains, gave advice, dispensed wisdom, was personally involved in the telling, but gave no explana-tion of the story. The spread of information demanded explanation and hence the death of story telling. Benjamin associates the art of story telling with the world of artisans: it is a craft like theirs. He then elaborates the contrast between story and novel: the novel does not come from oral tradition as the tale does. It is told by an individual and read in solitude. A novel searches for the meaning of life while a story conveys a moral. A novel concludes, while a story asks "How does it go on?" Benjamin quotes a saying of Moritz Heimann to the effect that "a man who dies at the age of 35 is at every point of his life a man who dies at the age of 35" in order to modify it by saying that a man who dies at 35 will appear to *remembrance* at every point of his life as a man who died at the age of 35 (I, 427). The novel is seen as an experience of death. "What draws the reader to the novel is the hope of warming his shivering life with a death he reads about" (I, 428). Oddly enough, a few pages before we are told that "death is the sanction that the story-teller can tell. He has borrowed his authority from death" (I, 421). Even if one can think of ways of reconciling these contradictions one can quote many counter-examples, not only of comic or humorous novels and stories, and one could easily reverse Benjamin's distinction between the novel and the story. Many novels do not conclude (not even with death). They also allow us to ask "How does it go on?" (think of *War and Peace*), while, on the contrary, most stories (Chekhov excepted) conclude, make a point, draw a moral, as Benjamin himself said before.

Also, the further reflections on the survival of the fairy tale in the story and the idea that the fairy tale is not a remnant of the myth but rather a revolt against it seem highly doubtful. Benjamin is thinking of rogues and fools who defy or cheat the powers of the mythic world. Leskov's characters are interpreted as fitting into this scheme. They magically escaped the early world (as Kafka's good people did). They are the righteous and have a maternal touch. Benjamin's one example, however, the hero of the story "Kotin the Provider and Platonida," is strangely misinterpreted. Benjamin speaks of him as a "hermaphrodite." For twelve years his mother raised him as a girl. "His male and female organs matured simultaneously" and his bisexuality "becomes the symbol of the God-Man" (I, 431). I have read the story attentively and cannot find a trace of Benjamin's view in the text: the only support is the fact that the mother of Kotin, left destitute after the death of her husband, seeks employment as a servant in a nunnery and, out of necessity, pretends that her baby is a girl rather than a boy. She leaves the nunnery when the boy is twelve, changes his clothes, and puts him into a boys' school. There is no suggestion of bisexuality or hermaphroditism and not a word about the God-Man. I am at a loss to imagine how Benjamin could have misread this harmless story so flagrantly. Nor can I find anything in the story "The

Alexandrite" which would prove the mystical as inherent in the nature of the story-teller. A gem engraver in Prague, a weird figure out
of E. T. A. Hoffmann, interprets the stone's changing color from green
to red as an allegory of the reign of Alexander II: from early hope to
the blood of the assassination. It seems to me sheer fancy to see some
connection between "soul, hand, and eye" in this story, to find mysterious support for the role of gesture and craft in the art of story
telling, and to conclude: "the story teller is the figure in which the
righteous man encounters himself" (I, 436). On occasion I confess I
do not understand the workings of Benjamin's mind, particularly in
this essay which has been considered his masterpiece.

The distinction between story and novel is of course a valid one: as
early as 1930 in a review of Döblin's *Alexanderplatz* (A, 437) Benjamin uses the contrast between Döblin's ambition of writing an epic
where montage and documents (a la Dos Passos) would replace the
formulas of the old epic with Gide's *Counterfeiters*, a "pure," written,
bookish novel, turned inward, elaborately reflected in Gide's own
Journal of the Counterfeiters (A, 438). Benjamin, however, denied
that Döblin succeeded in his intention: his novel remains a *Bildungs-
roman*, bourgeois in the German tradition (A, 442–3).

The only writer of the new proletarian dispensation whom Benjamin admired was Bertolt Brecht. Benjamin seems to have considered
himself an expounder and commentator of Brecht's, abdicating any
effort at criticism. The account of Brecht's *Dreigroschenroman*
(1934, published 1960) is mainly descriptive. It concludes that "satire is always a materialistic art" and that it becomes "dialectical" in
Brecht's hands (A, 301). The paper "What Is Epic Theater?" (1939)
is a straightforward exposition of Brecht's theories without any comment except two historical remarks: that Brecht's techniques descend
from medieval mysteries via the Baroque, and that Strindberg must
not be identified with romantic irony, which lacks Brecht's doctrinal
aim (A, 350). The accounts of first performances of *Die Mutter*
(1932) and of *Furcht und Elend des Dritten Reiches* (in Paris, May
1938) are merely approving reportage. The remark that German
émigré actors playing an SA man or a judge of the people's court are
faced with a different task from that of a kind-hearted man playing
Iago, supports Brecht's view that empathy is the wrong method of
acting. The comments on some of Brecht's poems (one published in
1939, the rest in *Schriften*, 1955) try "to bring out the political contents of purely lyrical passages" (A, 521) but do not seem to me to
go beyond the obvious. But the introductory reflections show that

Benjamin thought of a commentary as "assuming the classicity of a text" (A, 520) and of Brecht as the new classic (also A, 301). Benjamin certainly uses Brecht's political lyrics which, he says, combine consciousness and activism, to condemn the poetry of Erich Kästner as "left-wing melancholia" (1937, A, 457–61).

Further, Karl Kraus, who had appealed to Benjamin because of his attacks on journalism and his concern with the language, is ultimately condemned for his lack of understanding of economics and his social program which to Benjamin seemed to recommend only a return to the old bourgeoisie (I, 404). Kraus, as early as 1931, appears as the last bourgeois, defending the phantom of the unpolitical or "natural" man. Kraus's later defense of the Dollfusz regime shocked Benjamin deeply (see letter, Sept. 27, 1934, Br, 623) but could hardly have surprised him. He saw in Kraus a new Timon (Kraus's favorite play of Shakespeare) who "jeeringly distributes the acquisitions of his life among his false friends" (Sept. 15, 1934, Br, 620).

We are back to politics. Politics in a wide sense dominates the later writings of Benjamin as it dominated his life. Marxist ideas—the alienation of man, "reification," the work of art as commodity—permeate his later work. I am not qualified to decide whether Benjamin's application of these ideas is orthodox Marxism. Both Adorno and Scholem thought that it was not. Still, it was, it seems to me, Marxism in the sense expounded in Lukács's *History and Class Consciousness*. There alienation and reification appear, for the first time, as central concerns of Marxist theory, and appear as identical terms. Lukács's book was denounced by Zinoviev at the fifth Congress of the Third International in 1924, and it was attacked as "idealistic" by the Soviet philosopher, A. M. Deborin (see Parkinson, *Lukács*, p. 13). Lukács himself in the 1967 preface to the new edition condemned the identification of alienation and reification as a "fundamental and gross error" (see Luchterhand ed., 1968, p. 26). I suspect that Scholem was right when he predicted (Mar. 30, 1931, Br, 527) that within the Communist party Benjamin would soon have been "unmasked as a typical counterrevolutionary and bourgeois." But this would have been an even sillier label than that of orthodox Marxist. Benjamin had obviously transcended both these parties in his best criticism: in the essay on the *Elective Affinities*, in the book on German tragedy, and in the essays on Proust, Kafka, Leskov, and Baudelaire, not to speak of the many scattered articles and reviews which make him, almost incognito, what he wanted to be—"the first German critic" of his time.

Notes

As *Schriften* (2 volumes, Frankfurt, 1955) is out of print, I quote *Illuminations* (Frankfurt, 1961) as I; *Angelus Novus* (Frankfurt, 1966), as A; *Briefe* (2 volumes, Frankfurt, 1966), as Br; and *Charles Baudelaire* (Frankfurt, 1969), as B. *Versuche über Brecht* (Frankfurt, 1966) contains some unpublished or uncollected writings.

Rolf Tiedemann, *Studien zur Philosophie Walter Benjamins* (Frankfurt, 1965) contains an indispensable bibliography. *Über Walter Benjamin* (Frankfurt, 1968) lists the secondary literature.

LIST OF CONTRIBUTORS

FALK, EUGENE HANNES
Born August 10, 1913, in Czechoslovakia.
Studied at Charles University and German University, Prague, and the Sorbonne, Ph.D. University of Manchester, England, 1942.
Academic Honors: Ford Fellowship, 1952–53; Edward Tuck Professor of the French Language and Literature, Dartmouth College.
Present Position: Marcel Bataillon Professor of Comparative Literature, Professor of French, and Chairman of Curriculum in Comparative Literature, University of North Carolina at Chapel Hill.

Books: *Renunciation as a Tragic Focus*, Minneapolis 1954; *Types of Thematic Structure*, Chicago 1967; editor of the *University of North Carolina Studies in Comparative Literature*.

FIZER, JOHN
Born June 13, 1925, in Mircha, Ukraine.
Ph.D. in Psychology, Munich, 1949. Ph.D. in Slavic Languages and Literatures, Columbia University, 1960.
Present Position: Professor at Rutgers University.

IZUTSU, TOSHIHIKO
Born May 4, 1914, in Tokyo, Japan.
Litt. D. at Keio University, Tokyo.
Present position: Full Professor at McGill University, Montreal.

Books: *Language and Magic*, Toyko 1956; *God and Man in the Koran*, Tokyo 1964; *The Concept of Belief in Islamic Theology*, Tokyo 1965; *Ethico-Religious Concept in the Qur'ân*, Montreal 1966; *The Key Philosophical Concepts in Sufism* Tehran 1969; *The Concept and Reality of Existence*, collected papers, Tokyo 1971.

IZUTSU, TOYO
Born September 8, 1925, in Osaka, Japan.
Studied at Tokyo University, Tokyo, Japan.

Books: Collected short stories, *Hakuji Goshi (White Porcelain)*, Tokyo 1959 (in Japanese).

KRIEGER, MURRAY
Born November 27, 1923, in Newark, New Jersey.
Studied at the University of Chicago. Ph.D. Ohio State University, 1952.
Academic Honors: Guggenheim Fellowships in 1956–57 and 1961–62; ACLS Postdoctoral Fellowship in 1966–67; NEH Research Grant in 1971–72.
Present Position: Professor of English and Comparative Literature and Director of the Program in Critical Theory at the University of California at Irvine and Professor of English at the University of California, Los Angeles.

Books: *The New Apologists for Poetry*, Minneapolis 1956; *The Tragic Vision: Variations on a Theme in Literary Interpretation*, New York 1960; *A Window to Criticism: Shakespeare's Sonnets and Modern Poetics*, Princeton, 1964; *A Play and Place of Criticism*, Baltimore 1967; *The Classic Vision: The Retreat from Extremity*, Baltimore 1971. Editor of *The Problems of Aesthetics*, New York 1953; *Northrop Frye in Modern Criticism: Selected Papers from the English Institute*, New York 1966.

RAMSEY, PAUL
Born November 26, 1924, in Atlanta, Georgia.
Studied at the Universities of Chattanooga, North Carolina, and Minnesota. Ph.D. University of Minnesota, 1956.
Present Position: Poet-in-Residence and Alumni Distinguished Service Professor, University of Tennessee, Chattanooga.

Books: *The Lively and the Just: An Argument for Propriety*, Tuscaloosa 1965; *Triptych*, Stockton 1964; *In an Ordinary Place*, Raleigh 1965; *A Window for New York*, San Francisco 1968; *The Doors*, Tennessee 1968; *The Art of John Dryden*, Lexington 1969.

RICKETT, ADELE AUSTIN
Born July 9, 1919, in Yonkers, New York.
Studied at the University of North Carolina, Stanford University, University of Pennsylvania, and Tsinghua and Yenching Universities, Peking. Ph.D. University of Pennsylvania, 1967.
Academic Honors: Chinese Cultural Fellowship, 1945–46; Fulbright Scholarship, 1948–49.
Present Position: M. Mark and Esther K. Watkins Assistant Professor of Chinese Studies, University of Pennsylvania.

Books: Coauthor, *Prisoners of Liberation*, New York 1957, paperback 1973; editor, *Spectator Papers*, by Norman Whitney, Philadelphia 1971; *Wang Kuo-wei's Jen-chien tz'u-hua, A Study in Chinese Literary Criticism*, in press.

RUDNICK, HANS H.
Born November 1, 1935 in Belgard, Germany.
Studied at Kaiser-Karl-Schule. Ph.D. University of Freiburg, Germany, 1966.
Present Position: Assistant Professor of English, Southern Illinois University, Carbondale.

Books: *Das Verhältnis von logischer und aesthetischer Sprachbei den "New Critics" und das Problem der literarischen Wertung*, Freiburg 1966; *Two Planets*, by Kurd Lasswitz, translated from the German into English by Hans H. Rudnick, epilog by Wernher von Braun, afterword by Mark Hillegas, Carbondale 1971; editor of *Erläuterungen und Dokumente zu Shakespeares Hamlet*, critical commentary of the text, with a history of the sources, and critical voices from Goethe to Jan Kott, Stuttgart 1972.

SCHIMMEL, ANNEMARIE
Born April 7, 1922, in Erfurt, Germany.
Education: Ph.D. in Islamics, University of Berlin, 1941.
Habilitation in Arabistic and Islamology at the University of Marburg, 1946.
Academic Honors: M.A. hon. Harvard, 1971. Sitare-ye Quaid-i Azam (Pakistan), 1965. Friedrich Rückert-Preis, 1965.
Present Position: Professor of Indo-Muslim Culture, Harvard University.

Books: *Indices of the Chronicle of Ibn Iyas,* Istanbul 1945; *Lied der Rohrflöte, Deutsche Ghaselen,* Hameln 1948; *Die Bildersprache Dschelaladdin Rumis,* Walldorf 1949; *Dinler Tarihine Giris,* Ankara 1954; *Edition of the Siratj Ibnj al-Chafif, aš-Širazi,* Ankara 1955; *Gabriel's Wing. A Study into the religious ideas of Sir Muhammad Iqbal,* Leiden 1963; *Pakistan, Ein Schloss mit tausend Toren,* Zürich 1965; *Islamic Calligraphy,* Leiden 1970; *Orientalische Dichtung in Übersetzungen Friedrich Rückerts,* Bremen 1963.

Translations: *Lyrik des Ostens* (the Near Eastern part), München 1950; *Ausgewählte Abschnitte aus der Muqaddima,* Muhammad Iqbal, *Javidname-Buch der Ewigkeit* (German poetry), Munich 1957; *Javidname* (Turkish translation), Ankara 1958; Muhammad Iqbal, *Botschaft des Ostens* (German poetry), Wiesbaden 1963, Dschelaladdin Rumi, *Aus dem Divan,* Stuttgart 1964; Muhammad Iqbal, *Persicher Psalter* (Selections of his Persian, Urdu, and English writings), Köln 1968; al-Halladsch, *Märtyrer der Gottesliebe,* Köln 1969; John Donne, *Nacktes denkendes Herz,* Köln 1969.

Coeditor: Arabic Cultural Magazine *Fikrun Wa Fann,* Hamburg, since 1963.

WELLEK, RENÉ

Born 1903 in Vienna, Austria.

Education: Ph.D. Charles University, Prague, Czechoslovakia, 1926.

Academic Honors: Honorary Doctorates from Oxford, Harvard, Munich, and Rome universities, Lawrence College, the University of Maryland, Boston College, Columbia, University of Montreal, and University of Louvain. Guggenheim fellow 1951–52, 1956–57, and 1966–67; fellow, Silliman College; Fulbright resident professor universities of Florence and Rome 1959–60; Fulbright professor Mainz, Germany, 1969; Am. Counc. Learned Soc. distinguished scholar; Humanities award 1959; Bollingen Foundation award 1963.

Position: Sterling Professor of Comparative Literature, Yale University.

Books: *Kant in England,* Princeton 1931; *The Rise of English Literary History,* Chapel Hill 1941; *Theory of Literature,* with Austin Warren, New York 1949; *History of Modern Criticism 1750–1950:* volume I, *The Later Eighteenth Century,* New Haven 1955, volume II, *The Romantic Age,* New Haven 1955, volume III, *The Age of Transition,* New Haven 1965, volume IV, *The Later Nineteenth Century,* New Haven 1965; *Concepts of Criticism,* New Haven 1963, *Essays on Czech Literature,* The Hague 1963; *Confrontations,* Princeton 1965; *Discriminations,* New Haven 1970.

INDEX OF NAMES

Adorno, Theodor W., 173, 177
Ai (Emperor of China), 128
Aisha (wife of Mohammed), 160
Alexander II (tsar of Russia), 176
Alonso, Damaso, 34
Anawati G., 167
Arberry, A.J., 156
Aristotle, 34, 36, 76
Arnold, Matthew, 80–81, 92
Attar, Fariduddin, 157–58
Augustine, 76
Austen, Jane, 103

Bailey, W.G., 163
Balzac, Honoré de, 84
Basho, Matsuo, xii, 40, 41–50, 52–53, 62, 67–68
Bateson, Frederic W., viii–ix, xiv
Baudelaire, Charles, 169, 171–73, 177–78
Bausani, A., 157
Benjamin, Walter, xii, 168–78
Bergson, Henri, 92
Bertram, Ernst, 171
Bistami, Bayezid, 157
Blake, William, 83, 84
Blanqui, Louis Auguste, 172
Bloecker, Guenter, 37
Bloomfield, Morton W., viii, xiii–xiv
Brecht, Bertolt, 169, 174, 176–78
Brod, Max, 174
Browne, E.G., 156
Browne, William, 103
Buehler, Charlotte, xiii
Burke, Kenneth, 86
Butor, Michel, 4

Carlyle, Thomas, 140
Chang Hui-Yen, 118–19, 133
Chekhov, Anton Pavlovich, 175

Chia Tau, 125, 130
Chia-Ying Yeh, 119
Chiu-Fang Kao, 128–29
Cho O-kyo, 43
Chou Chi, 133
Chuang Tzu, 43
Chung Yung, 122
Chu Tung-Jun, 128, 130, 134
Ch'ü Yüan, 118, 133
Coleridge, Samuel Taylor, 78–79, 112, 173
Confucius, 124
Conrad, Joseph, 86
Corneille, Pierre, 6
Croce, Benedetto, ix, 79–80

Dard, Mir, 155, 163–64
Daumer, Georg Friedrich, 161
Deborin, A.M., 177
Dembo, L.S., 92
Demetz, Peter, xiv
Descartes, René, 6, 7, 148–49
Dilthey, Wilhelm, vii, x, xiii
Doeblin, Alfred, 176
Dogen (zenmaster), 66, 69
Doho, Hattori, 61, 69
Dollfusz, Engelbert, 177
Dos Passos, John, 176
Dryden, John, 99
Dubos, Jean Baptiste, 2–3, 5
Dufresne, Michel, 33

Eliot, Thomas Stearns, 3, 83, 155, 163
Engels, Friedrich, 169
Ermatinger, Emil, 171

Falk, Eugene, xii
Faulkner, William, 70, 103

Feng Yu-Lan, 124, 133
Finnerty, Pat, 92
Fizer, John, xii, 35
Fouchécour, G.F., 163
France, Anatole, 75
Frost, Robert, 96
Frye, Northrop, 83–84, 88, 154
Fuchs, Eduard, 169

Gardet, L., 167
Geiger, M., 35
Genshin, 68
Gentzler, Mason, 132
George, Stefan, 171
Ghalib, 164
Gide, André, 176
Goethe, Johann Wolfgang, 17, 140, 158–59, 161–62, 168
Graham, A.C., 134
Gramlich, A., 167
Greene, Thomas, xiv
Gundolf, Friedrich, 171
Gutenberg, Johannes, 171

Haecker, Theodor, 170
Hafiz, 158–62, 165
Hammer-Purgstall, Joseph von, 158–62, 165–66, 167
Hartmann, Nicolai, 34
Hegel, Georg Wilhelm Friedrich, 82–83
Hegemann, Werner, 170
Heidegger, Martin, 37, 144
Heimann, Moritz, 175
Hitler, Adolf, 170
Hoffmann, E.T.A., 176
Holzman, Donald, 132
Homer, 108–09
Horace, 2
Hsia, T.A., 113, 132
Hsiao T'ung, 122
Hsieh Tiao, 120
Hsien-Yi, 133
Hsü, 133
Huang T'ing-Chien, 114–15, 117
Hui-Hung, 117
Hulme, T.E., 85
Humboldt, Wilhelm von, 17
Humphrey, Robert, 35

Husserl, Edmund, xii, 6–7, 11–14, 17, 34–35
Hyman, Stanley Edgar, 86

Ingarden, Roman, vii, x, xii, 10–14, 16, 18, 20–25, 27, 29, 31, 33–35, 38–39
Izutsu, Toshihiko,, xii, 68–69
Izutsu, Toyo, xii, 68

James, William, 17, 20, 35
Johnson, Samuel, 78, 92
Joshu (zenmaster), 66
Joyce, James, 20
Junzo, Karaki, 57

Kaestner, Erich, 177
Kafka, Franz, 5, 174–75, 177
Kant, Immanuel, viii, xi, xii, 135–36, 138–54
Kenko, Kimura, 55, 69
Kifu, 64–65
Kikaku, 64–65, 69
Klabinsky, R., 68
Klemperer, Viktor, xiii
Kockelmans, J.J., 11, 34
Kraus, Karl, 177
Krieger, Murray, xii
K'uei-Chou, 115
Kuhns, Robert, 154
Kuo Shao-Yü, 111, 132
Kuo-Wei, 114

Lacan, Jean, vii
Latif, Schah Abdul, 166
Lauer, J.Q., 12, 34
Laugier de Beaureceuil, S., 167
Lawall, Sarah, 37
Leskov, Nikolay, 174–75, 177
Levy, Howard, 133
Li Hou-Chu, 121
Li, Mr., 125, 128, 131
Li Po, 112
Li Yü, 112
Lin Pu, 121
Liu Hsieh, 111–12, 116
Liu Tsung-Yüan, 132

Liu-Yi Yuh, Isabelle, 133
Longinus (= Pseudo-Longinus), 109
Lu Chi, 111
Lukács, Georg, 177

Mallarmé, Stéphane, 84
Malraux, André, 171
Maria Theresia (emperatrice of Germany), 158
Marmontel, Jean-François, 1–3, 6
Massignon, L., 167
Mayer, Hans, xiv
McLuhan, Marshall, 171
Mehring, Franz, 169
Mei Yao-Ch'en, 121
Miller, J. Hillis, xiv
Milton, John, 84
Minoru, Nishio, 68
Mototoshi, 55, 69
Mu (duke of Ch'in), 128
Mu (king of the Chou dynasty), 133

Napoleon III, 172
Nelson, Jr., Lowry, xiv
Nicholson, R.A., 156
Nwyia, P., 167

Otto, Karl, 37
Ou-Yang Hsiu, 118–19, 121

Parkinson, Thomas, 177
Paulhan, Jean, ix, xiv
Pepper, Stephen R., xiii
Platen, August Graf von, 160
Plato, 76
Po-Lo, 129
Pope, Alexander, 73, 77–78, 86, 106
Potebnia, Alexander, 17
Poulet, Georges, viii, xiv, 84, 92
Pound, Ezra, 85
Proust, Marcel, 173–74, 177

Ramsay, Paul, xii
Richards, Ivor Armstrong, vii, xiii, 141

Rickett, Adele, xii
Riichi, Kurimoto, 69
Ritter, Hellmut, 157–58
Robbe-Grillet, Alain, 4
Rueckert, Friedrich, 158–59, 161–62, 165–66
Rumi, Jalaluddin, 158, 160, 164, 166
Rychner, Max, 171
Ryokan (zenmaster), 66, 69
Rypka, J., 156–57

Sacy, Silvestre de, 158
Sadiq, M., 162–64
Saksena, R.B., 163
Salkever, Louis R., xiii
Saussure, Ferdinand de, ix
Scheler, Max, 6–7
Schimmel, Annemarie, xii
Schimmura, I., 68
Schleiermacher, Friedrich, x
Schmidt, Raymond, 154
Scholem, Gershom, 169–70, 177
Shakespeare, William, 70, 84, 92, 99, 109, 140
Shelley, Percy Bysshe, 79, 92
Shirota, T., 69
Sidney, Sir Philip, 76–77
Sievers, Eduard, xi
Solomon (king), 3
Spalek, John, xiii
Spitzer, Leo, x, 14, 34
Ssu-K'ung T'u, 116, 128–31, 133
Stammler, Wolfgang, 37
Stein, E., 35
Stevens, Wallace, 88
Strelka, Joseph, 36
Strich, Fritz, 34
Strindberg, August, 176
Sudi, 159
Su Shi, 114
Su Tung P'o, 68
Swift, Jonathan, 103

T'ao Chien, 115, 133
Tao-Ying, 129
Tassy, Garcin de, 163
Teika Fujiwara, 55, 69
Tennyson, Alfred Lord, 70, 86
Tholuck, H.G.F., 166
Tiedemann, Rolf, 178

Tolstoy, Leo, 18
Tretyakov, Sergey, 169
Trumpp, Ernst, 166
Ts'ao P'i, 111
Tu Fu, 115, 120
Tymieniecka, Anna-Teresa, 10–11, 17, 33–35

Veit, F., 160
Vorlaender, Karl, 154
Voszler, Karl, 14, 34

Waardenburg, J.O.J., 156
Wahle, J., xiii
Walzel, Oskar, xiii, 14, 171
Wang-Cho, 117
Wang Chü-Fu, 132
Wang Hsiang, 132
Wang Kuo-Wei, 113, 118, 123
Wang Wei, 125, 130

Warren, Austin, 33
Wei Ying-Wu, 125, 130
Wellek, René, vii, viii, x, xi, xii, xiii, xiv, 10, 33, 75
Wen T'ing-Yün, 112–14, 121
Wheelwright, Philip, viii, x, xiii
Williams, William Carlos, 103
Wimsatt, W.K., 85
Winckelmann, Johann Joachim, 17
Wordsworth, William, 91, 112
Wu-Tseng, 133

Yang, Gladys, 133
Yen Yü, 112, 116, 129
Yi-Ts'un, 129
Yoshinori, Onishi, 60, 67
Yü P'ing-Po, 113, 132

Zenchiku, Komparu, 43
Zinoviev, Grigori Evseyevich, 177